The Silent Game

David Stafford

the
SILENT
GAME

The Real World of Imaginary Spies

Revised Edition

The University of Georgia Press / Athens

To J. C., with love

© 1991 by David Stafford
All rights reserved
Published by the University of Georgia Press
Athens, Georgia 30602
The paper in this book meets the guidelines for
permanence and durability of the Committee on
Production Guidelines for Book Longevity of the
Council on Library Resources.

Printed in the United States of America

95 94 93 92 91 C 5 4 3 2 1
95 94 93 92 91 P 5 4 3 2 1

Library of Congress Cataloging in Publication Data

Stafford, David.
      The silent game : the real world of imaginary
spies / David Stafford. — Rev. ed.
          p.   cm.
      Includes bibliographical references and index.
      ISBN 0-8203-1342-4 (alk. paper), —
ISBN 0-8203-1343-2 (pbk. : alk. paper)
      1. Spy stories, English—History and criti-
cism.   2. Spy stories, American—History and
criticism.   3. English fiction—20th century—
History and criticism.   4. American fiction—
20th century—History and criticism.   5. Espionage—History—20th century.   I. Title.
PR888.S65S83   1991
823'.0872091—dc20   90-28594
                                                CIP

First published in 1988 by Lester & Orpen
Dennys Ltd., Toronto.

Contents

Preface

In Berlin, eager tourists congregate at the now deserted Checkpoint Charlie to hack off their own individual piece of the concrete wall that for a generation symbolized the division of Germany and Europe. In Moscow and Washington, leaders proclaim friendship and cooperation to solve international crises. The spectre of Communism that once haunted the West dissolves along with the Soviet Union itself.

In this new political landscape the world of secret intelligence has been turned upside down. The CIA and the KGB, once bitter rivals, now talk of sharing the struggle against international terrorism and drugs. Infected by *glasnost,* the KGB hosts a call-in radio show to humanize its image. Hundreds of spies and secret policemen from its former East European satellites are out of work, and in East Berlin one former secret police headquarters has become a popular café. Throughout Germany, the United States is cutting back on its espionage machine.

With the real world of espionage—like the Cold War itself—apparently on its deathbed, voices have inevitably been heard suggesting that the spy novel also is doomed. For without the Berlin Wall and the Iron Curtain, and without the daily tensions of outwitting the secret police in Warsaw, or Prague, or some seedy provincial Communist city, what are our fictional secret agents going to do in the future?

A glance at recent bestseller lists should reassure the fans of spy fiction. One of the most popular has been Tom Clancy's *The Cardinal of the Kremlin,* which concerns a high-placed American "mole" in Moscow. *The Russia House,* John le Carré's novel about a dissident Russian scientist seeking to send information to the West, and Frederick Forsyth's *The Negotiator,* about a conspiracy to derail détente between Moscow and Washington, easily moved up the lists in the very year that history swept away Communist regimes in Eastern Europe. Far from tiring of spy fiction, readers seem to be devouring it as eagerly as ever.

The reason is obvious. As this book shows, spy fiction long predates the Cold War, and those who envisage an unemployed army of spy writers resulting from the revolution of 1989 are ignoring history. Since the genre began in the late nineteenth century, spy writers have exploited national and international phobias of all kinds. As long as nation states exist in a dangerous world, their trade will survive. Writers have always been willing to take new paths when the international landscape changed, and they will do the same in the future.

When the genre began with British novelist William Le Queux the enemy spies were at first French, for France was the historical rival of the British Empire. Then they became Germans with the rise of German naval power under Kaiser William II. British secret agents added Bolsheviks to their list of villains after the First World War and, in the late 1930s, began to fight the Nazis. Since the 1940s fictional agents, British and American, have mostly fought for the West against the Soviet Union and its friends around the world.

The end of the Cold War merely means that the players, not the game itself, have changed. And who can better tell us this than one of the masters of the genre himself, John le Carré? "Do not imagine for one second that just because the Cold War is over the spooks are not having a ball," he said when the Berlin Wall was breached. "In times of such uncertainty as this, the world's intelligence industry will be beavering away like never before." As if to prove him right,

CIA director William H. Webster announced to an audience in Boston in the spring of 1990 that he had created a new directorate to "stay ahead of the curve" and track the changing intelligence requirements of the United States. "Nations around the world are building up their own arsenals," Webster told his audience; "the proliferation of nuclear, chemical, and biological weapons poses serious dangers to regional stability and to the interests of the United States." Washington decision makers, he announced, were relying more than ever on the CIA "to illuminate the playing field—and to understand the rules other nations are playing by."

So what Rudyard Kipling described several decades ago as "the great game" of intelligence goes on. As spy fiction adapts and changes, it too will undoubtedly continue to flourish. For that reason alone, the spy writers of the past have something to tell us.

The Silent Game explores spy novels and spy novelists, British and American, but is by no means a comprehensive guide. A recent bibliography of spy novels published since 1930 contains some thirty-five hundred entries, enough to kill off the enthusiasm and stamina of the most ardent explorer. Inevitably I have left many authors out, and this excursion visits only what I consider to be the major and most significant sites. For those who prefer different ones, there are other tours on the market.

After writing this book, I am not sure I would myself be a very good player in the silent game. When I embarked on the mission it seemed like a glamorous task. But like many a novitiate in the spy trade, I soon found my target elusive, the paperwork expanding, and the files growing exponentially. My publisher and John Duff, my agent, watched with the forbearance of hardened case officers, and then, when the target threatened to escape, brought me firmly back to the mission at hand. Betty Corson helped to make the manuscript read less like an internal CIA memorandum. Kate Hamilton and Ann Phelps decrypted the enigmas of my manuscript to put it all *en clair* for the printer. J.C., as usual, was my most creative debriefer and supportive companion along the way. Others helped, but rather than embark on the invidious task of singling out names I shall plead the privilege of not revealing my sources. But lest anyone suspect I am funded by either the CIA or the KGB, let me add that support in researching this book came mainly from the Ontario

Arts Council, with assistance also from the Social Sciences and Humanities Research Council of Canada.

A final note on terminology. Throughout I have used the terms *agent, secret agent,* and *confidential agent* as being more familiar to the general reader. In the twilight world of secret intelligence there is, in fact, an important technical distinction between an intelligence officer and an agent. The former usually operates under some kind of official cover and clandestinely runs one or many agents who are never allowed near the office. Kim Philby, for example, was an M.I.6 officer but a KGB agent. James Bond is only an agent carrying out orders and in real life would never meet Miss Moneypenny. But this is not a distinction I have drawn in the book. Instead I have followed most of my writers of fiction and, I suspect, the majority of their readers for whom the term *agent* has come to signify anyone who works in the mysterious world of the silent game. As for the British Secret Intelligence Service (SIS), I have on occasion referred to it as M.I.6—and, indeed, the terms are synonymous.

The Silent Game

Introduction

Let me lend you the History of Contemporary Society. It's in hundreds of volumes, but most of them are sold in cheap editions: *Death in Piccadilly, The Ambassador's Diamonds, The Theft of the Naval Papers....*

Graham Greene, *The Ministry of Fear*

I

Go into any bookstore, turn on the television, check out the weekend movies. There, promising suspense, sex, melodrama, and adventure, will be a generous choice of thrillers. On the bookshelves alone will be several hundred, and if it's a month or so since your last visit, there'll be at least a dozen new ones. Thrillers are one of the most popular forms of fiction in the world. They account for a quarter of all new books published in the United States. Of the world's fifty most translated authors in 1967, eleven were thriller writers—and two of them outnumbered Shakespeare and George Bernard Shaw in sales.

Why this popularity? Literary critics have pointed out that modern thrillers contain all the ingredients of epic poetry. They are essentially mythic stories about struggles between good and evil in which heroes hunt and are hunted in order to put the world to rights, contemporary versions of ancient tales that satisfy enduring human needs. "The thriller hero," writes Ralph Harper in *The World of the Thriller*, "is the hero in classical and recognizable form." In the thriller hero, Marshall McLuhan suggested, there is something for everyone to admire. Or, as Raymond Chandler unforgettably put it, "Down these mean streets a man must go who is not himself mean, who is neither tarnished nor afraid.... He is the hero, he is everything. He must be a complete man and yet an unusual man."

So far, so good. But if we want to know more about the particular type of thriller called the spy novel, we need to go further. Spy novels deal with archetypes, but they also mirror the time and place of their writing. Timeless in their appeal, they are time-bound in the language they employ, in the external fabric with which they are clothed. They involve heroes and villains, but they are particular types of heroes and villains—spies and secret agents—and they are set in the world of international intrigue. Those of us who have no interest in that world will probably not enjoy spy novels. Instead, we will find our need for fictional heroism satisfied elsewhere—in the western or the crime thriller, perhaps.

This book is about spy novels and the people who write them. When and why did these tales emerge as a best-selling form of fiction? Who were the writers who pioneered, established, and then perfected the genre? What was their motive? Were they spies themselves, and what did they really know about the craft of spying? These are not literary questions—they are but explorations of the people and the world that created spy fiction.

Spy novels are a twentieth-century phenomenon, set in the "real world" of contemporary international intrigue, violence, and espionage. The world they portray is one of danger, complexity, unpredictability, and—increasingly—imminent catastrophe and annihilation. If the finished canvas is often lurid, this is hardly because the artist has used synthetic materials. War, revolution, subversion, terror, genocide, and the threat of nuclear obliteration are the authentic experience of twentieth-century man. None of us is safe, wherever we are. No one who travels is secure from the random terrorist bomb in the bus station, the guerrilla attack at the airport, the hijacker with a beltful of grenades and a mouthful of slogans. No one who stays at home is immune from the possibility of the accidental or deliberate pressing of the nuclear button. Since the spy novel emerged at the beginning of this century, it has provided a barometer for measuring the fragility of our world. "Did you ever reflect, Mr. Leithen, how precarious is the tenure of the civilisation we boast about?" asks Lumley, the evil genius of John Buchan's *The Power-House*, published in 1916. Spy fiction has continued to ask that question ever since.

From the beginning, spy novels were, and have remained, novels of crisis. While secret agents and spies are at the centre of their plots, they are rarely, as Allen Dulles once lamented, about the "craft of intelligence". National vulnerabilities and fears symbolized by spies and spying are their principal concern. The plots paint a romanticized or highly dramatized picture of espionage. A novel depicting the true life of a secret agent would probably bore the reader to death. Instead, agents are portrayed in extraordinary moments of great national or international destiny: saving the country from invasion, protecting the vital plans of top-secret weapons, destroying the enemy's imminent conspiracies, and so on.

Because spy novels are set in the world of international rivalry and intrigue, they are, despite their escapism, highly political. They provide an obvious way to explore patriotism and loyalty, subversion and treason, paranoia and persecution. More than other forms of popular fiction they deal with national passions and phobias. Behind the surface melodrama lie the authors' beliefs about the world and their nations' place within it. They reflect, and respond to, the changing climate of international affairs.

Although spy novels seldom tell us much about the realities of espionage, they must seem plausible in order to carry conviction. The most successful spy novelists have often been spies, or at least have worked in professions closely involved with intelligence. This is almost a tradition in Britain, the original home of the spy novel, where the list is long and time-honoured. "All through its tortuous, dotty history," as spy writer John le Carré himself has put it, "British Intelligence has conducted a distraught, sometimes hilarious love affair with the British novelist." William Le Queux, who began it all, was a journalist who dabbled in amateur espionage. Both Valentine Williams and Ian Fleming were journalists, and the latter served in naval intelligence while the former worked in secret propaganda. John Buchan, A.E.W. Mason, Compton Mackenzie, Somerset Maugham, Graham Greene, and le Carré all had direct personal experience of intelligence work. Thanks to the establishment of the CIA, the United States is now building its own tradition of the agent-novelist.

The boundaries of fact and fiction in the world of espionage have often been blurred. If we are to believe one source, Soviet military intelligence was so impressed by the details of Somerset Maugham's secret service work during the Bolshevik Revolution provided in *Ashenden* in the 1930s that they advised that a special study be made of British spy fiction. And this was not so ridiculous as it sounds: *Ashenden* appears at one time to have been obligatory reading for noviciates into Britain's Secret Intelligence Service (SIS). During the Second World War, when the United States set up the OSS (Office of Strategic Services), Compton Mackenzie's novel *Water on the Brain* became background reading for trainees. Such examples give credence to an amusing story told by Hugh Greene in *The Spy's Bedside Book*, a classic anthology for the spy fiction *aficionado* he and his brother Graham edited in the 1950s. He tells of going into his favourite second-hand bookstore in London to add to his collection of spy fiction. To his surprise, he found the shelf empty, an embarrassed assistant explaining that a customer had recently bought the entire collection. The customer was none other than an attaché at one of the East European embassies.

If this seems like clumsy footwork by the KGB or its affiliates, consider the CIA. It once devised a plan to assassinate Fidel Castro by use of an exploding cigar—a lethal device introduced in 1899 by William Le Queux in *England's Peril*, one of the very first spy novels. Perhaps the CIA has its own experts on spy fiction who carefully scrutinize the booksellers' lists. If so, they will certainly come up with some familiar names. In former days, readers in the know could speculate about the real-life figures who inspired such characters as Richard Hannay or James Bond. In the 1980s the spy novel as *roman-à-clef* has entered the armoury of the spies themselves. The monumental struggle that factionalized the CIA in the 1970s on the issue of a Soviet super-mole within the agency led to the firing of James Jesus Angleton, arch-proponent of the KGB penetration theory, and to massive purges at lower levels. Ever since, disgruntled ex-employees and other interested parties have continued the struggle through fiction. Spy novels themselves have now become weapons in the silent game.

II

Kim, Rudyard Kipling's valedictory novel about India, first described espionage as a game—in his case, as "the great game". Published in 1901, when the immediate threat to the British Empire lay on India's north-west frontier, the novel tells the story of Kim, a young boy of Anglo-Irish origin, who is recruited by the secret service. Kim's adventures take him across India, keeping a close watch on enemy agents seeking to steal the jewel of the Empire. In the course of the book we learn one or two rules about espionage, rules that became axioms of all subsequent spy fiction: the Great Game never ceases day or night and will end only when everyone is dead; the players of the Great Game are beyond protection; and no man can follow the Game when he is pestered by women. We also taste the patriotic flavour characteristic of early spy fiction. Kipling was an ardent imperialist, his political sensibility finely tuned to the cadences of imperial decline and fall. In the Edwardian years he was on the radical right of British politics, vociferously supporting the introduction of conscription, enthusiastically praising the founding of the Boy Scouts by his friend Baden-Powell, and opposing reform of the House of Lords. A xenophobe, he saw the hand of foreign agents in many of Britain's pre-war strikes. Later he was briefly active in the Liberty League, whose purpose was to alert Britain to the dangers of Bolshevism. In general, he saw decline and fall all around him until his death in 1936.

None the less, *Kim* hardly qualifies as a spy novel. It is, as Kipling himself acknowledged, a plotless and picaresque novel, a magical evocation of youth and Kipling's beloved India. It was a spiritual godfather rather than a true begetter of the new genre.

Two other well-known novels of the same period are also relatives rather than parents. Baroness Emmuska Orczy's immensely popular *The Scarlet Pimpernel*, which appeared in 1905, is firmly set in the late eighteenth century, and makes no claim on the reader's knowledge of the contemporary world. But its hero, Sir Percy Blakeney, carries out his undercover missions with a distinctly modern flair. Indeed, Blakeney is remarkably like the later Bulldog Drummond created by "Sapper" (Herman Cyril McNeile) years later: tall, broad-shouldered, and "a year or two on the right side of thirty." The lazy expression in Blakeney's deep-set eyes and his reputation as an intellectual lightweight repeatedly fool those who underestimate his ingenuity in leading his compatriots against the murderous forces of the French revolutionary terror. Orczy's inspiration seems clear, but there its place in the history of the spy novel must end.

Joseph Conrad's *The Secret Agent* (1907), on the other hand, is set in the contemporary world. It is certainly a political novel, and a contemporary review noted that it contained "all the stuff whereof shilling shockers are made." But, as critic Julian Symons has rightly observed, it is far too concerned with characterization to be regarded as a thriller—a comment he also extends to Conrad's later novel *Under Western Eyes*. For all that, Conrad's works show distinct affinities of sentiment with spy novelists of his age, and the fear of chaos, social disintegration, and revolution lies close to the surface.

III

The spy novel emerged as a genre in its own right at the beginning of the twentieth century. The most important reason is indicated in one of its early examples, *Revelations of the Secret Service* (1911), in which the pioneer author William Le Queux introduced his protagonist, British secret agent Hugh Morrice. Morrice, Le Queux declared, is "a veritable prince of secret agents", and "many a time has secret information supplied by him turned the tide of political events in Great Britain's favour."

The belief that the intervention of secret agents was necessary for the tide of international affairs to flow in Britain's favour gives us the vital clue. For the appearance of the spy novel was inextricably linked with the crisis of confidence in British power and security that obsessed the Edwardian age. The doubts that had been growing during the last decade of Victoria's reign rose to a chorus of woes during the Boer War. On New Year's Eve, 1900, one of the country's most widely read dailies, Lord Northcliffe's *Daily Mail*, uttered an apocalyptic warning: "England is entering stormy seas and the time may be near when we shall have to fight for our life." This alarmist message shocked those accustomed to the securities of the Pax Britannica. Coming from a newspaper accustomed to delivering shrill boasts of imperial might, this pessimism was a clear sign of a new disquiet about Britain's security. Over the next decade, several measures were taken to strengthen Britain's defences. The Committee of Imperial Defence was created in 1903, and a series of diplomatic changes put an end to isolation, marked by the alliance with Japan in 1902, the Anglo-French Entente of 1904, and the Anglo-Russian agreement of 1907. From then on, Britain increasingly allied herself in the Triple Entente with France and Russia against the Dual Alliance of Germany and Austro-Hungary—alliance systems that eventually went to war against each other in 1914. These changes led to a shift of priority from Empire to Europe, and the gradual alignment of military planning with the French. The period, in short, was one of revolutionary change in Britain's external relations, overshadowed by the growing power of Germany.

Extreme forms of the increasing insecurity took shape in invasion scares. These had recurred at intervals ever since the Napoleonic wars, intensifying after the Franco-Prussian war of 1870–71. They had inspired a genre of fiction, the invasion novel, in which popular writers painted lurid pictures of Britain's fate at the hands of an invading—usually French—army. Discussions in 1882 over the proposed Channel Tunnel had created nightmares of Britain being infiltrated by French spies disguised as restaurant owners, waiters, bookmakers, and pastry cooks. Invasion fears grew even more pronounced in the 1890s as rapid advances in naval technology threatened Britain's maritime supremacy. Less than twelve months before the *Mail*'s warning about approaching stormy seas, the influential journalist W.T. Stead had suggested that Britain's preoccupation in South Africa made an invasion of Britain by Germany and France a real possibility. German waiters in London, he speculated, might act as saboteurs—a theme soon to be found in early spy fiction. The cry was taken up elsewhere. Lord Roberts of Kandahar, hero of the Boer War and Britain's most popular living general, campaigned energetically on behalf of the National Service League, a pressure group for conscription. The government discounted the threat, but predictably it inspired dramatic scare-mongering in the popular press.

What gave edge to this speculation was the belief that an invasion would be helped by foreign spies. Spy fever climaxed in 1908–09 during a national debate over the Anglo-German naval race, when public fears of German military might—stimulated by a vigorous campaign in the popular press—led to a flurry of reported sightings of spies. Lord Roberts, for one, solemnly told the House of Lords that there were some 80,000 German soldiers in various disguises already within the United Kingdom. In official quarters much of this was sensibly discounted as hysteria, and when war finally came in 1914 the government could find only twenty-one alleged German agents to arrest. Only one was brought to trial.

None the less, War Office and Whitehall bureaucrats seized the opportunity to establish the Secret Service Bureau, Britain's first organized intelligence service. It was divided into Home and Foreign sections, which eventually evolved into M.I.5 and M.I.6 respectively. Simultaneously, the government moved to strengthen the Official Secrets Act, rushing a new and more stringent bill through Parliament with indecent haste in 1911. With the formation of the Secret Service Bureau in 1909, Britain's rulers acknowledged the need for drastic measures to protect British security in the new century. Britain now formally joined other European powers such as France and Germany in playing the game of international espionage.

This contest—"this silent game of ours", as one of its earliest fictional protagonists called it—was by no means new. British players had been rehearsing on the margins of the Empire for several years, while the public had recently been entertained by some dramatic professional performances on the Continent. None the less the league that Britain joined was of relatively recent date. True, espionage is a time-honoured practice in international affairs—"the second oldest profession"—but it was only after the Franco-Prussian War of 1870–71 that the pressures of technological change made espionage a regular, institutionalized, and permanent feature of the European scene. Moving steadily towards the centre of the stage, its dramas and melodramas provided colourful copy for the rapidly expanding mass journalism of the *fin de siècle*. The best-remembered incident remains the Dreyfus Affair. For six years following 1894, when Captain Alfred Dreyfus of the French army was wrongly convicted by court martial of spying for Germany and exiled to Devil's Island, the *cause célèbre* threatened the survival of the Third French Republic. Supporters of Dreyfus, mostly radicals and progressives, accused the army and conservatives of indulging in a cover-up and plotting to overthrow the regime. There were press campaigns and violent street clashes, all of which served to highlight the powerful ramifications of international espionage.

The popular press exploited the story for all it was worth. In England the *Daily Mail* made such a feast of it that even Lord

Northcliffe wondered whether they were not overdoing it—to which the editor, Kennedy Jones, replied blandly that this was impossible. "This is the biggest newspaper story since the crucifixion of Jesus Christ," he told his boss. For most of the *Mail*'s readers, Jones claimed with undoubted truth, the affair was no more and no less than a daily whodunit. Its ingredients were irresistible, with "spies, stolen documents, foreign agents, suicides in jail, mysterious disappearances, veiled women, midnight visits, the whole bag of tricks." This particular bag of tricks certainly did the *Mail* no harm, and by 1900 its circulation reached a million. It was a lesson not lost on writers of popular fiction, and for spy writers such as Le Queux the Dreyfus Affair proved a goldmine.

IV

Recognition that spying was an integral part of British statecraft came slowly and reluctantly, disguised by many fictions. Much early espionage was amateurish and too often indistinguishable from eccentricities associated with representatives of Britain's upper classes. The importance of good intelligence in military matters had been recognized as early as 1873, with the establishment of an Intelligence Department of the army, and in the 1880s the navy followed suit. Most of their work was confined to the collation and evaluation of public intelligence. But the army sent out spies to explore particularly sensitive areas, mainly on the far-flung boundaries of the Empire. Carried out by officers ostensibly on leave, these explorations were never called espionage. After all, had not Lord Raglan in the official history of the Crimean War declared that the gathering of knowledge by clandestine means was repulsive to the feelings of an English gentleman? And were not the officers of the Empire all gentlemen?

One of the best known of these early spies was Robert Baden-Powell, hero of Mafeking and founder of the Boy Scouts. Under the guise of such typical English hobbies as butterfly-collecting, trout-fishing, partridge-shooting, landscape-painting, and hiking in remote and inaccessible areas, Baden-Powell conducted numerous secret missions in Kashmir, Turkey, Bosnia-Herzegovina, Dalmatia, and even Germany itself. Like Lord Roberts, Baden-Powell came to believe fervently in the non-existent German spy menace, and during the 1908 spy scare he added his voice to the chorus of Cassandras by speculating on the likelihood of a German landing during the August Bank Holiday weekend. The original idea behind the Boy Scouts was that they could act as a youthful counter-espionage force to detect German spies at work in Britain.

Baden-Powell's memoirs, *My Adventures as a Spy*, nicely capture the spirit of high-jinks and innocent adventure in which he clothed his exploits. A man who was constantly exhorting his fellow men to strengthen their moral fibre through physical fitness, Baden-Powell saw in espionage some of the same virtues he saw in cold baths and rigorous abstention from temptations of the flesh. "Spying," he robustly declared, "is a great recuperator for the man tired of life." But although he was bold enough to use the word "spying", he carefully demoted it to the respectable rank of routine military activity. "Spying," he assured his readers, "is in reality reconnaissance in disguise." Furthermore, he drew a firm distinction between "traitor spies", who were beyond the pale, and "unpaid men doing it for the love of the thing in the name of patriotic duty", for whom he had nothing but glowing praise.

Like Kipling, Baden-Powell saw espionage as a game—"the sport of spying", he enthusiastically dubbed it. And for the English gentleman sport was by definition amateur. This, of course, disguised its imperatives of deceit and trickery, which went against the grain of the nineteenth-century gentleman's code of behaviour—a code that had been reinforced by the values and ethos of the public schools of the Victorian age. By the end of the century, public-schoolboy morality was lending its unmistakable vocabulary to conventional views. "The very term 'spy' conveys to our mind something dishonourable and disloyal," wrote Colonel G.A. Furse in his handbook *Information in War*, published in 1895. "A spy, in the general acceptance of the term, is a low sneak...." Two years later, the critic Andrew Lang, commenting on spies employed during the Jacobite uprisings, told readers of *Cornhill Magazine* that "when one first meets a new, hitherto unmasked spy in manuscripts, one starts as from a rattlesnake. 'You, a gentleman,' one exclaims, 'you were, for years, a double-faced hired traitor.' "

Rattlesnakes and low sneaks spies may have been, but by the end of the nineteenth century they were becoming a regular part of international life. Attitudes adjusted slowly to practice. A variety of justifications, often accompanied by much verbal camouflage, began to appear. Patriotic duty provided the main one; by the beginning of the new century its requirements had considerably dented the code of Europe's gentlemen. This acceptance of the "gentleman spy" was rarely stated but was implicit in the denunciations of his antithesis, the "traitor spy", the man who betrayed his own country either by spying for others or by selling information. Baden-Powell spoke for many when he declared that for traitor spies there was absolutely no excuse, as their behaviour could only have mercenary motives. "Fortunately," he added sanctimoniously, "the Briton is not as a rule a corruptible character."

The most explicit argument in support of espionage was that it was legitimate self-defence in a hostile international world. Convincing arguments were found in analogies from the domestic sphere. Few gentlemen doubted that drastic measures were justified to defend society against revolutionaries. Irish terrorism had been a factor on the political scene for thirty years, and in the 1890s there was a wave of dramatic anarchist assassinations. The Special Branch had originated as the Special Irish Branch of the Metropolitan Police, and it was common knowledge that this secret police force was employing agents, informers, and *agents provocateurs*. While there were moral doubts about the latter, few voices were raised against "political spies". The *Quarterly Review* of 1893 endorsed their use when it declared that "There is no wickedness either in receiving and paying for the evidence of an informer, or in employing a secret emissary to discover the perpetrators of offences against the welfare of the State...the political spy and the plain-clothes constable are morally exactly on a level...the faithful political spy, like the faithful detective, deserves well of the State that employs him." If political spies were necessary to defend society against Irish nationalists, ni-hilists, and anarchists, then international spies were essential to defend Britain's interests against the predatory attentions of her increasingly powerful rivals.

By the beginning of the twentieth century the British public was ready to accept the need for secret intelligence agents. But their task was presented as mere counter-espionage, a purely defensive measure, a response to the aggressions of others. The moral obloquy attaching to espionage was transferred to the foreigners who made the activity necessary. Only *foreigners* used spies. The British were gentlemen acting secretly to defend their nation in an increasingly perfidious world.

V

Prominent in the chorus clamouring for Britain to arm itself with a secret service were popular novelists. Invasion novels had preached against British complacency in the face of threats from foreign powers. Often they were little more than thinly disguised propaganda for rearmament, paranoid tracts fuelled by the rela-tive decline of British power and the rise of powerful Continental rivals. As the machinations of enemy spies in preparing such imaginary invasions moved closer to the centre of these dramas, writers began to argue for an organized British secret service to counter the threat and compete with the services of the Continen-tal powers. As invasion novels turned into spy novels and merged with adventure stories, they continued the tradition of propa-ganda for a conservative cause. From the beginning they were designed not only to thrill and entertain but also to instruct and educate, delivering messages alerting their audience to dangers threatening the nation. Ever since, this has remained a powerful tradition within the genre.

CHAPTER ONE

Against the Grain

Even though it be against our grain, as Englishmen, to employ spies ourselves, yet it is daily becoming more necessary. Every nation in the world has its elaborate secret service; therefore England must not sleep and allow other nations to undermine her prestige.

William Le Queux, *Her Majesty's Minister*

For many years Britain's best-selling Edwardian spy author was the unwilling recipient of letters from a reader who regularly sent him long and elaborate criticisms. The critic read nothing but the author's novels and the Bible, and of the former he purchased every new book in several editions. Eventually he went mad and was removed to a lunatic asylum. When his books were counted, it was found that he possessed 418 volumes by William Le Queux.

Those who know their Le Queux will certainly understand the fate of this anonymous reader. Those who don't will surely be intrigued by a best-selling author who could so mesmerize a man otherwise solely addicted to the Scriptures.

William Tufnell Le Queux sprang to public fame with his highly successful invasion novel, *The Great War in England in 1897*, which rapidly passed through many editions and was translated into several languages. Setting the pattern for several of his later best-sellers, the novel appeared as a serial in *Answers*, Lord Northcliffe's first publishing venture, in 1893. Reflecting the deep concern about British security occasioned by the recently signed military convention between Britain's main imperial rivals, France and Russia, it remains one of the best-known fictions of imaginary war. But it is also a tale of spying, for the invasion is provoked by an act of espionage, and its central villain, Count von Beilstein, is an enemy spy.

Following the success of *The Great War*, Le Queux became a full-time writer of popular novels, producing over forty in the next ten years. They sold extremely well, and soon he was earning as much as H.G. Wells or Thomas Hardy for his writing. In 1903 a survey of the twenty-one largest public libraries in England indicated that among writers of the third rank—classified rather vaguely as "below standard"—Le Queux ranked third in popularity. By then he was known as the "Master of Mystery". Queen Alexandra was reputedly so enamoured of his work that she had placed a standing order for all new Le Queux novels. If so, the royal library must have expanded quickly. By the time of Edward VII's death in 1910 Le Queux had written another forty volumes, and by the outbreak of war he had published another dozen on top of that. Practically all were reissued as cheap editions, and many appeared in translation.

If *The Great War* was a spy novel in embryo, then in his next few novels Le Queux acted as chief midwife to the new genre. In *Whoso Findeth a Wife* (1897) the drama focuses on the Russian theft of Foreign Office secrets, while in *England's Peril* (published in 1899—only months after the Fashoda crisis, occasioned by imperial rivalry in Africa, had brought England

and France to the brink of war) the author introduced his audience to the devilish machinations of Gaston La Touche, head of the French secret service and a man of iron nerve and utter unscrupulousness. The novel contains murder, blackmail, and theft of highly sensitive documents, and—anticipating the CIA's campaign against Fidel Castro by some sixty years—introduces that deadly anti-personnel weapon, the exploding cigar. Only the French, the patriotic reader would conclude, could stoop so low as to use this weapon against an English Member of Parliament enjoying postprandial relaxation. Fortunately, protection lay close at hand in the shape of the British secret service. "It works in silence and secrecy," Le Queux assured his readers, "yet many are its successful counterplots against the machinations of England's enemies." *Of Royal Blood* (1900) expands on the threat to British secrets posed by the *cabinets noirs* of the European powers, while *Her Majesty's Minister* (1901) speaks directly to public anxiety arising from the Boer War. Le Queux depicted the dangers to Britain's position in the Mediterranean as a result of French intrigue, dangers caused this time by the tapping of secret telegraphic links between the Foreign Office and Windsor. Even more successful was *The Under-Secretary* (1902), in which a hapless under-secretary to the Prime Minister is "the unfortunate victim of as vile and ingenious a conspiracy as ever was formed against us by dastardly spies from across the Channel." French guile plays a prominent part, too, in *Secrets of the Foreign Office*, published the following year. This novel, describing the doings of Duckworth Drew of the Secret Service, has rightly become a classic. For Duckworth Drew presents us with the archetype of the gentleman secret agent who strides across the pages of generations of subsequent spy novels.

Let us pause for a moment and take a closer look at Drew. As chief confidential agent of the British government, and next to the Foreign Secretary one of the most powerful and important pillars of England's supremacy, he can boast of having had his skills recognized by no less a person than Bismarck. The Iron Chancellor, Le Queux tells us, once said of Drew that he had half a dozen nationalities and an equal number of personalities. We know that he has at least two, for it quickly emerges that the agent's real name is Dreux, and that his father was French. But although he is technically of French nationality and has had a foreign education, he is English to the backbone. He has been through Oxbridge, and when we encounter him, has been in England's service for at least fifteen years. Indeed, were he not prone to the rare confidence about his past, we would never dream of mistaking him for anything but English. There is a touch of Sherlock Holmes about this pipe-smoking bachelor with rooms in Guildford Street, Bloomsbury, who has a man, Boyd, to take care of most of his needs. Sent on numerous secret missions abroad, he is always thankful to return home to his grandfather chair and the comfort of a whisky and soda. This, he confesses, he prefers to the sloppy *cognac et siphon* of the continental café. In similar vein, he confesses that an English country house, with its old oak and silver and its air of solidity, is always delightful after the "flimsy gimcracks of Continental life." He is fond of riding to hounds, and when the occasion permits he rides with the Fitzwilliam. Although he is discreet about his age, we think of him as in his late thirties: old enough to have recovered from the heartache of a passionate and thwarted romance while a junior attaché, yet young enough to win the hearts of the many ladies he meets on his travels.

Drew knows Europe like the back of his hand, and the capitals of the Continent are as familiar to him as the clubs of the West End. If he is not at a president's reception in the Elysée, he is staying incognito at the Hotel de Rome on Berlin's Unter den Linden or at de Boek's on the corner of the Avenue Louise and the Boulevard de Waterloo in Brussels. And if he is not there, then we will probably find him catching the *wagon-lit* to Rome, the Sud-Express to Madrid, or on his way to an official ball at the Quirinal. He may even be on the Via Venti Settembre in Rome, walking to or from the British embassy. Our best bet, however, may be the small and discreet Hôtel de Nice in Paris or the Brasserie Universale on the Avenue de l'Opéra. For, as a man who can pass as a native Frenchman, Drew is particularly effective at secret service in France. And as the new century dawns, France still remains Britain's main Continental rival.

And what feats he accomplishes for the Crown! He is constantly called upon by the Foreign Secretary, the Earl of Macclesfield, to save the country from disaster. As his creator never ceases to remind us, the European powers are ever plotting against England, whose position is far from secure. "We are weak, Drew, terribly weak," reveals Macclesfield in a moment of appalling candour. For this is the era of the Boer War, and the conflict has attracted the predatory attention of jealous neighbours across the Channel.

With Drew at hand, however, we may rest unalarmed. It is thanks to his skill that plans for a German-Russian alliance to break Britain's power in the Far East and India are foiled, that foreign powers are prevented from intervening in South Africa, and that a Franco-Italian alliance that would destroy Britain's power in the Mediterranean is frustrated. It is also Drew's doing that the plans for a new Belgian rifle and a new French submarine find their way into the hands of the British military authorities, and it is with his assistance that the Italian secret service successfully deploys a sophisticated electric-eye detonating device that destroys the French naval defences at Villefranche. None of this is accomplished without Drew risking the gravest injury to life and limb: he escapes death from a deadly pin impregnated with a substance unknown to toxicologists, comes close to oblivion from an exploding cigar which at the last moment he deftly returns to his would-be assassin, is shot at point-blank range by a spy who fortunately has bad aim, and miraculously extricates himself from a cellar filled with poison gas.

In the face of such tribulations, we are grateful and indeed impressed to find that Drew retains at all times the sang-froid of the English gentleman. Of course, he has flattered us on numerous occasions by suggesting that we are intimately familiar with his Continental haunts, and we are inclined to be indulgent. "If you know Rome, you will recollect that half way up the Corso...there is a small white-painted shop where one can get English tea and cake at four o'clock," he says in introducing one of his adventures, and we certainly feel that we have been there, even if the nearest we have been to Rome is the closest pizza parlour.

With such flattery we can easily overlook the fact that, while he usually describes himself as a secret agent or a diplomatic freelancer, Drew is a spy. He says so himself. One day while strolling through Nice, enjoying the sensuous colours of the Mediterranean and the palms and oleanders, and apparently unconcerned about rumours of war between England and France circulating during the Fashoda crisis, he meets an old friend. It is the Marchese Meliani, sole surviving descendant of a noble Sicilian family and a serving officer in the Italian navy. Meliani confides that he has been entrusted by his government with a most important and secret mission. In the event of Britain and France engaging in war, the Italian navy will co-operate with the British to strike at French ports along the Mediterranean. He asks Drew for his assistance, but gives him an ominous warning: "Reflect well before you promise your help, for by assisting me you stand a good chance of arrest and deportation to Cayenne." Without fear or hesitation Drew responds to this challenge: "I am an Englishman, despite the fact that I am a spy. I promise you unreservedly all the assistance in my power."

"I am an Englishman, despite the fact that I am a spy"— the sentence has reverberated down through the decades since Drew proudly offered his assistance to Meliani. The superficial incompatibility of the profession of spy with the honourable avocation of English gentleman is boldly swept aside, rendering British espionage acceptable to the reader. At the same time we are reassured that English supremacy remains securely based on the broad shoulders of those entitled to rule, the gentlemen who inhabit its clublands.

In case there was any doubt about the matter, Le Queux rein-carnated Drew in a succession of characters who were patently chips off the same block. Published in the year following the appearance of Duckworth Drew, *The Man from Downing Street* features Jack Jardine—head of the British Secret Service and a book-collecting bachelor with rooms in Great Russell Street, an ancestral home in Cheshire, and a commission in the cavalry. Jardine was followed by Cuthbert Croom, the hero of *Confessions of a Ladies' Man*, a Wykehamist whose bookish personal inclinations are constantly frustrated by his patriotic duty, which demands that he mingle with the meretricious glitterati in order to pull the country back from the brink of danger. Above all, there is the unforgettable Hugh Morrice, chief travelling agent of the Confidential Department and hero of *Revelations of the Secret Service*. Morrice combines all the virtues of his predecessors: he is an accomplished linguist, a brilliant raconteur, an all-round sportsman, a polished diplomat, a born adventurer, "a cosmopolitan of cosmopolitans", and the personal friend of half a dozen sovereigns.

It is easy to underestimate Le Queux's appeal for unsophisticated readers: his "revelations" of the hidden corridors of international power, his reduction of complex events to dramatic duels between heroes and villains, and his repeated flattery of his "dear reader, who has so often strolled down the Champs Elysées..."—a reader who may well be an ill-paid clerk living in furnished rooms off the Edgware Road.

But what about the man himself? In feeding his readers' fantasies, Le Queux was also fuelling his own, and from an early stage led a Walter Mitty life saving Britain from imaginary perils. Duckworth Drew is but a transparent disguise for Le Queux. He claimed to be a secret agent of the British government, and to know the secrets of many others. In dismissing suggestions that he was a paid agent, he shrewdly encouraged speculation about the *unpaid* nature of his services to the Crown—claims he took very seriously indeed. He had, he said, been employed in a voluntary secret service set up by Lord Roberts while the latter was Commander-in-Chief, and in his service had carried out espionage tasks in the Near East and Italy. He had also spent much of his vast royalties travelling as a secret agent of the British government, which made him a target for the German secret service. In Berlin there was a price on his head, documents had been stolen from his London home, and his life had been threatened. In *Who's Who* he listed revolver practice as one of his main hobbies, and rumour had it that he was always armed. Distant relatives believe to this day that he perished at the hands of the Bolsheviks while working as a secret agent for Winston Churchill in the Soviet Union.

The truth bears little relation to any of these claims. His father, also called William Le Queux (the name, Le Queux claimed, meant "the king's head cook" in Norman)—a Frenchman from Châteauroux—was a lowly draper's assistant in Southwark, south of London, when his English wife, Henrietta Henson, gave birth to her first son in London on July 2, 1864. For reasons unknown, Le Queux spent his childhood travelling between England, France, and Italy, and, as his later *Who's Who* entry claimed, no doubt euphemistically, he was "educated privately" in London and at Pegli, near Genoa. After trying his hand as an artist and writer in the Latin Quarter in Paris, he eventually drifted into journalism via the English-language *Paris Morning News*. Then, in the late 1880s, he became a sub-editor on the London *Globe*, then its foreign editor, and from there he graduated to the mass-circulation popular press and the *Daily Mail*.

As a novelist who once proudly boasted that he had "never, in all the long list of novels that stand to [his] name, written a single line that a child of twelve could not understand," Le Queux was admirably suited to the brave new world of the popular press emerging in the 1890s. The *Daily Mail* had provided him with his breakthrough by serializing some of his earliest novels, and long after he assumed a full-time career as a novelist he kept close links with the newspaper, working, for example, as a correspondent for Northcliffe during the Balkan Wars of 1912–13.

Le Queux published his first novel in 1890. During the remainder of his life—he died in 1927—he produced novels at the average rate of over five a year, an output even more prolific than his better-known contemporary Edgar Wallace. By 1893 he was able to devote himself to a full-time writing career, and soon gave free rein to his insatiable wanderlust.

"I have led, and still lead," Le Queux confessed proudly in his later years, "a wandering life. My custom has been never to have even a *pied-à-terre* in one place longer than a year."

An habitual and indefatigable visitor to the capitals, spas, and resorts of Europe, the portly Le Queux became a familiar figure in the minor gentlemen's clubs of London catering to the capital's quasi-Bohemian and literary fringe, where, his biographer claimed, "he was outstandingly the life and soul of the party." He also spent a lot of time in Italy, and some time around 1900 acquired an Italian wife in Florence, where he was a well-known figure in the English colony. Like much else in his life, she remains a mystery. The marriage was never recorded in *Who's Who*, unlike most of his acquisitions, and she subsequently disappeared from view.

If his personal life remains elusive, however, Le Queux eagerly glamorized his more public activities. He was an untiring self-publicist, an early example of the man who became famous for being famous. "He has been associated with so many different kinds of people, ranging from Emperors to Paupers, from Saints to Scoundrels," blurted a typical dust-wrapper, "that he has practically experienced several lives in one...." Prodigiously energetic and self-important, he spent considerable time ingratiating himself with the minor aristocracy and second-rate royalty of the lesser European courts, and was an inveterate name-dropper. The gossip he collected later provided the bulk of his 1923 memoirs, *Things I Know about Kings, Celebrities, and Crooks*, a compendium of trivia sufficient to weary even the most ardent follower of royalty. Or, as the dust-wrapper ambiguously put it, "the whole book is a revelation of much that would otherwise remain unknown about many outstanding personalities and events." He sought social acceptance avidly, although his climbing was confined to the foothills of the social landscape. He was proud to declare himself a Knight Commander of the Order of San Marino, although this title was awarded merely for acting as the republic's honorary consul in London. He collected other orders, too—by 1909 he was Commander of the orders of St. Savia of Serbia, Danilo of Montenegro, and the Crown of Italy—and he prominently displayed these on his more than ample chest for portraits appearing in books and magazines. They had been awarded, he liked to suggest, for important secret service, and reflected his "intimate knowledge of the secret service of Continental powers."

His pretensions— or delusions—also extended into technical fields. His later spy stories often revolved around clandestine wireless transmissions by German spies from remote parts of

Britain, and he claimed to be an expert on the subject for he had dabbled in wireless transmission in these pioneer days. "I think I may justly claim," he told readers of *Radio Times* in 1923 with his usual lack of modesty, "to have been one of the earliest experimenters in the field of radio-telegraphy." Here again, he considerably embellished the truth. If he was prominent in the small circle of early wireless enthusiasts in England, it was merely as a novelist of wireless mysteries, not as a pioneer.

But Le Queux was a man of irrepressible boyish enthusiasms, and he quickly passed to the next, and last, great passion of his life: skiing. In the troubled years of post-war Europe he found solace on the slopes of Switzerland. There, he led his readers to believe, he graced the *piste* with that facility which came so effortlessly to him in all his undertakings. But this, too, was a fantasy. A man who had sought headlines much of his life, he can only have greeted with chagrin those in the *Daily News* of January 1923, which informed its readers of the "Novelist's Escape". But far from revealing some perilous skirmish with foreign spies, the article told how the intrepid hero, the worldwide adventurer, had fallen into a snowdrift "in such a position that he was helpless to rise", and had stayed there for several hours until help arrived. This was not at all dignified, and it portended his less than dignified death four years later. By this time he was nursing a deep grievance at official rejections of his pre-war allegations about the spy menace, and had little but contempt for the British secret service. Indeed, he went so far as to express regret publicly in 1923 that he had not adhered to his French nationality, which would have enabled him to "really be instrumental in strafing the Hun." Far from perishing in the Soviet Union on His Majesty's secret service, he died in bed from heart failure at the Links Hotel at Knokke-sur-Mer on the Belgian coast on October 13, 1927. Dying as he had lived, he had been recording the reminiscences of Princess Victoria, sister-in-law of the ex-Kaiser. He died alone. His funeral was attended by a mere handful of acquaintances.

Le Queux's main importance as a spy novelist was in popularizing the notion of a German spy menace in Britain and stirring

up anti-German feeling. Although this sentiment had been growing steadily as the German navy expanded, it was not until after
about 1905–06 that the Germans replaced the French as targets
of popular hostility. As befitted a popular author, Le Queux kept
a close eye on the shifting tides of public opinion, and rapidly
changed tack from his previous anti-French course.

"I think I can claim to be the first person," Le Queux declared
with typical panache in his memoirs, "to warn Great Britain that
the Kaiser was plotting a war against us. I discovered, as far
back as 1905, a great network of German espionage spread over
the United Kingdom." The discovery came, Le Queux asserted,
through the revelations of a close friend in Berlin, "who was at
the time under-director of the Kaiser's Spy Bureau.... As is usual
in Germany, his master did not exactly 'play the game' with him,
and therefore, in 1905, he told me frankly what was in progress."
This was all a fantasy, but Le Queux's "discovery" meant that
from then until his death he was a pathological Germanophobe.

He was not alone. "Yes, we detest the Germans, we detest
them cordially," Northcliffe told an interviewer in *Le Monde*
at the time of the signing of the Entente, "and I should not
like anything to appear in my paper that might be agreeable to
Germany." The *Daily Mail* now emerged as the chief mouthpiece
of Germanophobia, and Northcliffe commissioned Le Queux to
repeat the success of his first serialized invasion novel, this time
with material that would rally the population behind the anti-
German banner. Le Queux needed little encouragement, and *The
Invasion of 1910* began to appear, amidst a blaze of publicity, in
March 1906. When it later appeared in book form it sold over a
million copies and was translated into twenty-seven languages
including Arabic, Chinese, and Japanese.

Le Queux threw himself into the task with enthusiasm. In his
search for authenticity he spent several weeks touring England
by motor car in order to plot out the most plausible route for
the German invasion. This was then refined with the assistance
of Lord Roberts, eager to lend his hand to an enterprise that
promised increased public support for conscription. Alas, Le
Queux's diligence proved wasted. When he showed the first draft
to Northcliffe, the latter was quick to note that the invasion route

avoided all the big cities, and hence the bulk of *Mail* readers. He demanded that a new invasion route be planned and Le Queux, crestfallen, complied.

This sacrifice was more than compensated for by the series' vicarious horrors. Le Queux's description of the outrages committed by the invading Germans left little to the imagination, and on the morning London awoke to read of the Huns' arrival in the capital, *Daily Mail* street-sellers paraded down Oxford Street wearing spiked helmets and Prussian-blue uniforms. More important, the novel stressed that the invaders were helped by German spies throughout the British Isles. Although the Prime Minister denounced Le Queux in the House of Commons as a pernicious scare-monger, popular response was enthusiastic. Not surprisingly, Le Queux seized the chance to expound on his anti-German sentiments. "He had found a way," as Phillip Knightley has written in *The Second Oldest Profession*, "in which he could alert Britain to the danger from Germany and, at the same time, make a lot of money. From this moment on, the two motives, patriotism and profit, became inextricably linked in Le Queux's mind...."

Le Queux's most important contribution to spy phobia was his best-selling fiction *Spies of the Kaiser* (1909), which pitted two intrepid young Englishmen, facsimiles of Duckworth Drew, against the machinations of the German secret service in England. "What I have written in this present volume in the form of fiction," Le Queux solemnly told his readers, "is based on serious facts within my own personal knowledge.... As I write, I have before me a file of amazing documents, which plainly show the feverish activity with which this advance guard of our enemy is working to secure for their employers the most detailed information." *Spies of the Kaiser* describes a German network of some five thousand spies preparing the way for an invasion. Most of them, Le Queux "revealed", were resident German aliens masquerading as innocent landlords, waiters, and musicians. They were building secret wireless stations and establishing ammunition dumps, their underground work cunningly disguised by the music of German street bands. The villain of this classic piece of inspired lunacy is none other than the sinister and ubiquitous

Herman Hartmann, chief of the German secret service in Britain. Given his description as a "fat, flabby, sardonic man of about fifty-five, with grey eyes full of craft and cunning, a prominent nose, and short-cropped grey beard", it would take no particular astuteness on the reader's part to recognize Hartmann as a Jew, and indeed his cover identity in London is that of a Jewish money-lender.

That the enemy spy is a Jew is no accident. Le Queux's first villain, Count von Beilstein, was a Jew, and there were many others to follow, not only from Le Queux but from other authors. Anti-Semitic stereotypes enjoyed a long tradition in English culture and, at the time Le Queux was writing, were being reinforced by controversies over Jewish immigration from eastern Europe and the role played by Jewish-German financiers in Anglo-German relations. Negative stereotypes of the Jew provided the perfect antithesis to the English secret agent, who is invariably youthful, clean-cut, genteel, physically fit, with a liking for fresh air and sport, and an equally robust dislike for intellectuals, socialists, businessmen, artists, and foreigners in general. Rooted in the land and tradition as he is, his actions are motivated by the purest patriotism and irreproachable notions of duty. Inevitably, his opponent in the silent and deadly game should be his symbolic opposite: most certainly not a gentleman, lacking all notions of fair play, middle-aged or worse, deformed or ugly, deeply mired in the mercenary side of the modern urban world, and motivated by money, revenge, or some other low desire. Contemporary stereotypes that made the Jews a rootless and cosmopolitan people with no sense of national loyalty were tailor-made for a writer such as Le Queux, obsessed as he was by patriotism and national decline.

Spies of the Kaiser had a powerful effect on public opinion, by that time receptive to almost any idea, however far-fetched, of German perfidy. Le Queux was deluged with letters from people who claimed to have sighted spies. These he earnestly forwarded to the War Office, but soon became convinced that no one was taking him seriously. Like many writers since who have been obsessed by enemy spies, he attributed this to conspiracy. "The octopus hand of Germany was on every walk of life," he declared portentously, "and I knew myself to be a marked man." Although Le Queux remained aggrieved about this to the end of his life, ironically the real secret was that he had played a major part in forming the British secret service. The mass of frightened letters from patriotic Britons provided his friend, the head of the War Office counter-intelligence section, Lieutenant-Colonel James Edmonds, with sufficient ammunition finally to convince the government to establish Britain's official Secret Service Bureau in 1909.

Although Le Queux continued to claim that his was a voice crying in the wilderness, his novels had not only anticipated but also precipitated fact. Ever since the late 1890s he had been presenting his readers with the exploits of British secret agents in continental Europe—but there was not a single professional British secret agent stationed in Europe before 1907. Furthermore, the ubiquity and omniscience of Britain's secret service abroad was a myth widely believed by Continental governments as well as by British readers. It would be pleasing to think that this was because they had read their Le Queux.

From 1909 until war broke out Le Queux continued to bombard the government and the public with fictional and semi-fictional warnings about German spies, convinced that his warnings were being ignored because of the existence of German sympathizers in high places. "The whole situation," he said later, "was hopeless...one could write of spies in fiction, but to say there were spies in real life was almost an offence against King and Country." He frequently denounced the pre-war Liberal government for being soft on Germany, and this no doubt lay behind Arthur Balfour's claim that a Le Queux novel was worth several thousand votes for the Conservative Party.

When war came, Le Queux lost all restraint. "A veritable German Army, sixty thousand unscrupulous barbarians, well-equipped and eager," was already in their midst, he told readers of *The German Spy*, published shortly after the outbreak of war, while in his factoid exposure of 1915, *German Spies in England*, he claimed that "every German resident in this country may be classed as a spy, for he is, at all times, ready to assist in the work of the official secret agents of the Fatherland." Foreign nannies and the hall porters of the big London hotels were to be watched with particular care—a characteristic Le Queux touch, for few of his readers, predominantly lower middle class, were likely to have much contact with either, but it was flattering for them to think that they might.

Le Queux, like the Edwardian age itself, was uneasily poised between the security and relative innocence of the mid-Victorian age and the terrors of the twentieth century. His novels, as well as those of his many less prominent imitators, paint a scene in which elements of the new world are clearly present. There is a permanent and institutionalized secret service on the alert against Britain's enemies in both peace and war. Danger and violence for politically motivated reasons exist in the midst of English domesticity. Technical inventions are no sooner developed than men turn them to hostile purpose. Subversion by enemies, protected by powerful figures within the land, is rampant. And external danger is ever present—for the secure days of imperial hegemony are over, and Europe, with its powerful, intractable military superiority, is a constant threat. Suddenly Britain's fate rests upon decisions in Europe. Le Queux, however ineptly, played a part in educating the public to this revolutionary change of direction.

Yet, despite this, his novels retain an innocence and naïvety firmly anchored in the pre-war world. Le Queux remains ambivalent about the secret service: even when permanent, it remains amateur, and his agents have other things to do besides espionage, as though the need for their services might suddenly disappear. Indeed, his agents usually marry at the end of his novels, thus terminating their effectiveness; and Le Queux never produced a series of novels revolving around a single hero, such as was common with later writers like Buchan, Williams, Fleming, Deighton, and le Carré. Moreover, the action of a Le Queux novel rarely escapes the artificial bounds of Victorian melodrama. Heroes emerge unscathed, both physically and psychologically, from their adventures. They indulge in no introspection and suffer no doubt or hesitation. There are no existential dilemmas in a Le Queux novel. While there is subversion within the state, it can be rooted out—for it is specific and identifiable, embodied in the foreign and alien community. There are no traitors or "moles" in the world of Le Queux. The gentleman secret agent who defends his country knows who his enemies are, for the enemy spies carry their identification in their very looks—unshaven, beetlebrowed, stooped, ill-dressed—and they speak with accents. It may be a dangerous world, but it is still a world of moral certainty.

CHAPTER TWO

The Delicate Network of Empire

Believe it or not, but Germany detests you...a war between Germany and England is only a matter of time— of a few short years, perhaps even months....

E. Phillips Oppenheim, *Mysterious Mr. Sabin*

I

Although a royal favourite, Le Queux was readily dismissed by respectable opinion as a sensational hack not to be taken seriously. "The world read [me] eagerly," he complained, "but set me down as a second-class Jules Verne." It was a spy novel by a younger contemporary, also half-English, that really focused serious minds on the growing danger of Anglo-German rivalry.

"As a novel it is excellent, as a war plan it is rubbish," was the peremptory judgement of Lord Louis Battenberg, Director of Naval Intelligence, on the novel written by a thirty-two -year-old clerk of the House of Commons whose private hobby and passion was sailing around the Frisian and Baltic coasts in his thirty-foot cutter, *Vixen*. Published in May 1903, *The Riddle of the Sands: A Record of Secret Service Recently Achieved* has since become an espionage classic. Its author is Robert Erskine Childers, the Cambridge-educated son of a land-owning family of Anglo-Irish background whose cousin had been British Home Secretary under Gladstone. A man caught by dual loyalties to Ireland and England, Childers later achieved notoriety as a deeply committed supporter of Irish Home Rule. After a tour of western Ireland in 1908 he declared himself a convert to Home Rule, and gave up his clerkship shortly afterwards to become a propagandist for the cause. In 1911 he published *The Framework of Home Rule*, and shortly before the outbreak of war used his personal yacht to smuggle arms from Germany to Ireland for use by the Irish volunteers against the Ulster unionists in the north opposed to independence from Britain. Yet he served in the Royal Navy throughout the war, finishing in Operational Intelligence for the Royal Air Force. In 1918 he settled in Dublin and was principal secretary to the Irish delegation that negotiated independence from Britain in 1921. Still adamantly opposed to the exclusion of Ulster, he joined Eamon DeValera and the Republican army in the bitter civil war against the Irish Free State. Captured by government forces, he was court-martialled and executed by an Irish firing squad on November 24, 1922. Denounced by Winston Churchill—who ironically had greatly profited from Childers' pre-war warnings—for the "malignant hatred" he showed to the land of his birth, Childers none the less died "loving England", as he put it in a moving letter written to his American-born wife the night before his execution. His last act was to shake hands with each member of the firing squad. "Take a step or two forward, lads," he said after he was blindfolded. "It will be easier that way."

Childers' novel—the only work of fiction he ever wrote—was motivated by a fervent wish to protect England. Childers would have disliked Battenberg's judgement in particular, because he made no secret of the fact that he was writing more than a novel and wanted to educate his readers in the reality of power politics—propaganda disguised as fiction, as the novelist Geoffrey Household has called it. Indeed, to depoliticize *The Riddle of the Sands* is, as the critic Claude Cockburn once said, "like trying to take the incendiary matter out of an incendiary bomb." Like Le Queux, Childers wrote as a staunch patriot and imperialist.

Having thoroughly absorbed the ideal of service to one's country while at Haileybury School, the principal Victorian training ground for Britain's colonial civilian servants, Childers as the twentieth century began shared, in the words of his biographer, Andrew Boyle, "the conventional prejudices of an upper-middle-class Englishman still basking in the patriotic afterglow of Queen Victoria's Diamond Jubilee." At the time of the Kruger Telegram[1] he wrote to a friend, "What a damned insolent puppy that Emperor is," and three years later volunteered for service in the Boer War, with what Boyle describes as "the spontaneity of an incurable romantic." Inspired by his close friend Basil Williams, later to be Professor of History at Edinburgh University, he joined the City Imperial Volunteers, and when he returned from South Africa published *In the Ranks of the C.I.V.*, a collection of his letters home, which sold well and made his name known. The near-disaster of the Boer War, which came close to being Britain's Vietnam, outraged Childers, who was shocked by the mismanagement and inefficiency of Britain's forces and by the poor quality of British troops. The time had come, he decided, "for training all Englishmen either for the sea or for the rifle." He was also impressed by the universal hostility shown to Britain by other great powers during the war, and determined to waken the public to the dangers of invasion by sea. "The uneasy feeling that Britain, once the heart of a great and prosperous Empire, lay vulnerable...was the one message Erskine Childers badly wanted to shout from the rooftops," writes Andrew Boyle.

---

[1]The Kruger Telegram was a message sent by Kaiser William II to Boer President Kruger in 1896 congratulating him on the defeat of a British raid into Boer territory. Deeply resented in Britain, it turned public opinion against Germany and marked a milestone in the deterioration of Anglo-German relations.

"A yachting story, with a purpose"—Childers' own words—was the vehicle he chose. Correctly, he thought it would have more effect than if he tried to write an amateur strategic critique.

The Riddle of the Sands contains little original in its basic idea. Like other observers of the international scene, Childers suggested that the Germans were now the main danger, and that they would be likely to act against Britain in concert with other European powers. The novel's originality and impact lie in the skilfully developed build-up of suspense, the exciting power of its narrative, and the fact that it appealed to an audience in the higher reaches of British society who dismissed the effusions of Le Queux as cheap melodrama for the masses. John Buchan (later Baron Tweedsmuir), himself to make a major contribution to the spy genre, gave Childers' novel the generous accolade of being "the best story of adventure published in the last quarter of a century."

The Riddle of the Sands tells the tale of two young Englishmen on a sailing expedition who discover a German invasion fleet being secretly assembled behind the sand flats of the Frisian coast. The two young men are Arthur Davies, the owner of the yacht *Dulcibella*, and Carruthers, a junior diplomat from the Foreign Office. Davies is a somewhat disguised version of the author, an awkward and unsociable man but—like Childers himself—a first-class sailor and dedicated patriot. Carruthers, an Oxford acquaintance whom Davies chooses to accompany him because of his fluent command of German, is successful, elegant, and unselfconsciously arrogant. A perfect example of the amateur secret agent, he describes himself as "a young man of condition and fashion who knows the right people, belongs to the right class, and has a safe, possibly a brilliant future in the Foreign Office."

As these two innocents abroad navigate their way through the treacherous shallows of the north German coast, they slowly piece together the picture of the German threat. The villain of the story is the sinister "Herr Dollman", a self-proclaimed German who on a previous expedition has already tried to lure Davies to his death by providing him with false navigating directions. Davies is convinced that Dollman is really an Englishman, and in their attempt to discover the truth the sailing expedition turns slowly, but inevitably, into an espionage mission. At this point, conventional scruples temporarily raise their head. "Mightn't we become spies?" Carruthers asks cautiously, as Davies unfolds his plan for unmasking Dollman. But Davies dismisses such hesitations in the language of Baden-Powell: "I look at it like this. The man's an Englishman, and if he's in with Germany he's a traitor to us, and we as Englishmen have a right to expose him. If we can't do it without spying we've a right to spy..." Thus armed, the young men eventually expose Dollman as a former Royal Navy officer, cashiered for some heinous but unnamed offence and motivated in his work for the Kaiser by hatred for his former country. As the central villain, he runs true to form. On his first encounter Carruthers notes the "livid smiling mask" of Dollman's false amiability, and declares that he can "never efface the impression of malignant perfidy and base passion, exaggerated to caricature, that I received in those few instants." And he is a coward as well. Lured aboard Davies' yacht, his plans exposed and failed, he finally commits suicide by jumping overboard and drowning.

The book's overwhelming public reception took both author and publisher by surprise. Quickly reissued in a cheap edition, within a few months it sold several hundred thousand copies. Leading politicians rushed to compliment Childers on his work, and the eligible young bachelor was besieged by society hostesses eager to entice him to their soirées. Despite Battenberg's dismissal of the book, others in the corridors of power were less cavalier. Admiral Sir John Fisher, the First Sea Lord, later responsible for constructing Britain's Dreadnought fleet, was deeply impressed, while Lord Selborne, the First Lord of the Admiralty, initiated an inquiry into the feasibility of the invasion plan. Even with assurances of its impossibility, leading generals continued to assert that preparations against invasion were desperately required. "For the next ten years," Andrew Boyle notes, "Childers' book remained the most powerful contribution of any English writer to the debate on Britain's alleged military unpreparedness." It was, Claude Cockburn said, "the first explosive charge successfully detonated in the sporadic Cold War which preceded the war of 1914." It had its effects in Germany, too. The German government banned the book, and when Childers next went on a sailing holiday in the Baltic, German secret agents kept a close eye on him.

The enduring message of *The Riddle of the Sands* was the potential hostility of Germany. Carruthers describes Germany to his friend one evening while the two amateur spies pass the hours of darkness on their yacht: "...our great naval rival of the future, she grows and strengthens and waits, an ever more formidable factor in the future of our delicate network of Empire...radiating from an island whose commerce is its life and which depends even for its daily ration of bread on the free passage of the seas...."

Even as Childers put these words into Carruthers' mouth, the Admiralty was reaching similar conclusions. In the spring of 1902 it secretly decided to construct a naval base at Rosyth on the Scottish North Sea coast to protect against the threat posed by the new German High Seas Fleet. In March 1903, just two months before *The Riddle of the Sands* appeared in print, it made public its decision. No one aware of the implications could now doubt that Germany rather than France was the menace to Britain's fragile hold on world power. Childers' genius was to sense and to crystallize this new mood in a highly readable form just as it won converts among influential people in Britain. For that reason alone *The Riddle of the Sands* was the most important spy novel of the Edwardian years.

II

Le Queux's great rival as an Edwardian spy novelist was not, however, the modest and soft-spoken Childers, devoted to the service of his country, but a larger-than-life hedonist who began life as a successful businessman.

Back in July 1883 the headmaster of Wyggeston Grammar School in Leicester, bidding farewell to one of his less distinguished pupils leaving school early to help out with the struggling family leather business, had told the sixteen-year-old boy, "I hope that you will find a place for yourself in the world, and that your father will do better in the future and be able to help you, for I really cannot think of any profession in life in which you would be likely to earn your own living." The headmaster's prophecy was badly flawed. E. Phillips Oppenheim's entry into the family business was only the prelude to a career as one of the most financially successful British popular novelists of the twentieth century.

Oppenheim's first novel was financed by his parents when he was twenty-one and profits from the family business supported his writing career until he sold the firm to an American company when he was already in middle age. He began publishing prolifically in the mid-1890s, and by the end of the century was earning enough to live in considerable comfort. His royalties were helped by large sales in the United States, where he was a best-selling author for Little, Brown and Company. He also had a genuine affection for things American, and remained married for over fifty years to Elsie Clara Hopkins, an American from Boston whom he met on his first visit to the United States. He liked to drive an old Studebaker, and the regular transatlantic crossing to New York played an important part in the peripatetic rituals of his extravagant way of life. In the inter-war years Oppenheim reaped the full fruits of his rich literary harvest—he published well over a hundred novels—which quickly earned him the sobriquet "Prince of Storytellers". This referred to his narrative gifts, but was also suited to his ostentatious lifestyle in the fashionable lotus-eating resorts of the French Riviera, where, he happily confessed, "the elect of the world [mixed] freely with its most amiable profligates." Fellow spy novelist Valentine Williams, who became a close friend for the brief period when Williams himself lived on the Riviera, had this to say about him: "Anyone more thoroughly steeped in the Côte d'Azur atmosphere it is impossible to conceive...for all his three score years and ten he retains the incurably romantic mind of youth...he has the sweetest and gentlest of natures...yet...lives in a world of his own imagining peopled with potential assassins, with mystery behind every lighted window and violent death behind every bush. When 'Oppy' comes into the room, it's a party: his greatest happiness in life is to gather his friends about him and be gay."

For all his fictional fantasies, however, Oppenheim remained an observer on the sidelines, never quite belonging to the high society he so admired. For much of this period he lived in a modest villa at Cagnes-sur-mer, close to Cannes. When not writing or playing golf, he spent considerable time on his yacht, the *Echo*, which became irreverently known as the "floating double bed" due to its high turnover of female guests. A leading propagandist in the unsuccessful campaign to preserve Monte Carlo's monopoly on roulette, Oppenheim to the end remained a playboy at heart. With the collapse of France in 1940 most of the British colony on the Riviera returned home, but Oppenheim and his wife stayed behind, bemoaning the shortage of servants and the lack of petrol. In 1941 they finally crossed the border into Spain, and thence to England. At the Ministry of Information Oppenheim was disappointed to find a lack of interest in his recent impression of life in France, and soon declined into a melancholy, pathetic relic of a bygone age.

After the war he returned to a villa he owned in Guernsey, another haven for expatriates, and attempted to recapture the carefree lifestyle of former days. But it was too late. The Europe he had celebrated had gone for ever. Only a month after Oppenheim's own death early in 1946 at age seventy-nine, Churchill's Iron Curtain speech at Fulton, Missouri, marked the passage of the great capitals of central Europe into a darkness of their own. With the onset of the Cold War there was no room, and no need, for the synthetic melodramas of the Prince of Storytellers.

"So long as the world lasts," Oppenheim once said, "its secret international history will...suggest the most fascinating of all material for the writing of fiction." Oppenheim shared with Le Queux and Childers a concern about British preparedness in the jungle of international relations in the years prior to the First World War. He had a gladiatorial view of the world arena, once expressing the view that "so long as human nature remains what it is today...so long will military force be the natural, wholesome, and inevitable solution of international difficulties. The nation which ceases to breed warriors and sailors will be a nation without vital impulses." Like Le Queux, he supported Lord Roberts' campaign for peacetime conscription, and he joined the crusade against German militarism and espionage. In 1914 he volunteered for secret service, but to his chagrin was rejected for knowing insufficient German.

"It was not even much satisfaction to me," Oppenheim remembered later, "when I heard, some two months afterward, that the man who succeeded in obtaining the post...crossed the German frontier from Switzerland on a somewhat delicate mission only once and never returned." There was irony in his rejection, because to others Oppenheim appeared *too* German. Once, in Devonshire, he was accused by a local farmer of signalling to a non-existent German submarine from the window of his house. When asked to prove that his suspect was an alien, the farmer simply pointed to Oppenheim's name. For the rest of the war he carried his birth certificate to prove that he was born in Britain. Eventually he found propaganda work in the Ministry of Information, and in the latter part of the war helped escort neutral journalists around the battlefields of the Western Front. It was during this period that he wrote some of his most famous spy novels.

"The real centres of interest," Oppenheim believed, "are the places where human beings are gathered more closely, where the struggle for existence inevitably develops the whole capacity of a man and strips him bare to the looker-on." Yet it was the gathering places of pre-war European high society that Oppenheim chose as the sites for his dramas, for these were the centres of his own interest. This was a Europe, he lamented many years later in his memoirs, *The Pool of Memory*, written under the shadow of Hitler, "[where] beautiful and intriguing sirens whispered during the dance of secret houses where a fortune was to be made by easy gambling, or tried to excite curiosity concerning some mysterious personage behind the curtain, a personage of great power who was willing to purchase secrets, political, military or naval, of any country at a fabulous price." Whereas Le Queux's novels often descended to the lower abysses of society where alien spies might be found lurking, not so those of Oppenheim. He kept the mind's eye of his reader firmly fixed on the heights of suburban ambition, a promised land where the travails of daily life could be swept aside with the wave of a valet. This was how Oppenheim himself lived at the height of his fame and fortune, and his reliance on servants, secretaries, and chauffeurs, and his generous and lavish hospitality, were legendary.

"I am a maker of stories while you wait," he once said. "Sex is dropping a little. Crime is coming in again." Keeping such a keen eye on popular taste, he also exploited the growing public interest in espionage. But Oppenheim wrote more for profit than as a personal crusade, and his novels lack the visceral enthusiasm of Le Queux's admittedly cruder effusions. The library survey that placed Le Queux in the third rank of popular authors situated Oppenheim in the second rank—quite rightly, for Oppenheim had a better command of prose—but his work was less provocative. Whereas Le Queux's obsession with spies was served raw to the point of indigestibility, Oppenheim dispensed a blander menu, with espionage little more than a seasonable garnish for the main dish of romance and adventure. The reader with a strong stomach might dine nightly on Le Queux. A steady diet of Oppenheim would rapidly become tedious.

It was largely the success of his first spy novel, *Mysterious Mr. Sabin* (1898), that enabled Oppenheim to relinquish control over the family business and devote himself to a full-time writing career. "The first of my long stories dealing with that shadowy and mysterious world of diplomacy," wrote Oppenheim in his memoirs, the novel revolves around a plot to overthrow the Third French Republic. Its central figure, Monsieur Sabin, is none other than the Duc de Souspennier, a royalist nurturing ambitions of being a new Richelieu. The stratagem he devises for ridding France of the Republic is a German invasion, promised by Berlin provided that he deliver detailed plans of British coastal defences to the Germans. Sabin's attempts to steal such plans from Lord Deringham, a former high Admiralty official, form a major part of the drama, and are assisted by Lady Deringham, a former lover of the Frenchman. At the very moment of his success, however, Sabin is foiled by the intervention of some international secret society which forbids him to harm England (the nature of this society is unclear, but it is probably an order of Freemasonry).

Sabin, sworn to obey the society, dutifully burns the crucial secrets, and England is saved.

The idea of hidden agencies influencing the destiny of nations was to become a familiar theme of Oppenheim's novels, the agents often being members of a secret brotherhood or international financiers. And here too was a technique that Oppenheim—a voracious reader of newspapers—was to use on many future occasions: the exploitation of a thinly disguised recent international incident to provide topicality to his novels. In this novel a version of the Kruger Telegram incident provokes a warning about Germany which precedes that of Carruthers in Childers' novel by some five years. "Believe it or not," a Russian attaché tells one of the English characters, "but Germany detests you...a war between Germany and England is only a matter of time — of a few short years, perhaps even months...."

Despite this glimpse, the public was hardly ready for such pessimism in 1898, and Oppenheim's next major spy novel, *The Betrayal* (1904), was woven from traditional Francophobia. Again using a recent event, Oppenheim constructed his drama around the Committee of Imperial Defence, established only the year before, to present his readers with the theft of the committee's documents by the French secret service. The source of the leak turns out to be none other than the Duke of Rowchester, a distinguished member of the committee itself. The motive is money—for one of his business ventures has collapsed—and when he is discovered, the Duke commits suicide. "There," muses Lord Chelmsford, a fellow member of the committee, "was a man who to all appearances was a typical Englishman...he was willing to betray his country to justify his own sense of personal honour."

After this blunt and disturbing slur on the loyalties of an English gentleman, Oppenheim retreated to more secure territory in the following year. The 1904 Anglo-French Entente, with its reversal of diplomatic alignments, had sparked fears that Russia, still Britain's great imperial rival menacing the gateway to India, might ally itself with Germany. These fears peaked when the Russian fleet, on its way to the Far East, accidentally fired on some British trawlers in the North Sea. The crisis provided the backdrop for his next novel, the first of many in which he combined an anti-German theme with patent commitment to the health of Anglo-French friendship. *A Maker of History* (1905) tells of a young Englishman "caught in the heart of a European plot and stormcloud". Vacationing in Germany, Guy Royston accidentally stumbles on a secret meeting between the Czar and the Kaiser in a railway carriage deep in the forests of eastern Germany, where the two monarchs sign a treaty providing support in a war against Britain. A felicitous gust of wind places the crucial document in Guy's possession, and from there until the French secret service comes to his rescue Guy's life is in peril from spies of the Kaiser. The French government, convinced that Germany "plans [to become] the strongest nation on earth, able to dictate even to us", signs an alliance with Britain. "Remember," one of Guy's rescuers tells him, "that in the underground history of England you will be known always as the man who saved his country."

German spies in Britain itself dominated Oppenheim's next spy novel, for by now the author was convinced that the Kaiser was intent on ruling his empire from London. *The Secret* (1907), published in the aftermath of the spy paranoia generated by Le Queux's *The Invasion of 1910*, portrays the workings of a massive German spy ring, some 30,000 strong, operating in Britain under the cover of an apparently innocuous organization, the German Waiters' Union, with its headquarters in the Café Suisse in Soho. The waiters, who are being secretly trained to assist some future invasion of Britain, have put themselves at the service of the Kaiser, a man "chock full to the lips with personal jealousy, a madman posing as a genius...the man who believes that he hears voices from heaven." The novel also introduces a stock figure already made familiar by Le Queux and Childers: the skilful amateur agent. This is Hardross Courage, a bachelor of thirty-three who comes up to London to play cricket for his county, Medchestershire. Describing himself as Saxon to the backbone (it will be recalled that Drew described himself as an Englishman to the backbone), he lives at Saxby Hall, is a magistrate in two counties, and his grandfather was ambassador to France. Unintentionally precipitated into danger when he puts up at a hotel (managed by a Mr. Blumenstein) that turns out to be connected with sinister goings-on, he gradually assumes the role of a freelance secret agent. He penetrates the German network disguised as a waiter and finally persuades England's greatest popular daily newspaper to expose the Waiters' Union in print. As the news leaks out, hundreds of "aliens" mass in the streets below the offices of the paper, prompting one of those besieged to exclaim: "At last! The tocsin has sounded, and the rats have come out of their holes! Half a million and more of scum eating their way into the entrails of this great city of ours...who is going to keep them in check?"

Oppenheim provides several answers to this cry of anguish. The first is a government prepared to take a stronger stand against immigrants. The second is a proper secret service, one permitted to play a more active role than permitted by dilettantes in the highest reaches of government. The third is greater national military preparedness. And the fourth is the Entente with France, to be maintained at all costs. Only if it collapsed, *The Secret* concluded, could the Germans carry out a successful invasion.

The importance of the Anglo-French partnership inspired the motif for *The Double Four* (1911), Oppenheim's final excursion into the world of international intrigue before the outbreak of war. It tells of an eponymous secret society, with its headquarters in Paris, which claims—rather in the manner of Edgar Wallace's *The Four Just Men*—to draw the line between "moral theft and immoral honesty". The hero, Peter Ruff (alias Baron de Grost), is an international trouble shooter working on the society's behalf to aid France. His opponent in this deadly duel across frontiers is the Count von Hern-Bernardine, "the Teuton—muscle and bone and sinew...a German to the last drop of his heart's blood." "Think of yourself as a monk, dear Baron," says Ruff's chief lieutenant, "and Bernardine as the Devil Incarnate." Ruff's exploits do indeed assume the dimensions of a crusade, and evil is duly smitten. He saves Anglo-French plans for an expeditionary force across the Channel from falling into the hands of the Germans, and foils an ingenious German plan to purloin British military secrets from a number of high-ranking officers. His work reaches a satisfying conclusion with the self-inflicted death of Bernardine after Ruff has humiliated him on his own ground.

Oppenheim, writes a recent American author, "wrote lousy plots, wooden characters, clichéd dialogues, and bogus descriptions." All this is true. But "Oppy" deserves an honoured place in the pantheon of spy writers, for he played a major part in establishing what Eric Ambler later described as "the early cloak-and-dagger stereotypes—the black-velveted seductress, the British Secret Service numbskull hero, the omnipotent spymaster."

If the non-English, the non-Christian, and the non-U were automatically suspect in the world of the Edwardian spy novel, there was yet another category that included perhaps the most dangerous threat of all: the female.

Although those professionally concerned with espionage were sometimes prepared to accept that women could act as secret agents, the novelists of the era decided otherwise. At a time when the suffragettes were stepping up their campaign for a change in the role of women, both Oppenheim and Le Queux set their faces resolutely against change. Together they established the convention that secret agents, whether accidental or otherwise, should be single men operating in a man's world.

Women, their novels proclaim, are profoundly dangerous, for they dance to quite a different tune from that of men. Creatures of the heart, not of the head, their behaviour creates peril for men. Women's purity in the face of the world's tangled and complex affairs renders them incapable of operating according to the rules of the secret agent. Not that they are without patriotism; rather, they are moved by other values. "I, too, believe me, love my country and my people.... If I do not find them all-engrossing, you must remember that I am a woman, and I am young," declares one of the characters in Oppenheim's *Mysterious Mr. Sabin*. "I do not pretend to be capable only of impersonal and patriotic love." Or, as Adele von Hoyt in *The Secret* confesses to a mawkish Hardross Courage who has fallen for her charms, "It is only the woman who realizes what love is, who puts it before body and soul and honour. A man cannot do that." Le Queux understood the principle equally well. On the embossed cover of one of his earliest spy novels, the title—*England's Peril*—is juxtaposed with the figure of a woman. This is undoubtedly Lady Castleton, who falls in love with Gaston La Touche and attempts to murder her husband. It is never clear from the plot whether France or the female sex is the greater peril—la France or *la femme*?

This convention is followed consistently by Le Queux. The fortunes of his heroes rise and fall according to their success in meeting and overcoming the female challenge. "While diplomacy and flirtation are sister arts, diplomacy and love never run hand in hand," proclaims one of the protagonists in *Her Majesty's Minister*. But of course love constantly rears its head, and the mix proves as volatile as fire and gas. With their emotions women distract secret agents and make them vulnerable, while with their idle chatter they betray their secrets. "You've got a pretty difficult inquiry before you, so take the advice of an old diplomatic hand and avoid *la femme*," advises Jack Jardine, head of the British secret service, in *The Man from Downing Street*. Although the agent, being human, often ignores the advice—thus precipitating crises in which he can display his skills—none the less he is fundamentally a sound chap. He has usually avoided the ultimate trap of marriage for a good many years, and never marries before or during his mission. Only when he has completed his task is he free to marry, for marriage is a metaphorical death.

But when the woman is on the enemy side, her natural female characteristics make her even more dangerous. Here we see a cunning deployment of feminine guile, "the indefatigable exercise of ingenuity in the way of evading, stooping, conciliating, deceiving," as Le Queux so succinctly puts it. As our secret agents criss-cross Europe in pursuit of the foe—as they board the night express to Rome or stroll along the Promenade des Anglais—they are constantly tangling with enemy Mata Haris, figures known to fiction long before the First World War. "Women are always more successful as spies than men," Le Queux explains, "that is why so many are employed by both Germany and France." Throughout this period female spies, as Patricia Craig and Mary Cadogan have put it in their study of women detectives and spies in fiction, *The Lady Investigates*, "were synonymous with seduction, ruthlessness, and betrayal." Successfully worming their way into our agents' hearts, these *femmes fatales* continually threaten to dig out secrets that not even the most ingenious mechanical device could extract. Ultimately our agents are never destroyed by such women, just as they are never defeated by their male counterparts. But whenever a woman appears, the reader's heart beats a little faster, for danger is at hand.

Ironically, these deep forebodings were provoked by a fundamentally conservative view of women. Danger arises when women seek to cross the boundaries of the "legitimate" male world; if they stayed in the place nature had carved out for them, all would be well. This has remained the view of most fictional secret agents ever since. Duckworth Drew or Hardross Courage would identify immediately with James Bond's heartfelt lament in *Casino Royale*: "Women were for recreation. On a job, they got in the way and fogged things up with sex and hurt feelings and all the emotional baggage they carried around. One had to look out for them and take care of them." From Drew to Bond, British secret agents have done their best to travel without this particular form of baggage.

Although mainly focused on foreign threats, Edwardian spy novels were also deeply concerned with the social order. Secret agents like Duckworth Drew and Hardross Courage were not only heroes in their own right but also guardians of the social hierarchy, members of an élite with a traditional right to bear the burden of power and responsibility. Watching them at work, the reader knows that they will sniff out subversion within the nation just as readily as plots from across the Channel.

The conservatives of Edwardian England were mesmerized by images of decline, frequently drawing analogies with the fall of the Roman Empire. They saw one of its principal causes in the vast and anonymous urban masses, who threatened to undermine the social hierarchies that had controlled the expansion of England's wealth in the nineteenth century. The working class they viewed as a mysterious and frightening force, concentrated in sunless squalor and inhaling "twice-breathed air" (as one critic shudderingly noted), liable not only to physical degeneration but also to seduction by alien ideologies such as socialism.

The election victory of a reform-minded Liberal government in 1905 intensified such fears. Le Queux, for one, was quick to link the threat of domestic change with fears of international danger. In *The Invasion of 1910* the Germans find their way paved not only by the work of spies but by the weakness of the working class, which has lost the ability to fight. "The peasantry," Le Queux laments, "which had formed the backbone of the nation, had vanished and been replaced by the weak and excitable population of the towns." In 1910 he became more explicit. In a novel entitled *The Unknown Tomorrow*, he presented a nightmare vision of England in 1935, ruled by socialism, with mobs sacking London and burning temples of high culture such as the British Museum and the Bodleian Library. Le Queux had obviously been reading his Hansard. In 1908 Lord Malmesbury had warned the House of Lords that "socialism, narcotic-like, has drugged the spirit of patriotism into forced slumber", while in the next year Lord Curzon had predicted that a German invasion would unchain forces of disorder throughout the land and lead to the utter subversion of the old order of things.

Foreign danger and internal revolt thus coalesced in the conservative mind into a peril to the very fabric of society. The gentleman secret agent promised safety not just from foreigners but from basic threats to the social order.

CHAPTER THREE

The Thin Protection

You think that a wall as solid as the earth separates civilisation from barbarism. I tell you the division is a thread, a sheet of glass. A touch here, a push there, and you bring back the reign of Saturn.

John Buchan, *The Power-House*

The outbreak of the Great War produced an enthusiastic rush to join the colours in Britain. There was an equally zealous desire to punish the country's large population of German residents. In October 1914 an anti-German mob swept through the streets of Aberystwyth in search of Germans, while in Deptford there were three nights of looting against German-owned shops. After the sinking of the *Lusitania*, anti-German riots convulsed Liverpool, Birkenhead, and the East End of London, and the Cabinet was finally forced to intern all enemy aliens of military age. By this time, everything associated with Germans or Germany had suffered: German brass bands had disappeared, German music at concerts was banned, pet dachshunds were stoned in the streets, and the British royal family changed its title from Saxe-Coburg to the House of Windsor.

Such bitter sentiment demonstrated the power of pre-war stereotypes showing Germans as arrogant, aggressive, at the instant service of the Kaiser, and motivated by a deep and primordial hatred of all things British. It also showed how much the Germans were feared. "Every German, old or young, is a potential spy," the *Daily Mail* told its readers on October 26, 1914, in a comment on the alleged presence of 40,000 Germans in Britain. A few days later, it singled out German waiters as particularly dangerous: "Refuse to be served by an Austrian or German waiter. If your waiter says he is Swiss, ask to see his passport." In the first six weeks of war some 9,000 reports were received from members of the public about spies in London alone; practically all proved to be groundless.

This anti-German fervour was strongly nourished by the popular press, and especially by the Northcliffe press, which continued its pre-war crusade. Northcliffe himself, who by the end of the war was Director of Propaganda to Enemy Countries, was personally convinced both of the dangers from enemy aliens and of the insidious threat posed by their alleged sympathizers in high places in English society. He gave his newspapers appropriate instructions, and the *Daily Mail* became the main platform for this campaign. In July 1918, after an official Aliens Committee set up by Lloyd George had recommended yet further measures against enemy aliens, the *Mail* bitterly protested that they did not go far enough. As its editorial noted, "There is a sinister absence of protest from the Parliamentary friends of the Hun." Mass meetings throughout the country demanded the extension of internment to women aliens and naturalized Germans alike, climaxing in late August 1918 with a petition bearing over a million signatures. Only the prospect of impending victory finally dissipated this xenophobic hysteria.

I

In the vanguard of the anti-German crusade marched the tireless Le Queux. Acting as a drummer to popular Germanophobia for the past decade, he now became one of its most prominent buglers. The boundaries between fact, fiction, and fantasy—which he never drew firmly at the best of times—now virtually disappeared. In *German Spies in England* (1915) he claimed that every German resident of England should be treated as a spy because Germans, wherever they were, retained their loyalty to the Fatherland. Within three days of publication he received over three hundred letters from readers denouncing spies in their presence. Even on Le Queux's own admission, only three proved "useful" to the authorities to whom he forwarded this intelligence. "Once a German always a German" was also the message of his next publication, *Britain's Deadly Peril*, and of his numerous public lectures and articles in the jingoist press. While his novels *The Spy Hunter* (1916) and *Number 70, Berlin* (1916) demonstrated his fascination with the radio and wireless interception as weapons in the espionage armoury, and *The Zeppelin Destroyer* (1916) showed his interest in the new technology of air warfare, the dominating theme of all his wartime spy fiction was the danger from German espionage networks operating under the protection of highly placed elements in society. Probably the most paranoid of the novels written in this period was also the most blatantly anti-Semitic. *The Catspaw* appeared in the final year of the war, and portrayed the threat to Britain at the hands of Salmon, the leading London artistic agent, a German Jew heading the spy network in the capital. In all of these novels, Le Queux did little more than play variations on old themes. His heroes and villains were as predictable as the tempo of a military band.

Since the spy novel with its crude xenophobia was so well suited to the temper of the times, it is hardly surprising that another popular author of pronounced patriotic views entered the field as well. Edgar Wallace, already established as a writer of crime novels, rivalled Le Queux in the sheer productivity of his output; he wrote 173 novels in twenty-seven years. Graham Greene once described him as a "human book factory". Like Le Queux, Wallace came to fiction through journalism—he, too, had worked for Northcliffe and the *Daily Mail*—and to the end of his life he preferred to be known as a journalist rather than a novelist.

As a correspondent during the Boer War Wallace had struck a highly jingoist note. In an infamous article entitled "Women—The Enemy", he had advocated the out-of-hand shooting of Boer women behind British lines for their espionage and treachery. While in South Africa he had met Rudyard Kipling, who advised him that if he took up a literary career he would find it a good mistress but a bad wife. In later years Kipling provided George V, on his sickbed, with parcels of Wallace novels to read.

Also like Le Queux, Wallace was a passionate conservative. Having clambered up from the bottom of the social heap himself—he had been abandoned as an infant by his actress mother in the London slums—he had little but contempt for those who had failed to do the same. He once declared that he hated the average British working man, and he could see nothing wrong with a society in which he had managed to better himself.

Wallace first came to public prominence in 1905 with his novel of an international plot to overthrow the government, *The Four Just Men*, and his forte was to remain crime and mystery. None the less, to a man with a keen eye for the main financial chance, there was money in spies. With the coming of war, Wallace quickly adopted the most extreme aspects of popular patriotism, calling all Germans "Huns" and describing them as decadent apes. In a series of short stories later published as *The Adventures of Heine*, Wallace used ridicule to portray the stereotype of the stupid, arrogant German. The stories are recounted through the mouth of their eponymous protagonist, Germany's chief spy in Britain. The preposterously boastful Heine is constantly outwitted by the British, especially by the suave, ubiquitous, and omniscient secret agent Major Haynes. "We Germans," proclaims Heine at one point, "have a passion for detail and thoroughness, and for this reason (apart from the inherent qualities of simplicity and honesty, apart from the superiority of our *Kultur* and our lofty idealism) we have been unconquerable throughout the ages." The boast is followed by the immediate destruction of his plans by the British secret service, and the obtuse Heine is left wondering how he has been duped. The series flourished on such heavy-handed ironies, comforting its readers with the assurance that the Huns would be confounded not only by Major Haynes and his like but also by their own unmistakable national failings.

E. Phillips Oppenheim also flourished during the war, despite his quasi-official duties. His first two wartime spy novels, *The Vanished Messenger* (1914) and *Mr. Grex of Monte Carlo* (1915), played on his familiar themes of the dangers to the Anglo-French and Anglo-Russian alliances, and of the importance of Anglo-American friendship. The latter book was vintage Oppenheim, set in the hothouse climate of pre-war Monte Carlo. It pits the slim and athletic Sir Henry Hunterlys, "Emperor of his country's secret service", against the sinister and duplicitous Herr Draconmeyer, acting as agent of Germany despite a professed love for England, his adopted land.

That blood was thicker than water, and that those of German origin, however remote, were bound to serve the Reich, was a theme explored further in *The Kingdom of the Blind* (1916), the best of Oppenheim's wartime novels. Sir Alfred Anselman is a powerful London banker close to high circles in government, and his nephew, Ronald Granet, is a distinguished young officer in the British army. Yet both have German blood, and are thus fated to serve the Reich. "It's English air that I breathe but it's a German heart I still carry with me," Anselman confesses. The two engage in espionage, their prime target being a new British anti-submarine device. But their efforts are foiled by Major Hugh Thomson, chief of military intelligence. Ronald, in an act of poetic justice, is killed by a German bomb during a Zeppelin raid on London that he himself helped to arrange. Anselman's financial power, however, provides him with some protection. Concerned that his unmasking will discredit the government and create a catastrophic financial crisis, the Cabinet decides against his arrest and merely places him under surveillance.

By 1918, Oppenheim's novels were displaying much less enthusiasm for the war effort and an increased appreciation of the human costs to all the combatants. By this time he had experienced the war at first hand. Although his official job mostly involved preventing journalists from getting close to the battlefields, there were exceptions. One, which left a strong impression on him, was at Vimy Ridge, captured by Canadian troops after a bloody battle in 1917. Oppenheim was in the first group of journalists to arrive. "There were burying parties every few hundred yards dotted all over the hillside," he wrote later, "and nearly all the barns and houses that were left were in flames." So in *The Pawns Count*, in which John Lutchester of the British secret service foils the plans of Oskar Fischer, a German-American, to undermine America's policy of friendly neutrality towards Britain, the tone noticeably lacks the militant vigour of its predecessors. In his final wartime spy novel Oppenheim strikes an even more divergent tone. *Mr. Lessingham Goes Home* (published in America as *The Zeppelin's Passenger*) contains a distinct note of war weariness, with the author distancing himself from popular anti-German sentiment. A German spy (alias Mr. Lessingham), dropped into England to obtain vital British naval plans, is detected but allowed to escape, for he is a gentleman, well born and Oxford-educated, and class speaks louder than country. "You are about as fit to be a spy as Philippa, my wife here, is to be a detective," his English captor tells him. "You possess the one insuperable obstacle of having the instincts of a gentleman." In an avowal that would have horrified Le Queux, the spy himself declares that there are times when individuality is far stronger than nationality: "I am just a human being, born into the same world, and warmed by the same sun as you. Nothing can alter the fact that we are fellow creatures."

This was a temporary lapse. In the climate of anti-Germanism resuscitated by the Versailles treaty, Oppenheim wrote his major post-war spy novel, *The Great Impersonation* (1920). Set in 1914, it tells the story of Sir Everard Dominey, exiled by scandal and alcohol to East Africa. Here he meets an old school-friend from Eton, Major-General Baron von Ragastein. The two men bear a close physical resemblance, and von Ragastein, a secret agent of the Kaiser, conceives the idea of impersonating

Dominey, returning to England, and thus penetrating the highest level of British society. Implausible though the plot is, Allen Dulles, head of the CIA, once said that he would give the novel "the prize for cleverness among all novels about espionage"— which tells us as much about Dulles as it does about Oppenheim. Otherwise, *The Great Impersonation* was vintage Oppenheim, with its portrait of a German master plan for the domination of Europe and descriptions of the Kaiser as "a diseased personality". It was Oppenheim's most successful novel to date, and within a year Paramount made it into a movie. Two further movie versions, both made by Universal, appeared over the next twenty years, the second starring Ralph Bellamy and set in the Second World War.

But like most popular spy novelists, Oppenheim transferred his anxious post-war gaze to Bolshevism. One of the more readable novels of this period is *Miss Brown of X.Y.O.* Written against the backdrop of the 1926 General Strike, it exploits the theme of Bolshevik agitation and labour grievances. Communists have deeply penetrated political parties and the trade unions, and the basic strategy of the secret service (X.Y.O.) is to detach the Labour Party from foreign (that is, Communist) influence. The task accomplished, X.Y.O. is disbanded, and Miss Brown is left swooning in the arms of the secret agent. This is typical Oppenheim, and we can safely leave him here, secure in the knowledge that his later novels contain no surprises and contribute nothing new to the genre.

II

Far and away the most important writer of spy novels during the First World War was John Buchan. His impact on the genre was profound, and he left a mark that has remained strong to this day.

"Canada, as well as the whole Empire, is mourning Lord Tweedsmuir, its Governor-General, and the world in general has lost a brilliant author who wrote under the name of John Buchan," wrote Clara Milburn, an English housewife whose ordinary reflections were published many years later, on February 12, 1940. "In memory I see myself leaning against a haycock on a rough lawn one August afternoon some twenty or more years ago with the hot sun tempered by a delicate breeze. I was lost to everything but the story of *The Thirty-Nine Steps*.... After that one always asked for the new John Buchans as they came out, eager to read anything written by his clever pen."

The man whose storytelling entranced millions of readers like Clara Milburn, and who ended a distinguished life in 1940 as Lord Tweedsmuir of Elsfield, Governor General of Canada, was born in Perth, Scotland, in 1875. His father was a minister in the Free Church of Scotland, and Buchan's life was deeply marked by his Calvinist upbringing. "I had an acute sense of sin," Buchan confessed in *Memory Hold-the-Door*, his autobiography (significantly entitled *Pilgrim's Way* in the United States, and reportedly much admired by John F. Kennedy), "and a strong hatred of whatever debased human nature." Following three years at Glasgow University, he went on to Oxford and an outstanding student career. A phenomenally hard worker whose relentless drive for success caused recurrent battles with stomach ulcers, the young Scotsman not only won two of Oxford's most distinguished awards, the Stanhope and Newdigate prizes, and became president of the Union, but by the time he left had published five books and numerous literary articles, made his name in London as a talented and rising star in many fields, and earned a precocious entry into *Who's Who*. "His powers of work...inspire awe in his friends," commented *Isis*, the Oxford magazine, "and he confesses a deep-seated loathing for what is called leisure."

There was no letting up of the pace. Moving to London, he was soon called to the Bar, while continuing to write leading articles for the *Spectator*, to publish short stories, and to lead an active and strenuous social life. From 1901 to 1903 he served as a political private secretary to Lord Milner, High Commissioner to South Africa, becoming deeply involved in solving refugee and repatriation problems following the Boer War. This experience of practical action, combined with a strong faith in the British Empire, affected Buchan deeply, and he returned to England convinced of the moral imperative of serving the public good and determined to be a man of action as well as a writer of books. "Even a perverse course of action," he wrote, "seemed to me better than a tippling of ale in the shade." To some extent, he succeeded, although he never reached Cabinet rank, and remained something of an imperialist dreamer for the rest of his life.

Nor did he adapt well to twentieth-century life. As William Buchan, his youngest son, recalls, his father never learned to drive a car and steadfastly refused to install a telephone in the family home at Elsfield, outside of Oxford. Prior to going as the King's representative to Canada in 1935, he served for several years as a Member of Parliament for the Scottish Universities, and was a High Commissioner to the General Assembly of the Church of Scotland. Throughout, in addition to being deeply involved as a director in the affairs of the Thomas Nelson publishing house, he sustained his phenomenal output of essays, novels, histories, and biographies, including studies of Sir Walter Scott, Oliver Cromwell, and Julius Caesar. Only a man ruthless in organizing his time could have achieved so much. Even holidays were occasions for strenuous effort, for Buchan was a serious hiker, rock-climber, and mountaineer. His physical appearance mirrored his character. Catherine Carswell observed him thus: "His face was revealed as 'fine-drawn'," she noted, "in lines of energy and fatigue, sensibility and asceticism, recklessness and reserve.... The scar from an accident in childhood drew attention to the strikingly noble contours of his head. The long, queer nose, questing and sagacious as a terrier's, was in odd contrast with the lean, scholarly cheeks and with the mouth narrowed as by concentration or the limit of pain subdued."

For all his life of public service, Buchan is now remembered as a storyteller—"Teller of Tales", as Plains Indians called him when he crossed the Canadian prairies in 1936. Above all, he is celebrated for his spy stories. It was in 1913, while recuperating from his first ulcer attack, that Buchan decided to write a "shocker", something to both amuse him and provide an additional source of income. With a nice touch of irony, he told his friend Hugh Walpole that he was modelling himself on E. Phillips Oppenheim, "my master in fiction."

The novel was *The Power-House*, first published as a serial in 1913 in *Blackwood's Magazine*. It tells the story of Edward Leithen, a respectable young London barrister, who has an accident while motoring in the country and is taken in by a Mr. Andrew Lumley, an elderly and dignified host. Lumley, it transpires, is a member of the Athaeneum and Carlton clubs, and moves in the highest circles of London society. But events soon take a sinister turn. As the two men converse politely after an excellent meal, Leithen's host gradually reveals an acute knowledge of foreign affairs and a disquieting interest in the vulnerability of civilization. This, he points out to Leithen, is fragile, being essentially a conspiracy of the conventional. "You think that a wall as solid as the earth separates civilisation from barbarism. I tell you the division is a thread, a sheet of glass. A touch here, a push there, and you bring back the reign of Saturn." And suppose, he asks Leithen, some of the most powerful scientific brains full of the "knowledge which makes possible great engines of destruction", at present scattered across the globe, were to unite in a Power-House to destroy "the conspiracy we call civilisation"?

Leithen, horrified, soon finds that Lumley intends to realize this manic vision, and that his own life is threatened in the very midst of normality—in a restaurant, in Hyde Park, even outside his own club, as he is trailed by agents of "the most dangerous secret organisation in the world." "Now I saw how thin is the protection of civilisation," he muses, as he contemplates his vulnerability amid the bustle of civilized society. "An accident and a bogus ambulance—a false charge and a bogus arrest—there were a dozen ways of spiriting me out of this gay, bustling world." It was a theme, along with that of evil disguised as the respectable and the benevolent, that was to recur throughout Buchan's spy fiction. "John Buchan," Graham Greene has written, "was the first to realize the enormous dramatic value of adventure in familiar surroundings happening to unadventurous men."

None the less, it is Buchan's second "shocker", written in the first months of the war and published in 1915, that is best remembered. "A romance where the incidents defy the probabilities, and march just inside the borders of the possible," as Buchan described it, *The Thirty-Nine Steps*, a best-seller as soon as it appeared, is often described as the first British spy novel, and its hero, Richard Hannay, as the prototype of the fictional secret agent. While these claims are excessive, there is little doubt that this, and the three subsequent Hannay adventures, set their stamp on the imagination of a generation. Few British schoolchildren of the post–World War One era missed Hannay and company, for Buchan was a favourite of schoolmasters. One earnest teacher from the Lake District confessed to Buchan that he had read *The Thirty-Nine Steps* and *Greenmantle* (which sold even better than its predecessor) aloud to the boys in his preparatory school at least four times, and *Mr. Standfast*, a longer and more complicated book, at least once and possibly twice. As the critic Richard Usborne noted in *Clubland Heroes*, "if not exactly the author set for homework, Buchan was certainly strongly recommended to the schoolboy by parent, uncle, guardian, pastor and master.... Buchan was good for you."

Nor were Buchan's readers confined to the school population: A.J. Balfour, the Conservative leader, was a keen Buchan fan, and so were Clement Attlee, Britain's post-war Prime Minister, and King George V. Sir Robert Baden-Powell found reading *Greenmantle* "the greatest possible solace" while recuperating from an operation, a sentiment later echoed by another great exponent of the hearty outdoors, President Theodore Roosevelt, who was comforted in convalescence by *The Thirty-Nine Steps*. Stanley Baldwin, twice British Prime Minister, the very embodiment of inter-war British conservatism, declared that Buchan was "a ruddy miracle". In the far-flung reaches of Empire, Buchan also made his mark, most remarkably on a woman in the Australian outback who wrote and told him that reading *Mr. Standfast* while making jam had been so thrilling that it caused her singlet to run up and down her back "like a roller blind".

In grimmer and even more benighted circumstances, too, the Hannay stories have helped quicken the spirit. When the *City of Benares*, an evacuee ship carrying children from Britain to North America, was torpedoed in the North Atlantic in 1940, the adult in charge of a lifeboat full of children adrift for eight days kept up morale by reading from *The Thirty-Nine Steps*. As a movie, it has also done well. Hitchcock directed the classic 1935 version with Robert Donat, Peggy Ashcroft, and Madeleine Carroll. Kenneth More starred in a 1960 remake by 20th Century-Fox, and the most recent version dates from 1978. Sales of the Hannay books in the English-speaking world remain impressive. They all have sold several hundred thousand copies, with *The Thirty-Nine Steps* topping the list at over a million and a half.

The adventures of Richard Hannay, Sandy Arbuthnot, John Scantlebury Blenkiron, and Archie Roylance undoubtedly served as models and inspiration for those brought up in the inter-war years. They were stereotypes of the clubland hero; their values became conscious standards for action. Richard Usborne affords an example. During the Second World War he worked for the Special Operations Executive, which dropped secret agents into occupied Europe. "Practically every officer I met in that concern at home and abroad," he recalled not implausibly, "was, like me, imagining himself as Hannay or Sandy Arbuthnot."

Anthony Masters, author of *The Man Who Was M*, the biography of Britain's best-known inter-war M.I.5 agent, Maxwell Knight, provides another. Knight, a teenager when the war began, served on a naval training ship. "The war was tinged with romantic heroism," Masters notes. "It introduced him to the ever-resourceful Hannay in *The Thirty-Nine Steps* and *Greenmantle*. He fell in love with Buchan's racy, jingoistic writing and, in his fantasy world, he too raced through the Scottish heather with Richard Hannay, bent on routing all foreigners and keeping the Union Jack flying over good English soil." Later on, Knight tried his own hand at thrillers, his first, *Crime Cargo* (1934), being described by Masters as "a dire mixture of Dashiell Hammett and Mickey Spillane, tinged with John Buchan."

The opening of Buchan's own novel carries strong echoes of Childers' best-seller, *The Riddle of the Sands*, for as *The Thirty-Nine Steps* begins we find Hannay, like Carruthers, at loose ends, tired of London, and "with no real pal to go about with." His subsequent adventures provide a much-needed antidote to unhealthy introspection, and a tonic to a man yearning for action rather than reflection.

Upon returning home one night he encounters the occupant of an adjacent flat, an American, who is convinced he has stumbled on a massive conspiracy to provoke world war. Frightened, the American takes refuge with Hannay. Four days later our hero finds his guest dead in the smoking room, a dagger in his heart. He immediately flees, realizing that he will be the principal suspect. "I got out an atlas and looked at a big map of the British Isles. My notion was to get off to some wild district...for I would be like a trapped rat in a city. I considered that Scotland would be best...." For the rest of the novel Hannay is on the run, pursued and pursuer, gradually uncovering a sinister conspiracy that reaches close to the very heart of government. "For sheer versatility and non-stop thrills," writes Donald McCormick in *Who's Who in Spy Fiction*, "perhaps no fictional escape can compare with that of Hannay."

Hannay when we meet him is on the right side of forty (thirty-seven) and unmarried, and (in the Childers and Oppenheim tradition) not only an amateur agent but an "accidental" one. Beginning as an outsider on the English scene, having spent his youth in South Africa, he moves steadily in the course of the quartet from the periphery to the centre. From Richard Hannay of an anonymous London flat he eventually becomes General Sir Richard Hannay, DSO, CB, gentleman farmer and squire of Fosse Manor in the Cotswolds—"the essential England", as Buchan once described it, after he had successfully completed his own journey to the heart of English society. The crucial moment of transformation comes in *Mr. Standfast*. Clearing his mind, in true Buchan fashion, by a bracing walk, Hannay pauses to look down on Fosse Manor and its peaceful valley with church and village nestling in the folds of the green woods. He experiences a revelation: "I had a vision of what I had been fighting for, what we were all fighting for. It was peace, deep and holy and ancient, peace older than the oldest wars, peace which would endure when all our swords were hammered into ploughshares. It was more; for in that hour England first took hold of me."

As an English gentleman, of course, Hannay cannot be a professional spy. Throughout the series he is presented as a patriotic adventurer called to do his duty, sometimes reluctantly, on a purely ad hoc basis. After each exploit he returns to his natural role as landed squire or officer in the regular army. This explains why it is hard to accept him as a plausible secret agent. Modelling his hero on "Tiny" Ironside, the six-foot-four soldier he first met in South Africa while engaged in intelligence work, who went on to become Britain's youngest major-general, Buchan gave Hannay some remarkable qualities: an intelligence officer in the Boer War; skilled in the art of disguise; fluent in German, Dutch, French, and a couple of South African languages; fit and patriotic, with a healthy disrespect for over-intellectualization; and used to coping on his own.

Yet the pipe-smoking Hannay makes some very inept moves. The entire plot of *The Thirty-Nine Steps* rests upon his irrational notion that he can best conceal himself from his enemies by taking to the exposed hills of Scotland. Once there, he forgets, on more than one occasion, that his pursuers have a monoplane and can spot him against the heather as clearly as a hawk spots its prey. (This did not bother Clara Milburn. "Even now," she wrote in her diary, "I remember glancing up from the haycock [and wondering] whether it would *really* be possible for an aeroplane to seek out a fugitive who in desperation had taken to the heather, so that the hunted one felt there was no possible escape from the all-seeing eye overhead.") In *Greenmantle* he prissily rejects a chance to bribe his way to safety, and almost loses his life as a result. His obstinate adherence to the code of an English gentleman has graver consequences in *Mr. Standfast*. With Moxon Ivery, the evil genius master-minding Germany's plot against Britain, in the sights of his gun at a range of six feet, Hannay refuses to shoot because Ivery's back is turned, thereby letting his opponent escape to commit yet more evil.

In other ways, however, he follows convention, especially where women are concerned. "Women had never much come his way," we learn in *Greenmantle*, thus putting them in the same category as the occasional springbok encountered during a brisk walk across the veld. He meets the woman he will marry only in *Mr. Standfast*, the third of the quartet, and he marries her in the interlude between that tale and *The Three Hostages*. For three of the four books, then, Hannay is single. And what do we find when we encounter Mary Lamington, the future Lady Hannay? She is not only half Hannay's age, pretty, virginal, and demure, but "she moved with the free grace of an athletic boy"; and not only is she the most ravishing thing you ever saw, but "her laughing eyes were amazingly intelligent." Boyish, intelligent, and with a healthy liking for physical exercise, Mary Lamington is an ideal partner. More, she is a member of the secret service, and within an hour of their meeting has given Hannay his orders. For a submissive fellow with no real pal to go about with, Mary is quite a find.

Despite Mary's absence of cloying femininity, and her admirably slim hips, marriage dooms Hannay as a secret agent. In *The Three Hostages* he is dragged unwillingly into secret service, and only because he is shamed into it by his wife's sympathy for one of the victims; it is his last exploit as a secret agent. After that, he is fit only to record the adventures of his friends, as he does in *The Courts of the Morning*. The life of the secret agent is for single men.

As for female enemy spies, they are just as dangerous as in the world of Le Queux or Oppenheim. Fortunately they are rarely encountered. It is only in *Greenmantle* that Buchan conjures one up, the unforgettable Hilda von Einem, the master-mind behind Germany's plot to raise the Islamic world against the British Empire, described variously as a "female devil", "the most dangerous woman on earth", and "a devil incarnate". The first time Hannay meets her she is wearing a mantilla of black lace over her head and shoulders, and he notes her clear, soft voice, her slender, jewelled hands, and her beautiful, grey-blue eyes. As she appraises Hannay in turn, he is "shy and perturbed, but horribly fascinated. This slim woman, poised exquisitely like some statue between the pillared lights, with her fair cloud of hair, her long delicate face, and her pale bright eyes, had the glamour of a wild dream." Later on, in a climactic scene at the end of the novel, and surrounded by the enemy at Ezerum, the Hannay band is approached by Hilda with an offer of armistice. Observing her in spurred boots and breeches, a riding whip as her sole weapon, Hannay, with appalling candour, admits to her beauty. "She might be a devil," he confesses, "but she was also a queen.... I considered that there might be merits in the prospect of riding by her side into Jerusalem." (Curiously, as critic Howard Swiggett noted in his introduction to Buchan's last novel, *Sick Heart River*, published posthumously in 1941, Hilda von Einem was not the last of her ilk to work for the German secret service. On May 30, 1940, a French court martial began the trial—according to a United Press dispatch published in the *New York Times*—of Baroness von Einem, the former Reissa von Scheurnschloss, "on charges of attempting to organise a fifth column in France as personal emissary of German Propaganda Minister Goebbels.")

The von Einem episode is Buchan's most explicit statement of the threat of the feminine to the hard-edged masculine world of the secret service. He also implies it by attributing femininity to male enemy agents. Colonel von Stumm, the German officer who comes very close to thwarting Hannay in *Greenmantle*, is a case in point. "Hideous as a hippopotamus," he is a caricature of a Prussian officer, but what most disgusts Hannay is the German's "perverted taste for soft delicate things". Alone with von Stumm in the latter's room, Hannay quickly observes the thick carpet of velvet pile, the upholstered chairs, the fragrant incense, and the embroidered screens, and sees "the queer other side in my host, that evil side which gossip had spoken of as not unknown in the German army." There is nothing so explicitly homosexual about Dominic Medina, the villain of *The Three Hostages*. Yet Hannay finds himself fascinated by him "as a man is fascinated by a pretty woman." This effect is magnified by Hannay's reaction to Medina's mother, a blind woman who possesses considerable influence over her son. He finds her both wonderful and dangerous. "I realized that it was the most wonderful face of a woman I had ever looked on. And I realized in the same moment that I hated it, that the beauty of it was devilish, and the soul within it was on fire with all the hatred of Hell."

A common charge levelled against Buchan's spy novels is that they are anti-Semitic—Mordecai Richler, for example, has described Buchan as a "nasty-minded anti-Semite". Was Buchan following convention here as well?

Such accusations usually start with the first chapter of *The Thirty-Nine Steps*, when Franklin P. Scudder, the frightened American who is murdered in Hannay's flat, expounds on the nature of the international conspiracy threatening world peace. It consists, he says, of revolutionary anarchists and financiers who hope to reap the harvest of revolution, while "the capitalists would rake in the shekels...by buying up wreckage." "Capital...had no conscience," Hannay recalls Scudder telling him, "and no fatherland. Besides, the Jew was behind it, and the Jew hated Russia worse than hell." Scudder explains it as the reaction to years of repression. "The Jew is everywhere," he continues, "...if you're on the biggest kind of job and are bound to get to the real boss, ten to one you are brought up against a little white-faced Jew in a bath chair with an eye like a rattlesnake. Yes, sir, he is the man who is ruling the world just now...."

While Hannay noticeably refrains from responding to these views, in *Greenmantle* we find him musing briefly on the state of Germany and the fact that "the Jew is at the back of most German enterprises." It generally remains for others, however, to analyse the power of the Jews. Dr. Greenslade, who delivers a lecture on the state of the world to Hannay at the beginning of *The Three Hostages*, remarks with interest how "all the places with names like spells—Bokhara, Samarkand [—are] run by seedy little gangs of communist Jews." McGillivray of Scotland Yard makes a similar remark to a receptive Hannay. The world is full of moral imbeciles wedded to violence, he asserts, among whom are "the young Bolshevik Jews".

So conspiracy theories and anti-Semitic remarks abound in the Hannay novels. But then so do disclaimers—a point often overlooked. For example, Scudder's Jewish world conspiracy theory is immediately dismissed by Sir Walter Bullivant, a good, bluff, Foreign Office man who considers the American Scudder unbalanced in his views. "He had a lot of odd biases," Bullivant tells Hannay. "Jews, for example, made him see red. Jews and the high finance." And the fact remains that in *The Thirty-Nine Steps* we find a conventional spy plot master-minded by an enigmatic figure whose pseudonym, "Moxon Ivery", conceals a German aristocrat, the Graf von Schwabing, about whose Aryan origin there is no doubt. The notion of a Jewish world conspiracy is clearly peculiar to Scudder.

The Hannay novels do, however, assign Jews to a different universe from that of the English gentleman, depicting them as revolutionaries, businessmen, or financiers, alien in their values from the clean and robust clubland world of Hannay and his friends. If they are not Bolsheviks turning the world upside down, they are at least men of wealth pulling the strings of power. Classic stereotypes of the period, they reflect contemporary prejudice. "Thirty years before Hitler," writes Janet Adam Smith in her biography of Buchan, "people felt little self-consciousness in talking about Jews they disliked, and the Jews whom the upper-class Briton particularly disliked were Jews who were successful, rich, and well able to take care of themselves." Buchan fully shared this prejudice. Equally, he liked and respected individual Jews. *Prester John*, one of his most successful boys' adventure stories, is dedicated to his close friend Lionel Phillips, a Jew. He greatly admired Chaim Weizmann as a practical idealist, and was accepted by Jews as a genuine friend of Zionism, his name being inscribed in the Golden Book of the Jewish National Fund of Israel. Buchan, in short, shared common prejudices of his time. But what he did *not* do was make his spy villains invariably Jewish, or his Jews invariably villains, either in fiction or in fact.

The Hannay novels also lack the crude jingoism and xenophobia exploited by Le Queux. Here, Buchan shared more with Oppenheim, for both men directly experienced the reality of war. Buchan also learned something about espionage. He was, in fact, the first in the long line of British spy novelists to have direct professional involvement in the silent game.

"One side of my duties," wrote Buchan elliptically about his First World War experiences in *Memory Hold-the-Door*, "brought me into touch with the queer subterranean world of the Secret Service.... I have some queer *macabre* recollections of those years—of meetings with odd people in odd places, of fantastic duties which a romancer would have rejected as beyond probability."

Mystery still surrounds Buchan's secret service work. But although opinion differs as to whether he was directly involved, it is clear that he had plenty to do with those who were. "Correspondents and secret agents till all hours," he noted in a letter of May 1917. Philip Knightley, in *The Second Oldest Profession*, claims that Buchan's intelligence work lasted long after the war. "SIS in the 1930s was heavily penetrated," he writes, "by officers who had been talent spotted and signed up by...Buchan."

Buchan's contact with the secret service almost certainly began in 1916, when he began to work on unspecified duties for the Foreign Secretary, Sir Edward Grey. By then, the war had already extensively stretched his energies. Disqualified for combat on medical grounds, he had thrown himself into writing a month-by-month history of the war, had written about the Flanders battlefields as a special correspondent for the *Times*, and had officially reported on the Battle of Loos for the War Office. By early 1916 he was a major in the Intelligence Corps working at GHQ France on press liaison matters, and like Oppenheim, occasionally taking visitors on tours of the Western Front. The Battle of the Somme saw him close behind the lines preparing daily summaries for General Sir Douglas Haig and writing letters home which were increasingly filled with revulsion at what he saw. Not long after being invalided home with ulcer trouble, he found himself appointed by Lloyd George as director of the newly created propaganda organization, the Department of Information. One side of its activity was propaganda to enemy and neutral countries, and it was undoubtedly here that Buchan worked closely with the secret service.

According to Anthony Masters, Vernon Kell, the first head of M.I.5, Britain's counter-espionage service, had a hand in his appointment. Admiral Sir Reginald "Blinker" Hall, the legendary head of British Naval Intelligence, clearly entered Buchan's life in some way at this time, probably through Hall's interest in propaganda to the United States. In *Greenmantle*, Blenkiron, the

American engineer with the duodenal ulcer, swears that if he had a big job to handle and could pick his helpers he'd plump for the British Admiralty's Intelligence Department. And in "The Loathly Opposite", one of his post-war short stories published in *The Runagates Club* (1928), Buchan displayed a knowledge of wartime cipher-breaking techniques suggesting considerable familiarity with Hall's wartime operations.

Closer to Buchan's heart than that cloak-and-dagger side of his work abroad was the task of propaganda at home, the need to maintain national unity, and the vital necessity of gaining American support. For this, his spy fiction was as powerful a tool as anything else Buchan devised.

The Thirty-Nine Steps captured the romantic patriotism of the "days of August" in 1914, when crowds volunteered enthusiastically to fight for King and Country. *Greenmantle* was written while he was serving in France at GHQ, one of his declared motives being "simply to entertain the troops." But in doing so, he also instructed. His private letters increasingly referring to "this bloody war", he sought to cool the facile jingoism of his readers. In a climactic scene, while Hannay is being hunted in Germany by the police, he takes shelter with a woodcutter's wife. Observing her simple humility and suffering while her husband is fighting on the Eastern Front, Hannay is moved to renounce the popular anti-Germanism he learned at home. "I used to want to see the whole land of the Boche given up to fire and sword," he confesses, "...but that woodcutter's cottage cured me of such nightmares. I was for punishing the guilty but letting the innocent go free." It is in *Greenmantle*, too, that Hannay meets Gaudian, a German engineer, "clearly a good fellow, a white man, and a gentleman."

Mr. Standfast accomplished an even more difficult task. Written during the months that Buchan was actually in charge of domestic propaganda, it acknowledges with honesty the depth of war weariness, and expresses the collective grief and anger that set in after the bloodletting of the Battle of the Somme. Buchan's personal losses in the war added emotional power to this third Hannay story. "I acquired a bitter detestation of war," Buchan remembered of this period, "less for its horrors than for its boredom and futility, and a contempt for its panache." Tommy Nelson, his close friend since Oxford days—to whom he had dedicated *The Thirty-Nine Steps*—was killed at Arras in March 1917.

His own younger brother died of wounds in the following month. Raymond Asquith, another Oxford friend, had been killed on the Somme in September 1916, another, Bron Herbert, over enemy lines the same year, and Basil Blackwood, with whom Buchan had shared a house in South Africa, was killed at Ypres in July 1917. *Mr. Standfast* is a lament for his dead companions, for his own youth, and for an entire generation. At the same time, as its title indicated, it provides reasons to continue the struggle. Against the backdrop of labour unrest and pacifist agitation, Hannay struggles not only against Moxon Ivery and his penetration of English society, but also against the pacifist Launcelot Wake. Wake ends up dying heroically in the trenches, while Hannay comes to respect his opinions. For soldiers who had experienced trench warfare, Wake's discovery of fear, and of the courage to overcome it, echoed their own lives, and many of them wrote to Buchan expressing their gratitude.

"Sincere and honourable, if abnormal beings," was how Hannay described pacifists in *Mr. Standfast*. Ever alert to abnormality of whatever sort, the M.I.5 man within Buchan gave Hannay and his band the principal task of rooting out subversion at home.

"I began to have an ugly feeling that the Empire might decay at the heart," wrote Buchan of his reaction on returning to London after serving with Milner. This fear of decay at the heart, of an internal collapse caused by a subversion of will, haunted his spy fiction. Germany might temporarily be the enemy but the real threat in the Hannay novels exists beyond nationality. It is in the universal forces of evil, in a spiritual emptiness threatening western Christian values. "The free peoples have been challenged by the serfs," Buchan wrote in *Memory Hold-the-Door*. "The gutters have exuded a poison which bids fair to infect the world.... The European tradition has been confronted with an Asiatic revolt...as if a mature society were being assailed by diseased and vicious children."

With the exception of *Greenmantle* all the Hannay works, like the first "shocker", *The Power-House*, have as their central

antagonist someone close to the very centre of English society. In
The Thirty-Nine Steps the arch-villain successfully impersonates
both an eccentric archaeologist and—more impressively, if quite
implausibly—the First Sea Lord, in whose guise he attends a
Cabinet meeting. Trafalgar Lodge, the nest of spies with the
thirty-nine steps down to the sea, is a red brick villa with
a tennis court, "as orthodox in its quintessential Englishness
as an Anglican church"; and the three men Hannay confronts
within it appear to be "three ordinary, game-playing, suburban
Englishmen, wearisome if you like, but sordidly innocent." In
Mr. Standfast Moxon Ivery, although in reality a German, is a
public figure on the boards of many of England's most respected
institutions, a man on intimate terms with a number of leading
politicians, and apparently as English as the Norfolk countryside.
His integration into English society thus presents a danger of
terrifying dimensions. "It's as if the Chief of the Intelligence
Department were suddenly to desert to the enemy," Sir Walter
Bullivant, no alarmist, confides to Hannay. "This man knows our
life and our way of thinking and everything about us." The same
is true, but even more so, in *The Three Hostages* (1924), in which
Buchan finally turned his attention directly to Communism.

Dominic Medina, the villain of the novel, is in many respects
a facsimile of Hannay himself: youthful, athletic, a fine shot, and
an intrepid explorer. A Member of Parliament, he moves in the
highest circles. He also meets Hannay's more personal gauge
of acceptability, dressing conservatively in an old and well-cut
brown tweed suit, a soft shirt and collar, and a russet tie, "the
very beau ideal of the courteous, kindly, open-air Englishman."

Like Andrew Lumley before him, however, Medina is the
powerful and evil force behind a conspiracy—and beyond it lies
Communism. "Bolshevism," Medina confides to Hannay at a
climactic moment in the novel, "is a form of Shamanism," to be
welcomed for the weakening of civilization that it represents.

The novel provides an extended metaphor for the struggle
of the West against the forces of disorder unleashed by the
Bolshevik Revolution. The thinly disguised voice of intelligent
conservatism, it is the sophisticated man's alternative to the
cruder effusions of "Sapper" and Bulldog Drummond's struggles

against Carl Peterson and the Bolsheviks. The target of Drummond's campaign to save Britain is personified in the form of Peterson and other evil foreigners. Buchan, true to his Calvinist forebodings, sees a threat not only in Medina but in Hannay's own vulnerability to Medina's fascination. The danger has thus penetrated to the very heart of British society, to be resisted only by a determined reassertion of traditional values. In a world of flux and challenge, the Hannay novels tell us, the best we can do is remember the code of the gentleman.

Shortly after British publication of *The Three Hostages*, Buchan sailed on the *Empress of France* for the United States. Landing in Quebec, he spent a few days in Ottawa as a guest of Mackenzie King, the Canadian Prime Minister, and then travelled on to Boston. Like Oppenheim, Buchan had acquired a Boston publisher, in his case Houghton Mifflin, and there was business to discuss. From there, he travelled to Washington, had a personal interview with President Wilson at the White House, and then set off on the real purpose of his trip: a ten-day tour of the Civil War battlefields of Virginia.

The first of several visits to the United States, this trip made impressions on Buchan that never left him. The pioneer spirit appealed to his romantic temperament, and he was greatly attracted to his educated east coast hosts. "You have to go to America," he said in his memoirs, "...for the wholly civilised man who has not lost his natural vigour or agreeable idiosyncrasies, but who sees life in its true proportions and has a fine balance of mind and spirit." From an early age Buchan had been strongly pro-American, immersing himself in Thoreau and Whitman, reading intensively in American history, and conceiving the ambition (never realized) of writing a major biography of Lee. Lincoln was one of his great heroes.

"The alliance of America and Britain," he wrote during the First World War, "will be the greatest safeguard for the peaceful ordering of the world." "To [America's] hands," he wrote at the beginning of the Second, "is chiefly entrusted the shaping of the future."

This message about the United States is embedded in the Hannay novels, for wherever an American appears he is a sympathetic character. Hannay takes quickly to Scudder, his unfortunate neighbour in *The Thirty-Nine Steps*. Blenkiron, a central character in *Greenmantle* and *Mr. Standfast*, may be a millionaire with a Yankee accent, but he is as committed to western civilization in general, and the preservation of the British Empire in particular, as Hannay or Sir Walter Bullivant. Indeed, he works in tandem with the secret service, and often seems to be the real master-mind behind Hannay's successes.

Founding an informal Anglo-American society in London at a time when Britain's ruling class was still either indifferent or hostile to the United States, Buchan once declared that America and Britain shared "common ideals and common instincts, as well as common traditions." It was a sentiment he shared not only with Oppenheim, his contemporary. Later it was to be amplified even further and with dramatically greater success to a new generation by the spy writer once described as "a supersonic Buchan": Ian Fleming, the creator of James Bond.

In looking back on his literary career, Buchan once mused that he was "a natural story-teller, the kind of man who for the sake of his yarns would in prehistoric days have been given a seat by the fire and a special chunk of mammoth." Folk tales, he believed, were an important vehicle of popular philosophy, portraying attempts to overcome the hardships of the world and enjoining action rather than passivity. They had "a dominant purpose, a lesson, if you like, to teach, a creed to suggest...that the weak things of the earth can confound the strong; that nothing is impossible to the courageous and simple hearted; that the unfittest in the worldly sense can survive if he is fitted in more important respects. They are a glorification of the soul in man, an epic of the resurgence of the divine in human nature." To this universal formula, Buchan's spy fiction added a prophetic twentieth-century obsession: the fear of the destruction of civilization. T.E. Lawrence once wondered if some future age might recognize Buchan as "the great romancer of our blind and undeserving generation." In 1941, as German bombs blitzed

London, destroying so much of the city Buchan loved, Graham Greene, deeply influenced in his own spy fiction by Hannay and company, provided an answer. "Let us gratefully admit," he wrote, "that, in one way at any rate, Buchan prepared us in his thrillers better than he knew for the death that may come to any of us...by the railings of the Park or the doorway of the mews. For certainly we can all see now 'how thin is the protection of civilization'."

CHAPTER FOUR

"A Rather Jolly Pull-Together"

"Yes, but they couldn't very well do their hotel work and go
spying about all over Mendacia at the same time," Blenkinsop
objected.

"I say, don't use that word, if you don't mind, when you're
talking about our own people. We only use it of foreign agents....
There's always a slight stigma attached to that word, and since the
war we've really worked up a rather jolly pull-together spirit in
the Secret Service.... As a matter of fact, in ordinary conversation,
we always call the word 'plumbing'...."

Compton Mackenzie, *Water on the Brain*

The massive expansion of the intelligence services during the
First World War created a new breed of espionage writers and
changed the relationship between fact and fiction. In the pre-
war years, as writers imagined possible perils and weaknesses,
their fiction helped to shape the facts of counter-espionage and
defence. But after war broke out many writers and playwrights

became involved in the British war effort; a number helped in propaganda campaigns, while others entered the realm of intelligence work. Once the war was over, they could draw on personal experience in the writing of spy fiction. Three authors who profited from their direct experience in the silent game were A.E.W. Mason, Somerset Maugham, and Compton Mackenzie. All were popular and widely read in the inter-war years.

I

Alfred Edward Woodley Mason might have stepped directly from the pages of one of his own thrilling novels of adventure and romance. Watching him as a Liberal Member of Parliament in the House of Commons just before the First World War, one contemporary remembered that "he was one of the most boyish-looking members in the House—blue-eyed, clean-shaven, fresh-coloured, and slim." Another described him as the perfect clubman, a man with no domestic ties to keep him home at night, as good a listener as a talker, and a man who "never by any chance looked at the clock". This tall and cheerful extrovert, a lifelong cigar-smoking bachelor who was always impeccably dressed and invariably wore an eyeglass, had a zest for travel and adventure that lasted for all his eighty-three years. Firmly convinced that "travelling keeps your mind fresh", Mason was a wanderer with a lust for the exotic. He visited Omdurman only two years after Kitchener had finally subdued the Sudan, and travelling to a Morocco in rebellion came close to being shot by a tribesman. He kept himself in physical trim by mountain-climbing. An inveterate visitor to Switzerland, he scaled Mont Blanc five times from five different directions, and always, his biographer tells us, took a bottle of champagne to break open on the summit. The son of an accountant, Mason never fully satisfied his ambition to enter the landed gentry. But he came close. Frequently invited to fashionable dinners and country-house parties, he hunted, shot, and rode with Britain's élite. A polymath of a now-vanished breed, he was also an actor, novelist, and playwright, "a leading light at the Beefsteak and Garrick clubs in the days when Bohemianism still flourished".

Mason was born in London in 1865 and educated at Dulwich and Trinity College, Oxford. After a not very successful spell as an actor he turned to writing. With the publication of *The Courtship of Morrice Buckler* (1896) he entered the ranks of cloak-and-dagger writers, and *The Four Feathers* (1902) established his reputation as a writer of adventure stories, which he continued to produce successfully over the next thirty years.

The most famous and popular of his later adventure stories was *Fire Over England* (1936), a historical romance set in Elizabethan days and almost immediately made into a major movie directed by Alexander Korda and starring Laurence Olivier and Vivien Leigh. The hero is Robin Aubrey, a young Englishman sent out to Spain on a secret mission by Sir Francis Walsingham, the legendary founder of Britain's first secret service. It is Walsingham who finally tells Aubrey the truth about his long-lost father's past, revealing that the hero will be treading in his father's footsteps in the service of his country. "He did the great service to the realm, the service which earns no honours—nay, which may stain the name with infamy."

Mason knew what Walsingham was talking about. Desperate to serve his country in 1914, Mason had first gone off on a propaganda tour to the United States and then lied about his age to join the infantry. But a year later the fifty-year-old Captain Mason set out on the path he later mapped for Robin Aubrey. Mysteriously summoned to a dingy office in the neighbourhood of Charing Cross, he found himself in the presence of one of Britain's great twentieth-century spymasters, "Blinker" Hall.

As director of Naval Intelligence throughout the First World War, Admiral Hall was responsible for "Room 40", Britain's code-breaking operation, whose most famous triumph was the interception of the Zimmerman telegram. This message, sent in January 1917 by the German Foreign Minister to the German minister in Mexico, urging a German-Mexican alliance against the United States, greatly contributed to American entry into the war against the Germans. "Hall is the one genius that the War has developed," the American ambassador in London told President Woodrow Wilson in 1918. "Neither in fiction nor in fact can you find any such man to match him...all other secret service men are amateurs by comparison." One of Hall's side-shows was running cloak-and-dagger operations. It was for one of these that he had summoned Mason, whom he later described as his "star turn".

Hall's concern was German U-boat operations off the Spanish Mediterranean coast. Mason, a successful middle-aged novelist with an independent income and a love for yachting and adventure, was the perfect spy for the job. For most of the next two years he wandered around the western Mediterranean, to all the world an innocent Englishman simply messing about with boats. In fact, he was picking up information about German submarines surreptitiously refuelling in Spanish ports, and keeping an eye on the work of German spies in and around Gibraltar. In 1916 he spent some time in Morocco, where he helped to sabotage German attempts to stir up rebellion by Riff tribesmen against the French by blocking off their flow of funds into the country. Later he was involved in a bizarre incident in Spain, where he claimed to have intercepted a consignment of shaving brushes that the Germans had infected with anthrax in order to spread an epidemic among Allied troops on the Western Front. Subsequent evidence turned up by historians suggests that this was a product of Mason's imagination.

After Mason's cover was blown—the Germans eventually became suspicious of his yacht—he was transferred to Mexico. Here he adopted yet another disguise—that clichéd one of the wandering butterfly collector (obviously he had read his Baden-Powell). Improbable though it now sounds, the trick appears to have worked. Mason successfully put out of action the wireless station at Ixtapalapa, thereby making it more complicated for the principal German agent in the country to receive messages from Berlin. He also helped American authorities to track down German agents active in the United States. One of them, responsible for the sabotage of American munitions plants, visited Mexico to plan more destruction with the German minister in Mexico City. "I ran him to ground," Mason later told a friend, "and pushed him over into the United States, where he was court-martialled [and] sentenced to be shot...."

Major Mason of the secret service thus had direct front-line experience of espionage. He had no illusions about its dangers, and was well aware that agents in adversity were on their own. On one of his journeys to and from Spain he had witnessed the execution of Mata Hari as a spy in Paris, he carried a poison vial with him in case of arrest, and he was capable of disposing of his opponents in a chilling manner. Telling a friend after the war how he had prevented a party of Germans from setting up a secret transmitter in some remote mountain area of Mexico, Mason hinted at deadly work. "What did you do?" asked the friend. "Oh," replied Mason, "I spread it around that they were carrying diamonds. No more was heard about them." A similarly ruthless quality is evident in at least one of his short stories, "Pfeiffer" (1917). The eponymous German spy, who has set up a bombing attack on Gibraltar, is imprisoned by the British on the Rock without being told that his plan has been uncovered. The reader is invited to share a sadistic relish in Pfeiffer's discomfort as he believes he awaits death at the hands of his own side.

Much of this, of course, was post-war fantasy used by Mason to embellish his fiction. On the whole, he preferred to present secret service work as clean, thrilling, and innocent adventure in the service of King and Country.

As in the case of both Le Queux and Buchan, royalty loved such stirring patriotism. King George V was a keen fan of Mason's works, receiving specially inscribed copies directly from the author. Queen Mary visited the Denham film studio in person to see one of Mason's stories being filmed, and in 1937 he was offered a knighthood. But he declined, saying that for a childless man it was an empty honour.

Most of Mason's spy fiction is fairly thinly disguised autobiography. A case in point is the short story "One of Three" (1916), which might equally have been written by Childers or Buchan. (Indeed, when it came to writers in his own genre, Buchan once confessed that he enjoyed Mason as much as any.) Drawing heavily on Mason's experience in the western Mediterranean, it tells the tale of Anthony Strange, an Englishman unwittingly drawn into counter-espionage work, who helps sink a German U-boat off the coast of Spain. Illness has prevented the young man from fighting actively on the Western Front. But in joining the silent game he is "admitted to the band of the young strong men who serve, like a novice into the communion of a church."

This fairly obvious projection of Mason's own experience is elaborated at length in his novel *The Summons* (1920). Martin Hillyard, just down from Oxford, is recruited by a thinly disguised Sir Reginald Hall in the shape of Commodore Graham—"a thin man with the face of a French abbé"—and wanders around the coast of Spain foiling German conspiracies. If the physical landscape is familiar Mason territory, the mental maps are firmly within the tradition of the genre. Hillyard, the gentleman amateur, appreciates not only "the cunning of Berlin with its long-deliberated plans and its concocted ingenuity of method" but also "the white skin and clean-limbed boyishness of English girls".

Mason's novel *The Winding Stair* (1923) foreshadows Buchan's *A Prince of the Captivity* in presenting patriotic se- cret service as a form of redemption. Paul Ravenal overcomes past family dishonour by undertaking intelligence missions for the French in Morocco: "Far away from the main shock of the battles many curious and romantic episodes were occurring, many strange epics of prowess and adventure." Paul is in their midst, sabotaging German efforts to stir up the Moors against the French. Once he has proven his worth, the Anglo-French hero can assume the full British nationality he is so desperate to acquire. We hear Mason's voice in the words of Paul's old fam- ily friend: "Philosophers and Labour leaders talk very placidly about throwing down the walls between nation and nation, but the walls aren't of our building...to the men with anything, the soil cries...." Most patriotic Englishmen would have applauded such sentiments in the aftermath of the First World War. They might also have concluded, from reading Mason, that spying for King and Country was a travel adventure from which gentlemen returned unscathed and refreshed. Like Baden-Powell, Mason believed that espionage could be a great recuperator.

II

The romanticized view of espionage was finally challenged in 1928, with the appearance of Somerset Maugham's *Ashenden*. It was a milestone in the history of spy fiction, and appropriately enough, it was published a few months after Le Queux's death. Eric Ambler, who would emerge as the most important spy writer of the 1930s, was strongly influenced by *Ashenden*, following Maugham in creating characters far removed from the gentleman-agent heroes of the Edwardian tradition. John le Carré has said that Maugham was the first person to write about espionage in a mood of disenchantment and prosaic reality. Raymond Chandler paid his own compliment to the man he called "the lonely old eagle" when he asked Maugham for an inscribed copy of *Ashenden*; it was, he said, far ahead of any other spy novel ever written. The modern spy novel, Julian Symons has said, began with *Ashenden*.

Ashenden consists of a series of episodes in which the central character—clearly based on Maugham himself—is seen operating networks as an intelligence officer in Switzerland and Russia during the First World War. Maugham may well have believed, as he once claimed, that fact was a poor storyteller, yet *Ashenden* is a remarkably accurate description of his own experiences—sufficiently so that he was at first told that it breached the Official Secrets Act. He burned several of the episodes and had to wait for official clearance before publishing the remainder.

In 1914 Maugham was at the peak of his success as a playwright, much interviewed and discussed in London circles. It may seem odd that such a public figure would become involved in spying. But, like Mason's, his international reputation provided an excellent cover when he was first sent to Switzerland, and the tasks he assumed there were well suited to his experience and qualifications.

Maugham was born in 1874 in the British embassy in Paris, where his father worked as a solicitor, and he spent the first ten years of his life in France, speaking French more easily than English. He decided as an adolescent to become a writer, but first qualified as a doctor, obtaining his medical degree in London in

1897. He then began to write, and a decade later was both famous and successful. In a long career that lasted until his death in 1965, he became the best-selling English novelist of the century; one estimate suggests his books have sold 64 million copies. The hallmark of his fiction lies in the detached irony and precision of his observations on the human comedy, qualities well suited to the kind of intelligence work he would undertake.

When war broke out, Maugham volunteered for duty and was assigned to an ambulance unit on the Western Front. A year later he returned to London on leave, and through his mistress, Mrs. Syrie Wellcome, met Captain John Wallinger of the Indian Police, who was running secret operations in France and Switzerland. Wallinger suggested that with his knowledge of languages, Maugham could play a more useful role. Writing a play in the peace and quiet of Switzerland would, he pointed out, provide excellent cover for intelligence work.

"If you do well you'll get no thanks," Wallinger told Maugham, "and if you get into trouble you'll get no help." Far from getting into trouble, Maugham found that life as a secret agent was rather monotonous and, he said later, "uncommonly senseless". His first mission was to Lucerne, where he spied on an Englishman with a German wife suspected of working for the German secret service. He then set up his headquarters at a hotel in Geneva. Maugham's job was to service a network of agents working in Germany itself. Some of them turned out to be frauds, and the novelist's tasks turned out to be prosaic. Once a week he crossed to the French side of Lake Geneva, delivered his reports, and received instructions that he relayed back to his field agents. The job quickly palled, and after a year he returned to London to resume his writing career.

Then, in May 1917—despite the fact that he had already met Gerald Haxton, the American who was to be his lover for the next thirty years—Maugham married Syrie Wellcome. The daughter of Dr. Barnardo, founder of the Barnardo Homes for Orphan Children, she had borne Maugham a child the year before. The marriage was disastrous from the beginning, and soon Maugham was anxious to find an excuse to get away. So when Sir William Wiseman, head of British Intelligence in the

United States, phoned him in Jersey City (where he married Syrie) and asked him to go to Russia on another secret mission, he quickly accepted. The job offered not only escape from his new wife, but also adventure, service to his country, and, in contrast to his Swiss service for which he was not paid, money. On July 28, 1917, Maugham sailed from San Francisco for Tokyo and Vladivostok, using the cover name Somerville. "I was exhilarated...," he later remembered. "I went as a private agent, who could be disavowed if necessary, with instructions to get in touch with parties hostile to the government and devise a scheme that would keep Russia in the war and prevent the Bolsheviks, supported by the Central Powers, from seizing power."

It was a mission doomed from the start, although Maugham claimed that had he begun earlier it might have been successful. The Czar had abdicated in March and Kerensky was in charge of the new provisional government, but it was a fragile construction with Bolshevik and German propaganda rapidly eroding its authority. Wiseman hoped to counter this by rallying pro-Allied forces inside the country, including the Mensheviks, several thousand Czechs, and an assortment of other Slavic groups from Eastern Europe eager to defeat Germany and Austro-Hungary for their national liberation. Maugham also sent back intelligence reports on the deteriorating Russian situation. But events overtook him. In late October he returned to England to deliver an urgent and secret message from Kerensky to Lloyd George, pleading for guns and ammunition. Lloyd George refused. A few days later, on November 7, the Bolsheviks seized power, and soon afterwards signed a separate peace with Germany.

Maugham's career in intelligence was not quite over. Shortly after the Bolshevik victory, he was briefly involved in Allied plans to use Cossack forces to overthrow the Bolsheviks, and a short time later Wiseman asked him to go out on a mission to Romania. But by this time he had contracted tuberculosis, and he declined the offer in order to enter a sanatorium in Scotland. That seems to have ended his career as a secret agent.

Maugham's achievements in the silent game were relatively minor, but their impact on the spy novel was immense. For the reader accustomed to the patriotic melodramas of Le Queux and

Oppenheim, or even to the adventures of A.E.W. Mason, *Ashenden* must have appeared revolutionary. For the most important message of the novel is that in most respects espionage is like any other job, consisting of tedium, routine, and boredom. Ashenden, like any other government employee, does what he is told by his superiors. Some of it is unsavoury, and often it leads to tragic consequences. In "Giulia Lazzari", for example, Ashenden exploits a man's love for a woman to lure him into Allied hands, where he commits suicide; in "The Traitor" the love between the Englishman Caypor and his German wife is destroyed when Ashenden leads the man into British custody, where he is shot. The episode most likely to have caused offence, however, is "The Flip of a Coin"—significantly omitted from some later editions of the book. In this tale, one of Ashenden's agents, a Galician Pole, is involved in a scheme to blow up a munitions plant in Austria-Hungary, a plan that will inevitably lead to the deaths of many of his countrymen. Both the agent and Ashenden think the action necessary but distasteful. Ashenden has no desire to take responsibility, so they make the decision by flipping a coin. The moral indifference of the story is heightened by the fact that we are not told the result: as they both look at the coin, the agent draws in his breath, while Ashenden says dispassionately, "Well, that's that."

After the resolute morality and patriotism of earlier heroes, it is no wonder that, as Julian Symons says, the *Ashenden* stories have all the reality of a cold bath. But Maugham went even further. It was not only that the agent himself disclaimed moral responsibility for the consequences of his action, but that he was merely copying the behaviour of his superiors. "Though ready enough to profit by the activities of obscure agents of whom they had never heard," Ashenden reflects cynically, "they shut their eyes to the dirty work so that they could put their clean hands on their hearts and congratulate themselves that they had never done anything that was unbecoming to men of honour."

Ashenden also recalls reporting to "R", his immediate superior, that he has found an agent willing to assassinate the ruler of a Balkan state that is about to declare war against the Allies. "It's not the kind of thing we can have anything to do with," replies

R, in a tone of outrage. "We don't wage war by those methods. We leave them to the Germans. Damn it all, we are gentlemen." But it soon becomes clear to Ashenden that R's objection to the assassination lies in the decision rather than the act; he will be happy if the scheme succeeds, provided that he himself need not shoulder the responsibility. "They were all like that," observes Ashenden. "They desired the end, but hesitated at the means. They were willing to take advantage of an accomplished fact, but wanted to shift onto someone else the responsibility of bringing it about."

In his portrait of R, Maugham expressed a hard-nosed realism that set the tone for an entirely new generation of espionage writing. "Of course a lot of nonsense is talked about the value of human life," R says at one point. "You might just as well say that the counters you use at poker have an intrinsic value. Their value is what you like to make it; for a general giving battle, men are merely counters and he's a fool if he allows himself for sentimental reasons to look upon them as human beings." This was not a sentiment that any gentleman would have voiced in a novel from the pen of Le Queux, Oppenheim, or even Buchan. The *Times Literary Supplement* was quick to seize upon the point. "Never before," said its anonymous reviewer, "has it been so categorically demonstrated that counter-intelligence work consists of morally indefensible jobs not to be undertaken by the squeamish or the conscience-stricken."

For all the cynicism to be found in *Ashenden*, it contains a strong undercurrent of traditional patriotism. There is no doubt, for example, that Ashenden regards traitors as people of particular infamy. Spying for one's own country and spying for the enemy are morally two quite different things. Ashenden is aware that his own activities have devastating human consequences, but he puts a clear distance between himself and the Englishman Caypor, who is working for the Germans, by describing the latter's work as "a base and dishonourable calling". Ultimately the justification for Ashenden's distasteful task remains his duty to his country. The book's significance lies not in a rejection of patriotism but in its realism, its recognition of the awful human costs of espionage. The cynicism comes in the evaluation of human motives, not in any judgement of the tasks themselves. Had it been otherwise, the book would hardly have become standard reading for new entrants into the British Secret Intelligence Service in the 1930s.

III

The publication of *Ashenden* overshadowed another spy novel that appeared in 1928. Its title was *Extremes Meet*, and its author, Compton Mackenzie, had also been professionally involved in wartime secret service work. Like *Ashenden*, the novel radically changed the traditional picture of espionage, although unlike Maugham's book this and its successors failed to receive the recognition they deserved.

Born in 1883, Edward Morgan Compton Mackenzie was the son of Edward Compton, a successful actor-manager, and his wife, Virginia Bateman, an American actress. The family was wealthy enough to send him to St. Paul's public school in London and then to Magdalen College, Oxford, where he took a degree in modern history in 1904. His early writing career was a dazzling success, and after the publication of his 1914 novel, *Sinister Street*, Henry James hailed him as "by far the greatest talent of the new generation". Although he subsequently fell out of favour with highbrow critics, he continued to attract millions of readers with an unceasing flow of books—by the time of his death in 1972 he had written well over a hundred, some forty of which were novels. A lifelong extrovert, he was an outspoken supporter of Scottish nationalism, a keen music connoisseur and gardener, a popular broadcaster, and a media celebrity. Described by an obituarist in the *Times* as "pugnacious, egotistic, and ebullient", Mackenzie was no stranger to controversy and never sought to hide his opinions. These were often savage and scathing. His writings about the secret service were no exception.

Whereas Maugham shocked people by painting espionage as a morally dubious activity carried out by bored and unglamorous people, Mackenzie showed it as largely unadorned farce. *Extremes Meet* drew heavily on the author's own experiences as a secret agent in wartime Greece. This occupation he had stumbled into almost by accident. After several unsuccessful attempts to volunteer for war service in 1914, Mackenzie finally found a job with the ill-fated Allied expedition to the Dardanelles in 1915. Invalided out of active service shortly afterwards, he worked briefly as a war correspondent, and here his writing talents were quickly spotted by British Intelligence in the eastern Mediterranean. Before long, he was in charge of counter-espionage for the Aegean region at Intelligence HQ in Athens. The situation was ripe for intrigue and ideal for an extrovert like Mackenzie. Greece was still neutral, but the King was pro-German while Venizelos, his Prime Minister, was strongly pro-Allied. Mackenzie was not content merely to devise and maintain a massive dossier on the multitude of German agents swarming through the area. Additionally, he threw himself into cloak-and-dagger intrigues for the Venizelist cause, and in 1917 personally took over control of the Cyclades Islands in the name of a provisional government established by Venizelos in Salonika. From this base on the island of Syra, Mackenzie sailed around the islands in his personal yacht, ruling the archipelago as a personal fiefdom until ill health finally forced him to return home.

Mackenzie drew very different conclusions than Maugham from his career as a secret agent. As representative in Athens of "C", the head of the British Secret Intelligence Service,[2] he had encountered sufficient human absurdity to last him a lifetime: the fantasies of over-imaginative agents manufacturing plots and conspiracies; the follies of inter-Allied relationships in which the British, French, Italians, and Russians often seemed more intent on outwitting each other than on defeating the enemy; and above all, the internecine warfare among different branches of British intelligence. For not the least of Mackenzie's problems in the midst of this maze had been that, as C's man, he was often at loggerheads with other divisions of military intelligence which regarded him as a menace. "This officer has

---

[2]The initial comes from the signature of Sir Mansfield Cumming, the Service's first head, who held the position from 1911 to 1923. Subsequent directors have always been referred to as "C".

too much initiative," noted one War Office file about Mackenzie, which only confirmed him in his view that he was dealing with fools. He even ran afoul of Cumming at first, but eventually developed a close and affectionate relationship with him. Indeed, on the basis of Mackenzie's brilliant performance in Greece, Cumming even went so far as to propose that Mackenzie become his second-in-command. "After the war's over," C told him, "we'll do some amusing secret service work together. It's capital sport." Mackenzie declined the offer. Instead, he built on his wartime experience to expose secret service as a Marx Brothers affair. With Cumming as his former boss, this was not difficult. Mackenzie once described him as a man with a pair of very bright eyes and "a Punch-like chin".

Frequently Cumming also exhibited a Punch-like character more suited to vaudeville than to secret intelligence. Fitted with a wooden leg after he lost a foot in a car accident, he used to propel himself at top speed down War Office corridors on a child's scooter, terrifying all those who got in his way. He had a passion for conjuring tricks, schoolboy jokes, and disguises, and a mystical affinity with inks. He always used green to write his official correspondence, and once, experimenting with secret inks, gleefully reported to a colleague that he had discovered that the best invisible ink was semen. In a world populated by eccentrics such as Cumming, fact and fiction seemed to merge, and farce was never far below the surface.

Extremes Meet combines cynicism about the value of most intelligence work with a fine sense of human folly. "A good agent," Roger Waterlow, head of the secret service in Greece, confides to his assistant at one point, "tells you that lack of coffee and contraceptives among the Turks will make them sue for peace in less than a month. The fighting arms are always thirsting for an intellectual tonic. That is what the secret service is intended to provide." It is Waterlow, too, who pronounces the following *bon mot*, which could continue to serve as a motto for the intelligence analyst: "A prudent man at the end of his life will have decided that most men are liars; a year's experience of the secret service will teach the most imprudent that all men are liars."

These views of the secret service did not endear Mackenzie to his former colleagues, and he compounded the offence by publishing an even more biting sequel on the surreal fantasies engendered by the hothouse climate of espionage. The enemy in *The Three Couriers* (1929) is less the Germans than the Gordian knot of British bureaucracy and red tape. The hapless Waterlow is constantly foiled by the inanities of his own side, whether it be the naval and military authorities, the diplomats, his own agents, or the French. And when he finally succeeds in intercepting a vital message being carried by the last of three enemy couriers, its contents are ignored by higher authority. "This is a Charlie Chaplin war," he sighs as he attempts to gain poise after yet another disaster.

As long as this was disguised as fiction, there was little anyone could do about it. But in 1931 Mackenzie, publishing the second volume of his war memoirs, *First Athenian Memories*, made it clear that the farce was by no means confined to fiction. He entitled one chapter "Early Absurdities of Secret Service", and made biting references throughout to the self-hypnotism induced by the "abracadabra" of the secret service. When the third volume, *Greek Memories*—an unadorned picture of Mackenzie's wartime exploits in Athens—appeared in October 1932, the wrath of officialdom, and of George V himself, was finally provoked. The publishers were forced to withdraw the book from circulation and Mackenzie was shortly afterwards prosecuted under the Official Secrets Act. The trial at the Old Bailey in January 1933 was held in camera, but sufficient details became known that it rebounded on those whom it was intended to protect. One of Mackenzie's main offences, it transpired, was to have named Sir Mansfield Cumming as head of the wartime secret service; that Cumming had been dead since 1923 was apparently of no significance. Mackenzie had also named other names and had given a detailed plan of various wartime intelligence organizations in Greece, observing that their "conflicting powers and contending ambitions made battered shuttlecocks of their junior officers." Furthermore, he made no attempt to conceal the rivalry between C and "Blinker" Hall, and he made many passing references to "obscurantist minds" and "bygone stupidities".

The trial represented malicious prosecution. The government failed to demonstrate that the revelations threatened the security of the realm, and it was obvious that Mackenzie was the victim of people who disliked their existence being treated with irreverence. The Attorney-General was reputed to have told the Cabinet that *Greek Memories* had destroyed the secret service—which was patently ridiculous—and a friendly secret-service contact told Mackenzie that its establishment was out for his blood. In the end the case collapsed under the weight of its own weakness. Mackenzie was found guilty on an essentially technical count, and the judge made it clear in imposing a minimum fine that he thought the prosecution had been a waste of time. All the same, the legal costs left the author several hundred pounds poorer.

The trial might have destroyed or deterred a different person. But Mackenzie's combative instinct, combined with his acute financial need, led him to strike back. Less than a year later he published *Water on the Brain*, which remains to this day one of the most caustic satires on the British secret service. Although less effective because more overblown than *Extremes Meet* or *The Three Couriers*, *Water on the Brain* captured the high farce and low comedy produced by the secret service's obsession with secrecy, its pathological jealousy of other services, and the peculiar faith held by certain of its senior officers in the possibilities of disguise.

The plot of *Water on the Brain* is one of Byzantine complexity. Major Blenkinsop, with some post-war business experience of Mendacia, one of the new nations of south-east Europe, is summoned by the British secret service to help restore Mendacia's king to the throne. Impressed deeply with the need for secrecy and stealth, Blenkinsop tells his wife that he has taken a job in a business involving the waste products of bananas. Shortly thereafter, Blenkinsop meets Arthur Hudson, who really is in the banana business but who, in order to impress *his* wife, pretends he is in the secret service. Indeed in his spare time Hudson writes spy novels under the pseudonym "Yorke Lankester" ("who," his publisher's blurb announces, "has a knowledge of the underworld of diplomacy which recalls that of the late William Le Queux"). Blenkinsop is ordered to Paris to meet the head of the secret service, N, a man much given to mysterious rendezvous and disguise. (On this occasion, N is disguised as Captain Winston Churchill.) Having received his instructions, Blenkinsop returns to London and is initiated into the secrets of Pomona Lodge, the headquarters of the service. There he meets a bizarre menagerie of creatures who roam the labyrinths of the secret worlds of espionage, from Major Claude Hunter-Hunt, his immediate superior, who as a precaution always sleeps with a respirator, to Miss Glidden, N's private secretary, who carries the secrets she knows "as multitudinously, as easily, as safely, and as neatly packed away as the female herring carries her roe." Blenkinsop heads north to Scotland to make contact with Madame Tekta, a beguiling and attractive Mendacian agent, but he is followed by at least two people—a private detective hired by his wife, who suspects him of having an affair with Madame Tekta, and a British counter-espionage agent who reports that Blenkinsop is involved in a Scottish Nationalist uprising backed by Moscow gold. At this point Hudson's next novel is announced, entitled—apparently by coincidence—*The Secret of Pomona Lodge—A Thrilling Romance of the Secret Service.* N and his headquarters are thrown into apoplexy by this apparent breach of security, and Pomona Lodge is hastily transformed into an asylum for bureaucrats driven mad in the service of their country—a cover which, as one character points out, is foolproof.

None of this farcical behaviour affects events in Mendacia: the King returns to power, Blenkinsop—relieved of his duties and miraculously back in marital favour—returns to Mendacia, and we leave him running a resort hotel where guests take the waters of the Island of Parvo, waters that "possess that indispensable quality of clarifying the stomach and obfuscating at the same time the brains of its devotees."

Such a summary hardly does justice to the novel's rich texture of farce, but it captures the essential themes that Mackenzie was at pains to convey: the obsession with secrecy of a bureaucracy out of touch with reality and usually working at cross purposes with those who should be its allies. "Although [it] is a deliberate caricature of Intelligence," Mackenzie told Sir Robert Rait, the principal of Glasgow University to whom he dedicated the book, "there are features in the system which will be recognised even by those with a good deal less humour and knowledge than yourself." One can only wonder whether the secret service now regretted its persecution of Mackenzie: N was a thinly disguised portrait of Admiral Sir Hugh Sinclair, Cumming's successor as C, and behind Major Claude Hunter-Hunt could be recognized the man whom Kim Philby would describe as "cringing and ineffectual", Major Valentine (Vee-Vee) Vivian, head of the secret service's counter-espionage section.

Water on the Brain was a savage revenge on those who had suppressed Mackenzie's memoirs and contributed to the nonsense of his trial. It was even more satisfying when *Greek Memories* was reissued, albeit with some cuts omitting details about the intelligence network in Athens and the names of British secret service personnel, in 1939. In the preface the author commented, "For the moment, we are making a parade of our freedom. Nevertheless the tendency of our democratic rulers moves steadily towards repression, and the Official Secrets Act is a convenient weapon for repression."

For Mackenzie's target was not only the secret service but the more general abuses of bureaucracy and the centralization of the modern state. Like many "mere entertainers", he had a serious message to deliver. Edmund Wilson once perceptively remarked that Mackenzie had never fully received the critical acclaim due him because he "was always at an angle to English society." Indeed, Mackenzie's heritage—Scottish on his father's side and American on his mother's—made him an uncomfortable figure on the English scene, and as early as the 1920s he had become a supporter of the Scottish Nationalist cause. Once describing himself as a "Jacobite Tory", he felt instinctive sympathy for the rights of small nations and cultural minorities. Above all, however, he had nothing but contempt for the bureaucratic mind and for those who defended and were protected by it. In the secret service he found bureaucracy at its most obsessive. "Alas," he said when summing up his lifetime experiences, "no insecticide has ever been discovered for the parasites of bureaucracy." In his spy fiction he tried hard to provide one.

CHAPTER FIVE

The Silent Game...

The Secret Service has its fighting line, too, though the war
correspondents don't write about it. It never gets a mention
in despatches, and Victoria Crosses don't come its way. The
newspapers don't publish its casualty list, though you and I know
it's a long one. A man slips quietly away and never comes back,
and after a certain lapse of time we just mark him off the books
and there's an end of it. But it's a great service.

Valentine Williams, *The Man with the Clubfoot*

Early in the Second World War, Kim Philby found himself travelling by official Rolls-Royce in the company of an important
figure in British "black" (secret) propaganda to Germany. "I
would have liked to talk to him about Clubfoot," Moscow's
super-spy later recalled, "but he had lunched well and he slept all
the way." Philby's dormant companion was Valentine Williams.
Clubfoot was the nickname of the German master spy Dr.
Grundt, the villain of a series of spy novels that Williams wrote

between 1918 and the end of the Second World War. Like the novels of Buchan and Sapper, they were often an unofficial part of the curriculum at private schools, where they were read out loud to the boys. Many, like Philby, could not hear enough about the evil Clubfoot.

"I was a newspaper man, then a soldier, and now I am a novelist, whose feet still turn to Fleet Street as inevitably as a river to the sea," wrote Williams in his 1938 autobiography, *The World of Action*. Indeed, Williams, like Le Queux, had experienced the adventure and ordeal of serving Lord Northcliffe. From 1910 to 1922 he had worked for the *Daily Mail*, first as correspondent in Paris, where one of his earliest tasks was to help Norman Angell, the managing editor, correct the proofs of Angell's best-selling anti-war polemic, *The Great Illusion*. He reported from Lisbon on the Portuguese revolution of 1910, and then travelled to south-east Europe to cover the Balkan Wars. After the First World War, he became the newspaper's foreign editor. Even after resigning to concentrate on his fiction, Williams frequently accepted special foreign assignments—covering the discovery by Howard Carter of Tutankhamun's tomb, reporting on the Riff rebellion in Morocco, visiting New York at the height of Prohibition. This was Williams' "world of action" that provided the raw material for his spy novels. "I can trace back the plot and characters in my novels to incidents and encounters of my newspaper days," he recalled, "when, with a belt of golden sovereigns round my waist, I would leave at an hour's notice for Spain, or the Balkans or Italy...."

Born in London in 1883, Williams was the seventh child of a comfortable, late Victorian, middle-class professional family. His mother was Irish, from Galway, although for most of her pre-married life she had lived with relatives in Florence, Italy. There she had met and married George Douglas Williams, the young Reuters News Agency representative in what was then the capital of the newly united Italy. Two years later, in 1870, the young couple was in Paris for the Franco-Prussian War and the uprising of the Paris Commune. From there, George Williams rose steadily in Reuters until he became its chief editor, and when his son completed his education at England's leading Catholic public school, Downside, he found him a job as a sub-editor in the London office. Shortly afterwards, while most British eyes were turned to South Africa and the fight against the Boers, Valentine Williams found himself in Germany.

The experience proved decisive. He arrived just as Anglo-German rivalry was beginning to harden, and one of his earliest recollections was seeing President Kruger and his Boer generals being cheered by a crowd in Cologne. Later, after he had been appointed Reuters' Berlin correspondent, he became acutely aware of Germany's power, and the threat to Britain's maritime supremacy. The experience convinced Williams that Germans were fundamentally different in mentality from the English. "Their hypersensitiveness, their mandarin-like caste system and adherence to outward forms, their standardised mentality, produced an impression on my youthful mind which was to help me explain to my own satisfaction many seemingly inexplicable developments of the Teuton character in years to come." This belief remained with Williams to the end of his life, and shaped his view that the Nazi regime was nothing more than "Kaiserism" in its extreme form. It was a common enough opinion in Britain, and it lingered on until well after the Second World War.

In 1915, after having left Reuters to join forces with Northcliffe, Williams was sent, along with John Buchan, as one of the first official war correspondents to GHQ France. Shortly afterwards, seeking action, he joined the Irish Guards and fought on the Western Front, where he won the Military Cross. On September 25, 1916, while he was resting beside a shell hole after a successful advance during the Somme offensive, a six-inch shell landing close by blew him several feet into the air. "I went up an experienced newspaper man," he wrote, "and came down a budding novelist." In hospital, brooding over his situation as an unemployed special correspondent, he had a brainwave. Several times at the GHQ press château he'd had lengthy conversations with John Buchan, who had urged him to try his hand at writing a shocker. Buchan had written one when he was bored and ill, and had done very well out of it. Why shouldn't Williams do the same?

But what should he write about? It wasn't difficult to decide. While convalescing he suffered recurrent nightmares of being a British spy trapped in Berlin, pursued by the German police. "From such nightly horrors," he wrote, "I would awaken bathed in perspiration and screaming with fright." He turned the experience to good use. In 1918, under the pseudonym of Douglas Valentine, he published the first of his spy novels, "my shell-shocker" he quipped, *The Man with the Clubfoot*. An early success, it was followed shortly afterwards by *The Secret Hand*, *The Return of Clubfoot*, and *Clubfoot the Avenger*. All were quickly translated into foreign languages, and their sales were good enough for Williams to take himself off to live in style at Cannes. There he met and became friends with Oppenheim, who described him in *The Pool of Memory* as the "most immaculate and certainly the best-dressed of authors I ever knew." Williams returned the compliment. "Some of my most pleasant memories of the Riviera," he wrote, "are associated with the hours spent in company with 'the Opps'."

What Oppenheim thought of Williams' novels he did not say, although they struck a sympathetic chord with fellow Germanophobe Rudyard Kipling. "We all read your books with the greatest zeal," the creator of *Kim* wrote to Williams in 1922, "and they always thrill and interest me." Certainly they draw on Williams' pre-war experience. In Berlin several encounters with the Prussian secret police had introduced him to some picturesque minor players in the silent game. One was an agent who arrived at Williams' office unannounced one day, flourishing an extremely dirty visiting card, to question him about a retired Indian colonel living in Berlin who had voiced hostile opinions about the Kaiser. The agent was, Williams said, "straight out of Dickens, a shabby, shifty-looking individual clad in rusty black and clasping an enormous umbrella, with a pair of beady eyes peering suspiciously above a nose polished to a lovely and most expensive [sic] hue of red."

Later on, after war broke out, Williams used couriers to get news out of Europe. They travelled, he remembered, "in a regular William Le Queux atmosphere...always being tackled by mysterious nosy parties in the hotels of Rotterdam, Amsterdam,

The Hague, and on the boats." Mysterious strangers began to turn up at Williams' office claiming to be refugees or informants with news to sell. Some were plain rogues, others spies. And one such encounter, wherein Williams pinpointed a suspect, started a friendship between him and Sir Mansfield Cumming, the legendary "C", which lasted until the latter's death.

"I never worked for him and he gave no secrets away to me," Williams wrote, "but he told me many stories of secret service, including one or two of his own adventures before the war." Williams became a Cumming fan and a frequent visitor to the small wartime headquarters on the seventh floor of Whitehall Court, a residential block of flats just behind Charing Cross. Perfect raw material for the budding spy novelist, who cheerfully admitted that his stories contained a high degree of wish fulfilment, these glimpses of the inside convinced Williams of the omnipotence of Britain's secret service and its founder: "From his tranquil room high above the London streets a great web spread right across the enemy countries: he was the spider waiting with infinite patience for the flies." Not surprisingly, Williams was the first spy novelist to introduce C into spy fiction. The former sailor now commanding Britain's silent service made several brief cameo appearances as an avuncular and burly figure "with an odd flavour of the sea."

The novels themselves owe their flavour almost exclusively to the eponymous villain who so fascinated Philby. Williams had a long-standing obsession with villains, since as a young boy in London he'd been fascinated and horrified by the Ripper murders. Furthermore, he complained, "in fiction stained-glass heroes have a habit of staying put in their windows." If one could create a convincing villain, he believed, the hero would automatically come to life. Like many things, this worked better in theory than in practice; the hero of his early spy novels, Desmond Okewood, remains as leaden as any stained-glass saint.

Still, the villain alone makes these novels well worth at least one reading. "I decided that I would have to create a master spy," Williams later recalled, "one who should incorporate all I knew of Prussian efficiency and ruthlessness." Clubfoot is a symbol of all that Williams hated about Germany and the

Germans, lovingly embellished with the stock characteristics of villains throughout the ages. It is not just his twisted foot that repels and frightens—as a man similarly afflicted had scared Williams when he was a child—nor his other deformities either, although these are repulsive enough. It is the entire baggage of national hatreds that he carries with him as the stereotype of the wartime Beastly Hun. For Germanophobia had by no means ended with Germany's defeat. At the Paris peace conference, where Williams headed the *Daily Mail* team, the desire to punish the Germans had reached a frenzied climax. England could hardly have found a more welcome villain than Clubfoot, the psychologically maimed and physically crippled spymaster in the personal service of the Kaiser.

It's hard to forget our first introduction to Grundt. His name is appropriate: his guttural Teutonic imprecations—*Schweinhund! Herrgott! Himmelkreuzsakrament nochmal!*—provided generations of English schoolchildren with their first and most enduring introduction to the German language. Desmond Okewood studies the German master spy closely as he limps across the room to fetch one of his best Havanas:

> He was a vast man, not so much by reason of his height, which was below the medium, but his bulk, which was enormous. The span of his shoulders was immense, and, though a heavy paunch and a white flabbiness of face spoke of a gross, sedentary life, he was obviously a man of quite unusual strength. His arms particularly were out of proportion to his stature, being so long that his hands hung down on either side of him when he stood erect, like the paws of some giant ape. Altogether, there was something decidedly simian in his appearance...his squat nose with hairy, open nostrils, and the general hirsuteness of the man, his bushy eyebrows, the tufts of black hair on his cheekbones and on the backs of his big spade-like hands. And there was that in his eyes, dark and courageous beneath the shaggy brows, that hinted at excesses of ape-like fury, uncontrollable and ferocious.

Grundt also possesses that infallible clue to malevolence: the glitter of gold in his teeth. It accounts for the peculiar timbre of the dry and mirthless chuckles he utters when he has a victim in his clutches.

This is all horrifying enough, and it is small wonder that Kim Philby wanted to know more about him. But it leaves out Clubfoot's real vileness. Desmond's older brother, Francis Okewood, a secret service professional, explains: "There's a code of honour in our game, old man...we give and take plenty of hard knocks in the rough and tumble of the chase, but ambush and assassination are barred." Lots of Germans in the secret service live up to the code, he goes on—but not Clubfoot. *He doesn't play the game!* This, of course, damns him entirely, almost releasing Francis and Desmond from all manly inhibitions. At a climactic moment Francis shoots Grundt in cold blood. Then, the gun still smoking in his hand, he has qualms. "It seems rather like murder," he says unsteadily. "No, Francis," his brother replies, "it was justice." Unfortunately for our heroes and Britain, Francis has merely wounded Clubfoot, who returns to haunt Desmond in a subsequent exploit—now with a vivid red scar beneath his right eye which accentuates even more the leer of his menacing eyes and cruel mouth.

Through Clubfoot and his minions, Williams projected the image of a Germany dedicated to restoring its domination of Europe and destroying the British Empire. He portrays Germans either as cringing cowards or as bullying, sadistic brutes— or even both—thus reinforcing the popular British adage that Germans are always at your feet or at your throat. Collectively, they are shown as automatons. Desmond puts this nicely when musing on the pre-war German press. Clearly speaking with Williams' own voice, he sees "organization with a vengeance, the mobilisation of national thought, a series of gramophone records fed into a thousand different machines so that each may play the selfsame tune." Deliberating on the best disguise to adopt, he tells himself, "You've only got to be a parrot to the rest, and you'll be as good a Hun as Hindenburg." Notably, he does not say "as good a Hun as the Kaiser", for his otherwise unqualified Germanophobia spared the emperor. Indeed, in *The Man with the Clubfoot* Williams presented him as a tortured victim rather than the architect of Germany's militarism, a man who would have liked to back away from confrontation in 1914. In this he was following Buchan, both of them aware that the popular image of an all-powerful Kaiser concealed a weak, indecisive, and tragic figure.

Apart from Clubfoot, the main pleasure in Williams' novels comes from meeting familiar period stereotypes. Take our hero, Desmond Okewood, who appears in the first three adventures. As stalwart as the tree that gives him his name, Desmond is a twenty-seven-year-old captain in the British Army when we first encounter him. Fit and handsome, he has an Anglo-Irish background that provides him with just the element of Celtic verve and dash he needs in many a tight spot. He meets Clubfoot in the course of a foray into wartime Germany, where he is searching for his missing brother, Francis. Only after he is irrevocably committed to the venture does he learn that Francis is a member of the British secret service, and thus Desmond immediately enters the tradition of the amateur spy. He so impresses C that in the second adventure (*The Secret Hand*) the burly old man asks him to help the service out.

Soon he finds himself breaking up a German spy ring in Britain and becoming rather dangerously attracted to the mysterious, alluring Nur-el-Din, a dancer clearly modelled on Mata Hari, whose sinuous feminine wiles almost get him into deep trouble. True to the code, he resists, instead falling in love with Barbara Mackthwaite, C's secretary—the Miss Moneypenny of her day. Although Barbara has the disconcerting habit of fainting at moments of crisis, it is she, clearly speaking with the authentic voice of Cumming (so often heard by Williams above the rooftops of London), who educates Desmond in the stern and stirring realities of the silent game. After rescuing her from many heart-stopping perils, Desmond is about to propose marriage, but Barbara recalls him to his duty as a fighting man: "The Secret Service has its fighting line, too, though the war correspondents don't write about it. It never gets a mention in despatches, and Victoria Crosses don't come its way. The newspapers don't publish its casualty list, though you and I know it's a long one. A man slips quietly away and never comes back, and after a certain lapse of time we just mark him off the books and there's an end of it. But it's a great service...."

As Desmond hesitates, she clinches the matter: "What do you and I matter when the whole future of England is at stake? If you are to give of your best to this silent game of ours, you must be free, with no responsibilities and ties, with nothing that will ever make you hesitate to take a supreme risk...and I never met a man that dared more freely than you!" Could any man resist such appeals to patriotism, honour, and vanity? Certainly not Desmond. The novel ends with his leaving to take his instructions from the chief, and with Barbara awash in the tears of noble self-sacrifice.

This is not, however, quite the end of the woman business. In *The Return of Clubfoot* we find Desmond, still a bachelor, in Central America, where he quickly stumbles across Grundt's attempts to recover a fortune and put it at the disposal of the Reich. But more important for Desmond is his meeting with Marjorie Garth, daughter of a wealthy businessman. Marjorie is suitably androgynous, which is fortunate for Desmond, who confesses (with a candour he must have learned from Hannay) that he doesn't know much about women. He describes his ideal woman as "tall and slim and clean in mind and body"—he had clearly been in the Boy Scouts and read his Buchan and Mason—and when he looks at Marjorie he muses that "but for her softly rounded throat and the gentle swell of her bosom one might have taken her for a boy." During one of the many crises they face together, and after the requisite number of faintings on her part, she reproaches him for not taking her into his confidence because she is a woman. Under the sting of this rebuke, all the more potent because true, Desmond confesses that he feels "like a naughty little boy being reprimanded by his nanny." He marries her, of course, and that is the end of Desmond Okewood, secret agent.

Williams also remains true to type in his use of anti-Semitic stereotypes, despite the fact that he almost worshipped the Reuter family and was appalled by Nazi policy against the Jews in the 1930s. At one extreme we find Barney, an East End Jewish thief, squat, pudgy, and middle-aged, with "little black beady eyes, a round white fat face and a broad squabbly Mongol nose", who distinguishes himself in *The Secret Hand* by acting the cringing and cowardly Jew. Believing he is to be wrongly accused of murder, Barney flings himself to his knees and begs for mercy, and his face turns a distinct shade of green. When not on his knees, he sits with his hands on them, twisting and fiddling continuously, a characteristic that William Le Queux had already defined as essentially Jewish.

But Barney is a mere thief, small fry when compared to the dangerous Dr. Custrin who appears in *The Return of Clubfoot*. A sleek and smooth young man with hair "like black satin" and a beautifully trimmed small black moustache, he has, Desmond notices, small, well-made feet and hands verging on the feminine. More important, he betrays his Jewishness through a certain narrowness of the eyes and a curl of the nostrils. Custrin turns out to be the Trojan Horse of the enemy forces. Even worse, he attempts to seduce Marjorie—and in the course of a subsequent thrashing by Desmond he reveals himself as German. It is a duplicity that more than justifies his death at Desmond's hands.

Williams' anti-German sentiments are counterbalanced by his pro-American feelings. Like fellow spy novelists Buchan and Oppenheim, he was strongly attracted to the United States, where his books, published by Houghton Mifflin of Boston, sold well and increasingly embraced American characters and locales. In *The Man with the Clubfoot* Francis Okewood is married to a beautiful American woman, while the young English hero of *The Three of Clubs* (1924), Geoffrey Cairsdale, sets the seal on his secret mission to Hungary when he foils a plot to restore the Hapsburg monarchy by marrying Virginia Fitzgerald, the private secretary to a highly placed State Department official. The best man at this Anglo-American wedding is C, smelling, as always, of the sea.

Boyhood impressions, mainly derived from being taken by his father to see Barnum's *Greatest Show on Earth* at the Olympia Exhibition in London, and from once actually shaking hands with the great Bill himself during a British tour of *Buffalo Bill's*

Wild West Show, had early on convinced Williams that "the United States must be one of the most wonderful countries in the world." Friendships with American correspondents met while travelling around Europe before the war strengthened the belief. The appointment of his older brother Douglas as head of Reuters in New York provided him with the opportunity he had been waiting for. In 1924 he left Cannes for a seven-week whirlwind visit to the United States. It confirmed all his wildest dreams.

Arriving just as the great post-war boom was beginning, Williams stood in Times Square with a tumultuous crowd to welcome Coolidge's election victory, and soon after accompanied his brother for a personal White House interview with the President. In New York he spoke at the Dutch Treat, the famous writers' and authors' club; witnessed a lineup at police headquarters (he was writing *The Clock Ticks On*, a crime novel set in the States); and made a broadcast from one of the city's earliest radio stations. He was fêted in Boston by his publishers, dined with George Horace Latimer, editor of the *Saturday Evening Post*, in Philadelphia, spent a few days in Virginia fox-hunting country with friends, and was everywhere overwhelmed with Americans' generosity and hospitality. "When I finally left the States," he recorded, "it was in a state of blissful exhaustion." Six years later, just twelve months after the Wall Street crash, Williams returned with his wife, the actress Alice Crawford, for a stay that lasted, with interruptions, for almost seven years.

For Williams, Americans' reactions to the Depression confirmed all his previous beliefs in their resilience, their strength, and their determination. Opportunities still abounded, minds were still open, and for an intelligent and observant writer and journalist such as himself there was plenty to do. He wrote and broadcast a series of thrillers for NBC (one of them on Mata Hari); wrote a stage version with his wife of *The Crouching Beast*, one of his Clubfoot novels, which was briefly performed on Broadway; and travelled extensively on promotion tours throughout the country.

Above all, after January 1933 and the last of the Republican years, there was the New Deal to write about and admire. During a trip to the Gaspé Peninsula (the scene of his crime novel *Dead Man Manor*), he and his wife had met Eleanor Roosevelt at the Frontenac Hotel in Quebec City, where he was delighted to hear from the President's wife that her husband was an assiduous reader of his novels. Shortly afterwards, through Mrs. Roosevelt, he met the President for a personal talk at the White House. Immediately captivated by his charm, courage, and determination, Williams also saw him as a future world statesman and an ally of Britain in world affairs.

"In his appreciation of the role which the two great English-speaking peoples are called upon to fill in world affairs," he wrote in *The World of Action*, "his line of thought is indistinguishable from that of our own statesmen.... Dark clouds obscure the view as I pause on the long, steep road I have followed to look back. But two peaks rise in majesty through the mist—the British Commonwealth of Nations, emerging in greater strength and unity from the two most perilous crises in our history, and Anglo-American friendship, mighty mountain of the same range. I do not believe," Williams concluded, "that the life I have still to live will witness the growth of greater influences for good than these twin achievements."

Pearl Harbor four years later made the Anglo-American alliance a firm reality, and Williams quickly became more deeply involved in its promotion than he could ever have imagined while writing his memoirs. Although he denied that he had ever worked for SIS under Cumming, he admitted to having had "some fugitive contacts with that dramatic figure, Admiral Sir Reginald Hall." In reality, these were probably the normal contacts of a professional journalist with a director of Naval Intelligence. But the silent game quickly claimed Williams as a player in the Second World War, as fellow author and journalist Malcolm Muggeridge found out. Summoned by letter for an interview to see if he was suitable for some unspecified intelligence duties, Muggeridge complied.

"I went to London for my interview," he wrote in *Chronicles of Wasted Time*, "which turned out to be with a writer of thrillers named Williams, whom I met at his club, the Savage. Writers of thrillers," Muggeridge added caustically, "tend to gravitate to the Secret Service as surely as the mentally unstable become psychiatrists, or the impotent pornographers. Williams spoke darkly of the dangers involved in a service in which, by the nature of the case, a blown agent had to be discarded. After a year as IO [Intelligence Officer] at a corps headquarters, I said, this held no terrors for me."

After thus briefly playing the part of a character from his own novels, Williams was transferred to the United States, where for a time he worked on propaganda at the British embassy in Washington. Then, for two years, he was a leading figure at Political Warfare Executive Headquarters at Woburn Abbey outside London. It was here that Kim Philby encountered him asleep in the back of the Rolls-Royce. Had Williams been awake, he might have been able to give Philby some inside information of his own, for shortly afterwards he published the last of his Clubfoot spy novels, *Courier to Marrakesh*. Appropriately enough, it was a glorification of the transatlantic unity that Philby later tried so hard to destroy.

"Marrakesh, Naples and a villa outside enemy-occupied Rome; murders, abductions and SS executions; American and British secret agents, a countess, her son and other anti-Fascist Italians...journeys by air, in high-speed cars and even finally in a submarine; Allied air-raids, dinners with a sheik and with the notorious Clubfoot..." proclaims the dust-wrapper, depicting a profile of the deformed Dr. Grundt superimposed on a map of the western Mediterranean. The blurb nicely captures the flavour of Williams' wartime novel, in which he revived his old theme of the dangers of Prussian militarism. Clubfoot, now the Führer's personal emissary in North Africa and Italy, is on a mission to track down a secret dossier on his master's financial dealings which has fallen into the hands of the Dreiblatt Bund, or Trefoil League, a clique of Prussian generals plotting against him. The generals realize the war is lost, and are now trying to salvage something from the wreckage. Echoing wartime Allied propaganda, the novel tells us that they are as great a menace as Hitler, and certainly no friends of the Allies. "The reactionary elements are fighting a rearguard action to save the world from democracy," an Allied intelligence officer explains; "people who have this cockeyed idea that a military government in Germany, purged of the Nazis, is preferable to a victorious Russia."

Anglo-American unity and the fight for democracy, however, are the dominating themes of the novel, which is narrated by Andrea Hallam, a twenty-six-year-old folk singer from New York on an entertainment tour of North Africa for the troops. Convalescing in Marrakesh after a plane crash, she stumbles by accident onto Clubfoot and his mission to find the Führer's dossier, a bombshell in the hands of either the generals or the Allies. True to form, this accidental agent is at first reluctant but soon becomes deeply involved with the British and American intelligence services. The former is personified by Captain Nicholas Leigh, a tall young man with cool grey eyes who has won a Distinguished Service Order medal at Dunkirk, and the latter by Hank Lundgren, a blond and blue-eyed Scandinavian-American from Milwaukee. Also true to form, Andrea, as a woman, carelessly falls into Clubfoot's clutches, to be rescued after a series of hair-raising adventures by the two young men who by now are friendly rivals for her favours. It is the Englishman who wins her heart, but she tragically loses him when he is killed during the final showdown with Clubfoot, who also perishes. Nick, Andrea reflects several months later, safely back in her Manhattan apartment, was "one of the generation who, born during the First World War, hovered for a little like a butterfly in the sun and then was gone." But his spirit, and that of the transatlantic unity he embodied, lives on. Suddenly, out of the blue, Andrea receives an invitation to launch a liberty ship at Camden, New Jersey. As she stands on the launching platform she raises her eyes to see the name inscribed on the ship's hull—*Nicholas Leigh*. And, the ceremony over, she falls into the arms of Hank, "looking like a Viking in his uniform, fighting his way towards me through the crowd, his blue eyes shining."

After the war Williams returned to New York. For the previous three years he had travelled frequently between London and Hollywood working on screenplays with Alexander Korda, but now he was mortally ill. He booked passage on the first post-war luxury voyage of the liner *Queen Elizabeth* and arrived in New

York with his wife in October 1946. He immediately checked into the Gotham Hospital on East 76th Street, and four weeks later, aged sixty-three, he died.

CHAPTER SIX

...And Not So Silent

We had an amusing little show rounding up Communists and other unwashed people of that type. We called ourselves the Black Gang, and it was great sport while it lasted.

"Sapper", *The Black Gang*

I

Sometime in 1922, a group of ex-officers wrote to William Le Queux, whom they believed to be a secret agent. They thought they might be useful on confidential missions and asked his advice. "This letter is not written after a visit to 'Bulldog Drummond'," they assured him, "but after calm and mature thought. We, like Drummond, have no fear...."

Bulldog Drummond was the hero of a series of best-sellers published in Britain between the two world wars. Packed with action, they thrilled a generation of schoolboys of all ages, and their popularity lingered on until well after 1945. Their violence and jingoism were apparently quite acceptable to professional educators: as late as the mid-1950s the Athlone Press of the University of London still included Drummond adventures in a series of school editions, although by then they were being superseded by a more sophisticated and updated version of Drummond, James Bond. In his own day Drummond, like Bond, was also a hero of the movies. As early as 1922 he was played by British matinée idol Carlyle Blackwell, and Ralph Richardson played Drummond in a 1934 version of *The Return of Bull-dog Drummond*. But the most famous Drummond was Ronald Colman, who was first cast in the role in the 1929 United Artists production and in part built his screen popularity on his portrayal of the secret agent. Paramount Films began a series of eight Drummond films, starring John Howard, which appeared in rapid succession between 1937 and 1939. Drummond films continued to be made through the 1940s, then ceased until revived by the Bond mania, which inspired a 1966 Universal version starring Richard Johnson and Elke Sommer, *Deadlier Than the Male*. In the United States a popular half-hour radio series was broadcast during the 1940s.

Drummond was the creation of Herman Cyril McNeile, the son of a captain in the Royal Navy, who was born in 1888 at the Naval Prison in Bodmin, Cornwall, where his father was Governor, and educated at Cheltenham College and the Royal Military Academy at Woolwich. He married into a military family, and in 1907 entered the Royal Engineers.

Seven years later he found himself serving in the trenches of the Western Front, where he won the Military Cross, and writing short stories about his experiences. Northcliffe published a number of them in the *Daily Mail*, and because McNeile was a serving officer who could not use his own name, chose the pseudonym "Sapper" (from the term by which members of the Royal Engineers were known) for his new author. It stuck in the public mind, and this was how McNeile was known until his early death at age forty-eight in 1937.

McNeile—known to his friends as "Mac"—had much the same effect on people as the man whose name he made a household word. A robust and ebullient man of decided views who loved practical jokes, he spoke and laughed with a loud, confident voice. "He was loud in every possible way," wrote his friend Gerard Fairlie, who continued the Drummond series after McNeile's death, "in his voice, in his laugh, in his clothes, in the unconscious swagger with which he always motivated himself, in his whole approach to life...Mac loved the vivid colours, the strong smells, and the potent tastes. He loved all lustiness in life...." A dinner with McNeile was likely to be a strenuous affair: he preferred to eat at his club, in hearty masculine company, and was noted for his conspicuous consumption of caviar and port. He was not, as Fairlie drily noted, everyone's cup of tea.

Not surprisingly, McNeile's view of life was that observed from the officers' mess, and Drummond was more of a trouble-shooter and vigilante than player in the silent game. Recalling Bulldog Drummond's first appearance in 1920, McNeile said: "Troubles over demobilization were rife. Men were discontented, and the soil was ripe for agitators. Believing as I do that 90 per cent of agitators are concerned with their own pockets, and care no whit for their wretched dupes, I decided to make Carl Peterson an arch-Communist." Peterson, the villain of the first few Drummond novels, is the master-mind who does his best to disrupt post-war Britain, shown as a society yearning for normality but frustrated in its efforts by the machinations of foreigners in general and Jews in particular. These aliens are occasionally aided by willing dupes within Britain itself, usually recruited from the ranks of avaricious businessmen, discontented workers, scheming politicians, mad scientists, and—probably the most dangerous of the lot— effete intellectuals.

The fundamental threat comes from some unspecified revolution and often involves Bolsheviks, such as Yulowski in *The Black Gang*, one of the murderers of the Czar and a political commissar who advocates subversion through the introduction of socialist Sunday schools into Britain: "Blasphemy is instilled at once.... Get at the children.... They can be moulded like plastic clay.... We preach class hatred...." Carl Peterson himself, however, is more of a master criminal than an ideologically committed Communist. He's prepared to associate with Bolsheviks, but mainly because their subversive work will help further his own objective—usually some international conspiracy by unscrupulous foreign capitalists. Since both Bolsheviks and foreign capitalists wish to weaken Britain, they often work hand in hand—Sapper's political world bears a strong resemblance to the Fascist world view.

Bulldog Drummond, the man who confounds these foreign plots, belongs to a very special breed. He is a former army captain, holder of the DSO and Military Cross, and a demobilized officer who finds civilian life so tedious that he advertises for adventures in the newspaper. Sapper's description of the hero of one of his previous novels, Derek Vane of *Mufti* (1919), applies almost exactly to Drummond.

> [He] regarded his own country...whenever he thought about it...as being the supreme country in the world. He didn't force his opinion down anyone's throat; it simply was so. If the other fellow didn't agree, the funeral was his, not Vane's. He had to the full what the uninitiated regard as conceit; on matters connected with literature, or art, or music, his knowledge was microscopic. Moreover he regarded with suspicion anyone who talked intelligently on such subjects. On the other hand, he had been in the eleven at Eton, and was a scratch golfer. He had a fine seat on a horse and rode straight; he could play a passable game of polo, and was a good shot. Possessing as he did sufficient money to prevent the necessity of working, he had not taken the something he was supposed to be doing in the City very seriously.... He belonged, in fact, to the Breed; the Breed that has always existed in England, and will always exist to the world's end. You may meet its members in London and Fiji; in the lands that lie beyond the mountains and at Henley; in the swamps where the stagnant vegetation rots and stinks; in the great deserts where the night air strikes cold. They are always the same, and they are branded with the stamp of the Breed. They shake your hand as a man shakes it; they meet your eye as a man meets it.

Drummond shares nearly all these qualities. We never doubt his contempt for literature, art, music, conversation, productive labour, or foreigners, and if he gets entangled with the latter we are safe in the knowledge that he's impervious to their influence. For Drummond also despises foreign languages. His Italian is confined to *è pericoloso sporgersi*—a cautionary phrase he has seen on Italian trains—and his French is an extreme form of the franglais subsequently adopted and refined by Sir Winston Churchill; on one occasion, after he has crash-landed a plane into a field of onions in France, he tells a bewildered gendarme that he has *"craché dans les rognons."*

Among Drummond's other characteristics are physical size and strength, a powerful pair of fists and good boxing skills, a useful knowledge of ju-jitsu, and a steady hand with a revolver. He also has—like the Scarlet Pimpernel—an outward nonchalance and obtuseness that inevitably fools his opponents. They usually discover their error from a horizontal position, for Drummond's favourite method of resolving a dispute is a swift upper cut. While Sapper describes him as a sport and a gentleman, C. Day Lewis once preferred to call him "an unspeakable schoolboy bully". He and his friends act as a vigilante group, cleansing the country of rabble, and they have little respect for the law if it stops them giving an unwashed left-winger a good thrashing in the cause of King and Country. Furthermore, they have little to fear from the police, who accept their activities as essential to social hygiene. "We're a free country, Sir John," the director of Scotland Yard tells a Cabinet minister, "but the time is coming when freedom as we understood it in the past will have to cease. We can't go on as the cesspit of Europe, sheltering microbes who infect us as soon as they're here. We want disinfecting, we want it badly."

A clean nation delivered by a clean-cut patriot—that is the Drummond formula. Patriotism comes to him as naturally and spontaneously as his right arm moves to a tankard of British ale after a gruelling round with Peterson. He's prepared to accept that some things are wrong "in this jolly old country of ours", but nothing that can't be mended. As a platoon commander on the Western Front he inspired his men through courage and boldness and many remain loyal to him. "Which is why," Sapper tells us, "there are in England today quite a number of civilians who acknowledge only two rulers—the King and Hugh Drummond. And they would willingly die for either."

Drummond has no problem in getting his old wartime pals together to fight the arch-villain Peterson; like him, they seem to have no particular employment other than lunching at their clubs. They accept his leadership with unswerving loyalty and undertake his missions with considerable pleasure. Like their leader, they are concerned with the pests that threaten society: "All that mattered was that there should be a certain amount of sport in the collection of the specimens."

Loyalty and obedience also help sort out the desirable from the undesirable among the working class. The desirable immediately recognize Drummond's leadership qualities, and with instinctive respect for their social superiors unquestioningly defer to his command. Pity those who don't, for Drummond has a school prefect's view of class relations. As Richard Usborne notes in *Clubland Heroes*, Drummond "tended to carry the Fuehrer principle from the school playing-fields to St. James's Square", and a non-deferential member of the working class was likely to be thrashed as an "agitator". It's the need for leadership in dealing with agitators that produces the formation of the Black Gang by Drummond in his second round with Peterson in 1922. This was the year that Mussolini and his Fascist Blackshirts came to power in Italy. Sapper, like many of his class and persuasion, approved.

Defender of England and protector of its social hierarchies, Drummond is also thoroughly conservative in his views on women: they are purity enshrined. Their place is either to serve, like the faithful Mrs. Denny who prepares Drummond's breakfast, or to worship and be worshipped, like Phyllis, the girl Drummond saves from Peterson's clutches. Drummond eventually marries Phyllis—an apparent breach of the rule that men of action should not be married—but Phyllis is, like Richard Hannay's wife, a bit of a female chap anyway. She's described as a thoroughbred, and we're told that when she runs it's with "the steady run of a girl who beagles when she goes beagling, and doesn't sit on the top of the hill and watch." Sporting though she is, Phyllis quickly tires of the games with Peterson and urges

Drummond to give it all up. She is then captured by Peterson, which puts Drummond at his mercy, and even after her rescue she gets in the way by preventing Drummond from strangling his opponent. Drummond feels "like a dog must feel when called off his prey by his master." In later adventures, fortunately, Phyllis slips into the background.

Since women embody the more gentle and merciful qualities, they deserve chivalrous treatment, and mistreating them is a sure sign of a villain. In *The Final Count* (1926), Peterson's wickedness lies less in his plan to control the world through deployment of some deadly poison than in the fact that he is contemplating destroying an airship containing women. But then we know, of course, that Peterson is a blackguard: otherwise he'd have the decency to make his constant companion, Irma, his wife. As it is, she masquerades as his daughter, and there is the hideous unspoken possibility that perhaps she is. (Gad!) Since Irma is a woman, she does not entirely share Peterson's infamy; there are even hints that she has a weakness for our hero, but of course his heart beats true only for English girls.

In a post-war Britain characterized on the one hand by hard-faced men who had done well out of the war and on the other by increasingly radical labour demands that culminated in the General Strike of 1926, the Bulldog Drummond novels struck a responsive chord in a powerful middle class yearning for law and order. "He glorified, in peacetime, the comradeship, leadership and bravery of the days in the trenches," writes Richard Usborne; "it was salutary to read of sportsmen with money *and* guts, and still ready to fight for England. Sapper made hay while the sun still shone on the British Empire, and before the cold winds of overdrafts blew through London Clubland."

Behind the world of Drummond, of course, lay the menace of Communism. The Bolshevik Revolution was widely attributed on the political right, in England and Europe, to the conspiracies of Jews. Sapper's novels did nothing to dispel this view. In *The Final Count*, published during the year of the General Strike, the Bulldog Drummond fan was told, flatly, that Russia was ruled by a "clique of homicidal alien Jews." This merely echoed the *Morning Post*, national repository of High Toryism, which once described the Bolshevik regime as the "government of Jewry". *The Final Count*, it might be noted, went through forty editions in the next twenty-five years.

The Drummond novels were not only xenophobic, they were isolationist. If foreigners could be kept out of Britain, villains like Carl Peterson would have no minions to act as their agents, there would be no agitators to disturb the decent and loyal working man, and all would be well. If Britain as a nation did not get entangled abroad with foreign powers, things would be even better. For Britain was as isolationist towards Europe in the 1920s as was America. There was a powerful reaction to the Continental commitment that had seen the flower of Britain's youth slaughtered on the Western Front, and the revolutionary upheavals of post-war Europe intensified the resistance to any more involvement in Continental affairs. Many an Englishman found his own sentiments articulated in the testimony of Robin Gaunt, the gifted scientist captured by Peterson in *The Final Count*:

> The Armistice was signed: the war was over: an era of peace and plenty was to take place. So we thought—poor deluded fools. Six years later found Europe an armed camp with every nation snarling at every other nation. Scientific soldiers gave lectures in which they stated their ideas of the next war: civilised human beings talked glibly of raining down myriads of disease germs on huge cities. It was horrible—incredible: man had called in science to aid him in destroying his fellow man, and science had obeyed him—at a price. It was a price that had not been contemplated: it was a case of another Frankenstein's monster. Man had now to obey science, not science man: he had created a thing which he could not control.

The lesson was obvious. While Britain might well try to establish a system of international law and order through her God-given right to act as arbiter of international affairs, she should keep away from direct involvement in Europe. The Continent was a seething volcano where Germany's lust for revenge might erupt at any moment. Foreign powers were no more trustworthy than foreigners. Englishmen had everything to gain and nothing to lose by retreating into xenophobic insularity.

Sapper died in 1937, but Bulldog Drummond lived on. McNeile had agreed that Gerard Fairlie should continue the adventures. Fairlie was a military man, too, and after training at the Royal Military Academy at Sandhurst had served in the Scots Guards from 1918 to 1924 before becoming a successful author and London and Hollywood screenwriter in his own right. More to the point, he had partially provided a model for Drummond, having been army heavyweight champion in 1919. His Second World War career was one that Drummond would have envied: he was head of a commando training school, he broadcast to France on many occasions, and he capped this off by parachuting to the Maquis for secret service work.

The first Drummond book by Fairlie, *Bulldog Drummond on Dartmoor*, appeared in 1938, and the last, *The Return of the Black Gang*, in 1954. At the height of the Cold War, just a year after Stalin's death, *The Return* reintroduced Irma Peterson, still working hand in hand with the Communists to paralyse Britain through industrial action. The wheel had turned full circle since the early Drummond days when, in Sapper's words, "we had an amusing little show rounding up Communists and other unwashed people of that type. We called ourselves the Black Gang, and it was great sport while it lasted."

II

The main rival to Bulldog Drummond in the inter-war years was "Tiger" Standish, whose real name is Timothy Overbury Standish, son of the Earl of Quorn—a tall, strong, virile, and impeccably dressed gentleman agent who works freelance for "Q.1", British Intelligence, is the country's best amateur football player, and likes his glass of beer and a good pipe. Standish was the creation of Sydney Horler, a man who rivalled Edgar Wallace as a prolific writer of popular fiction. Indeed, Horler greatly admired Wallace, and after the latter's death in 1932 proudly purchased the chair in which Wallace had written so many best-sellers, seeking, no doubt, inspiration for his own efforts. Like Wallace, Horler had left school at fourteen and had been a journalist before the First World War—first in Bristol, where he grew up, then on the London *Daily Mail*. During the war he wrote propaganda for Air Force Intelligence, and first emerged in the 1920s as a writer of sports fiction, where his short stories appeared regularly in the tabloid *News of the World*.

He and his readership were well matched, for he fully shared its generous suburban prejudices. He freely confessed in *Excitement*, his autobiography, that he disliked most modern literature, especially that written by "half-baked Oxford undergraduates, man-obsessed old maids, homo-sexuals...and pinheads of all descriptions": if *Lady Chatterley's Lover* was art, he declared, then "every sanitary inspector should be able to turn out a literary classic." As for George Bernard Shaw, he detested him for criticizing Britain and scoffing at "our religion, our laws, the traditions which we admire and uphold." For this reason, he despised all things European. In the flush of his early financial success he had followed Oppenheim and Williams to the French Riviera. He had hated it and quickly returned, declaring that its attractions were a delusion and a snare and that he missed England.

Horler did his best to uphold these views through his spy fiction. Appropriately enough, he came to the genre after being involved in an intriguing incident with a man who claimed to have been a secret agent. The man, called Pardy, approached Horler claiming to be one of Britain's top three intelligence chiefs and asking the journalist to ghost-write his autobiography. Horler was duped for several weeks before Pardy was unmasked as a fraud. Undaunted, Horler used the material for his first mystery romance, *The Mystery of No. 1*, which was a pronounced success. From then, Horler was unstoppable. A great admirer of A.E.W. Mason and John Buchan, he nevertheless relied heavily on formulas derived from Sapper and Wallace, and although inferior to both, he made up in quantity what he lacked in quality: between 1920 and his death in 1954, he produced well over a hundred novels. They were enormously successful, and often extravagantly praised, especially for the lively pace at which they moved.

The promise held out by the books' garish yellow dust-wrappers, "Horler for Excitement", was fulfilled—provided the reader had no objection to implausible plots and cardboard characters. Standish, Horler's most important secret agent hero, is a freelance secret service man who spends his time saving virginal women and the nation from the plots of foreigners and cads, particularly brutal Prussians. He also grapples with treason. In *The Grim Game* (1936) we find Standish searching for an enemy spy within Q.1 itself, a man, it transpires, who has been selling British secrets for money. Such venal behaviour attracted the ire of Horler the moralist more than once. Brett Carstairs, another of his patriot-heroes, who joins British Intelligence for love of country and adventure, also tracks down a double agent betraying the country for money in *The Spy* (1931). But such creatures are there principally as counterpoints to the stereotyped amateur agents working for the love of the job alone. Pale imitations of Drummond, they deserve little more attention. And Horler, while curious as a type, was probably the least interesting of the spy writers of this period. He was certainly among the worst.

CHAPTER SEVEN

"Pretty Sinister"

"Do you want to serve, or will you try your hand among the sheepbreeders?"

Francis Beeding, *The Three Fishers*

In 1922—the year Sapper fans applauded the birth of the Black Gang—the Nobel Peace Prize was awarded to the Norwegian explorer and scientist Fridtjof Nansen. Since his famous expedition across the Arctic ice-field in the 1890s, Nansen had turned his attention to political and humanitarian work. Heading the Norwegian delegation to the first assembly of the League of Nations in Geneva, he then successfully helped repatriate some half-million prisoners of war from Soviet Russia. Subsequently the International Red Cross put him in charge of famine relief following the Russian Civil War. Shortly afterwards he devised the so-called "Nansen Passport", an identification card and travel document used by thousands of persons displaced by the redrawing of the European map after 1918. It was for this work among the human debris so despised by the likes of Sapper that Nansen received his Nobel prize, making him a symbol of the liberal idealism inspired by the League of Nations in the inter-war years.

One of Nansen's personal staff was a young Englishman called Hilary Aidan St. George Saunders. The son of an Anglican vicar, Saunders, born in 1898, had served in the Welsh Guards on the Western Front and received the Military Cross for gallantry. After post-war study at Balliol College, Oxford, he joined Nansen's team as a private secretary, for five years travelling with him all over Europe. He then stayed on in Geneva as a member of the League's secretariat, and there he met John Leslie Palmer, another Balliol man. Together, under the pseudonym "Francis Beeding", they began to write the Colonel Granby spy novels.

Older than Saunders by some thirteen years, Palmer had worked in the War Trade Intelligence Department and attended the Paris Peace Conference as a member of the British delegation. A writer and critic by profession, Palmer wrote books on literature, including studies of Shakespeare's comedies, George Bernard Shaw, Molière, and Kipling. His main contribution to the Beeding partnership was in character and dialogue, while that of Saunders was narrative and plot.

Not all the Beeding books were spy novels—indeed, not all the Saunders/Palmer collaborations were published under the Beeding pseudonym—but the nucleus of the collaboration was the spy series. It began in 1925, with *The Seven Sleepers*, and lasted until Palmer's death in 1944. Its central character was Colonel Alastair Granby, DSO, of the British Secret Service, a thoroughly decent Englishman of piercing blue eyes and unshakeable sang-froid. Had he not been a secret agent, he could well have been one of that new breed of detectives like Lord Peter Wimsey who in the same period amused a highbrow readership by investigating murder and mayhem among the rural gentry. Granby is a man of taste. He appreciates good food, has a discriminating palate for vintage wine, and is never short of a Shakespearean quotation to fit a crisis. Self-consciously flippant in tone, he tends to reduce any crisis to its right proportions by muttering, "Pretty sinister!" Possessing the traditional talent of British secret agents for disguises, he can be relied upon to turn up at just the right moment, though often with complete disregard for security or even credibility. In *The Ten Holy Terrors* (1939), for example, we find him masquerading as a German victim of Czech oppression—despite the fact that he is, by this time, P.B.3 (Head of the British Secret Service)—and even obtaining a personal hearing from an unsuspecting Adolf Hitler.

Although such implausibility was squarely in the Le Queux /Oppenheim tradition, Saunders and Palmer aimed at a more educated audience that would take pleasure in erudition and literary allusion, and studded the Granby novels with quotations from Dickens, Shelley, and Shakespeare. The *New York Herald Tribune* once declared that Francis Beeding was "a real godsend in the way of a thriller for persons who require good English and expert plotting in their mysteries." In short, Beeding helped to make the reading of spy novels respectable. In Granby the educated middle classes could see one of themselves. They could also take comfort in the general outlook of the novels, for the Beeding universe is the Britain of Stanley Baldwin and the growing prosperity of the suburban middle class.

Granby heads a service whose principal task is to preserve peace. It is taken for granted that this is in everyone's best interest. Certainly it was good for Britain: the British Empire reached its largest extent as a result of the Versailles settlement, and Britain's commitment to the ideals of the League of Nations was firmly underpinned by self-interest. But none of this is spelled out to the readers, who instinctively recognize that what is good for Britain is good for the world. What they do need to be reminded of is the cost of peace. Shortly after assuming the post of P.B.3, Granby muses on the fate of the young men who join the secret service:

> I receive callers at hours that are mostly inconvenient, men with lean brown faces, wearing their town clothes like a strange disguise, who look with puckered eyes on the pageant of cockney London. They have heard the avalanches crashing down the Karakaran, or the reed notes that the shepherds play in the hills about Delphi, or the drumming of bulls' hooves on the sierras of Andalusia, or the whispering dispute that precedes a knife thrust

in a Belleville Bouge or a Genoese doss-house. They come to me
from time to time for instructions or to make reports, and I send
them out again. Sometimes they fail to come back. Nothing more
is heard of them, and I draw a neat red line through an official
number and name in the secret registry of the Service, and look
through the window at the grey sky and the greyer streets and
wonder how it happened.

Who are these young men of the silent game who so often
make the supreme sacrifice? We don't see many of them because
Granby himself tackles most of the problems. But the few we
do glimpse are Granby facsimiles—gentlemen of good breeding
who maintain their stiff upper lips in the face of pretty sinister
things. For some of them, such as Ronald Briercliffe in *The Three
Fishers* (1931), secret service provides redemption—as it did in
A.E.W. Mason's *The Winding Stair*. Although cashiered from
the army (for an unfortunate drinking episode), Briercliffe is
of sound background and deserves a better future than disgrace
and obscurity. A sympathetic uncle, Colonel Calthorpe, gives
him a choice of emigration to New Zealand or secret service:
"Do you want to serve, or will you try your hand among the
sheepbreeders?" he asks. Ronald has little hesitation in opting
for the secret service. SIS thus appears, like the Empire in the
Victorian age, as a useful system of outdoor relief for the younger
sons of the gentry.

Ronald's induction into the service gives us a rare glimpse of
its inner workings, and we instantly find ourselves in the world of
Compton Mackenzie. Colonel Calthorpe, an old friend of P.B.3
from Sandhurst days, arranges for Granby to vet Ronald personally at his headquarters. Sitting ill at ease in the old man's
Battersea flat, Ronald passes the first test by revealing a sound
knowledge of regimental history and an adequate capacity for
holding his drink ("a couple of cocktails, half a bottle of Bur-
gundy, a glass or two of champagne, and a couple of brandies").
Suddenly, outside the door, there is a tremendous bang. Ronald
correctly identifies it as a revolver shot, and on being told that

Granby's valet occasionally goes berserk in the kitchen, he offers to disarm the man. Thus he passes the second test, for the incident has been staged to assess his ability to remain calm in a crisis.

That is all that is required for Ronald to become a secret agent—apart, of course, from the unromantic business of learning about codes, ciphers, and secret signals. P.B.3 tells Ronald that he must go to Paris and make contact with an informer in a bar called the Moine Gourmet; if he runs into trouble the service will be there to help him. How, asks Ronald, will he know his fellow agents? Simple, replies the old man. Whenever Ronald is in the Moine Gourmet and has occasion to light a cigarette, he must use his left hand and then pass the match over to his right before blowing it out. If anyone else in the bar does the same, he too is a member of the service.

We meet a few other junior members of the service as we proceed through the Beeding canon, but for the most part the heroes are the traditional accidental amateurs who date back to Childers, young and decent men thrown into adventure. Such is Thomas Preston, whom we meet in the first Beeding adventure, *The Seven Sleepers* (1925). A thirty-year-old bachelor with a good war record, Preston is travelling on the Continent for the family business, "a very ordinary sort of fellow...no special knowledge of what is styled foreign politics." He receives a quick and unwelcome lesson in international affairs, however, when he's mistaken for a member of a German conspiracy planning to launch a sudden attack on the West.

True to form, the Beeding heroes are single. Although the women who are both the incentive and the reward for their exploits lack the androgynous characteristics of Buchan's heroines, they are clean, vigorous, and healthy. Consider Beatrice, Preston's fiancée in *The Seven Sleepers*: "In mind, as in form and feature, she was compact and competent, her forearm drive at tennis having the same quality of precision and judgement as her observations on things and persons in general." Even Mrs. Granby is a sportswoman, with a passion for skiing. With female energies directed well away from the men, the latter can carry out their work unhampered by any tiresome emotional and sexual baggage.

Like Le Queux, Saunders and Palmer used the spy novel as a travelogue, leading their readers through druggings, knifings, and kidnappings in practically every city in Europe. Unlike Le Queux, however, they wrote for an audience who probably had some knowledge of the Continental scene. Nor, unlike Sapper or even Williams, were they xenophobes; their foreigners are quaint but not necessarily dangerous, and even the villains lack the unmitigated evil of Yulowski or Clubfoot. Where the Beeding novels try to imitate these—as with Dr. Kreutzemark, the evil scientist—the result lacks conviction. They even go so far as to cast an Englishman as a villain in several of the novels. This is Francis Wyndham, a debonair man of many talents and few scruples who acts as a freelancer on the international espionage market. He, too, is a half gentleman, for he was at Eton and Oxford and once even worked for the British secret service, but he has "a lazy passion for style" and is very particular about his clothing. This distinctly un-British trait not only betrays him as a wrong 'un, but points up the authors' secure complacency about the British way of life. Such insular smugness leads to a self-consciously flippant exchange in *The Five Flamboys* (1929). With the young King of Romania kidnapped, revolution and Soviet intervention in that Balkan trouble-spot seem imminent. John Baxter, a junior official of the League of Nations secretariat, recalls an exchange with Granby:

> "Why should you be interested in revolution?" I began. He looked at me a moment before answering.
>
> "Ever hear of a thing called Bolshevism?" he said at last.
>
> "Some sort of disease, isn't it?" I asked.
>
> "Epidemic in character," said Granby. "It nearly got into Italy some years ago, but they called in Dr. Mussolini. There was also an outbreak in Hungary. There have been one or two cases in our own country, but the British form is benignant."

Spanning a period of some twenty years, Granby's secret-service exploits mirror the decline and fall of liberal hopes in the League of Nations. The early novels present Granby, often closely assisted by secret agents of the French Deuxième Bureau, fighting to preserve the values and institutions of the League. As in much other popular fiction of the inter-war years, the enemy is portrayed not as some foreign power but as war itself—that unmitigated disaster, a monster created by the marriage of science and weaponry. Typical is Thomas Preston's reaction to Professor Kreutzemark's plans to destroy London and Paris with clouds of yellow poisonous gas.

> I saw, in my mind's eye, hovering silver specks, ten thousand feet up in the morning air, raining abruptly down invisible and remorseless death, making in a moment of that happy scene a desert and a shambles; and I felt incredulous wonder and a gratitude, impersonal and immense, that fate should have permitted me to assist in foiling the powers of malice and disorder which in every age must be encountered and freshly overcome if men are to keep and to increase their inheritance.

War is so terrible, indeed, that decent and rational men cannot contemplate it as a means of national policy. Hence it must be the tool of conspiracy. So conspiracy, by self-interested groups of evil men, is the opponent against which Granby struggles throughout the 1920s. In *The Six Proud Walkers* (1928) the several conspirators hope to profit from a war they will provoke between Italy and Yugoslavia: one will speculate on the financial markets, one will sell munitions, one will deal in drugs, and one, the Bolshevik, will ingratiate himself with his masters in Moscow—an inveterate enemy, of course, of the League in the 1920s. This was one of the most successful Granby novels. "If Francis Beeding has merely set out to show how little there may be to choose between the methods of High Finance, Communism and Commercialized Crime and how necessary for the well-being of mankind it is that the League of Nations should exist to restrain these dangerous forces," wrote a critic in the *Times Literary Supplement*, "he has succeeded amply. If his purpose were more novel, and he wished to deceive, harrow, shock, delight and generally interest the reader, his success is even more ample." Similar conspiratorial groups animate *The League of Discontent* (1930), *The Four Armourers* (1930), in which the arms merchants are the villains, and *The Three Fishers* (1931), which depicts an attempt to start a Franco-German war by financiers convinced that peace has an unfortunate effect on the markets.

The lack of any identifiable national enemy in this first Beeding period reflects the liberal mood of the time, when from the signing of the Locarno Pact in 1925 to the international economic breakdown of 1930–1931 it seemed possible that the peace would be permanent. In the rosy glow of this tragically brief period people could believe that international conflict was the deliberate creation of "merchants of death", individuals obsessed with wealth and power. The Covenant of the League of Nations had singled out private trade in armaments as a cause of war, and when the World Disarmament Conference met in Geneva in 1930 there were great hopes of progress. It's hardly surprising, therefore, to find arms merchants prominent in the Beeding gallery of villainy, along with those favourite scapegoats, financiers. But the new liberal-mindedness did nothing to diminish the anti-Semitic stereotypes; as usual, a high proportion of enemies were depicted as Jewish.

In the very first Granby adventure we meet the wretched Baumer, "a thin, undersized rat of a fellow", who later confirms his lack of gentlemanly attributes by weeping in a most unmasculine way. In *The Five Flamboys* a money-lender masquerades as Angus McGuffie, a Scotsman from Glasgow, but betrays his racial origin through a slightly too large diamond in his tie pin. Berglund, leader of the Six Proud Walkers, wears a subdued tie pin with a single pearl—but he schemes to smash the League of Nations so that he can speculate on fluctuating markets. Albert Wertheim, a conspirator in *The Three Fishers*, who is "the third, perhaps the second biggest man in Europe", is quite prepared to involve his own country with the eternal enemy across the Rhine as long as it furthers his business interests. While by no means all the Beeding villains are Jewish, the Jews who appear are nearly always villains.

By 1930 Beeding's faith in the League was in decline, giving way to an image of the "droning" and ineffectual Assembly at Geneva, as in *The Three Fishers* (1931). Within three years Hitler had taken Germany out of both the League and the Disarmament Conference. Now the Beeding novels begin to depict the world once again treading the path to war.

For one brief moment, Colonel Granby toys with the idea of revolution to stop the inevitable. *The One Sane Man*, published the year after Hitler's seizure of power, presents our hero, just appointed head of the secret service, contemplating disobedience to his political masters. The cause is a conspiracy, this time a "good-bad" one, aimed at forcing the world to accept a new and peaceful international order. The "one sane man" is a London financier, Sir Ernest Burstead, described as the greatest financial expert in England after the Governor of the Bank of England. He plans to marry finance and science—previously the villains of the Beeding novels—in a holy alliance to save the world from itself, master-minding from his hideaway in the Alps the kidnapping of experts to help implement his vision. Using the ultimate weapon of weather control, he succeeds in forcing the League Assembly to agree to his plan. At the last moment, doing his duty to King and Country, Granby locates Burstead's secret headquarters and neutralizes him. But he does so reluctantly and even appeals to the British Foreign Secretary to conceal Burstead's defeat and thus force the League to go ahead with the plan. Predictably, his plea is rejected. As the Assembly is told that the "one sane man" has been defeated, Granby reflects sadly that this will merely ensure "bigger and brighter cenotaphs in all the capitals of the world."

"Although it abounds in exciting adventures such as usually befall the men of the Secret Service," noted the *New York Times* on publication of *The One Sane Man*, "this is not so much a detective story as propaganda for a new social order." Beeding quickly stepped back from the revolutionary precipice, and for the remainder of his career carried on a thoroughly patriotic crusade, with Germany shown as the land of evil and malevolence. Although it is a new Germany, Hitler and his Nazi minions conjure up old stereotypes. By the time we reach *The Ten Holy Terrors* we are back in the world where England's innocence is menaced by the dark fanaticism of the Hun. The novel finds Granby arguing in vain with supporters of "appeasement", wryly describing himself as "one of those damned fools who are usually right in the end." The next book in the series, *Eleven Were Brave*, published after the outbreak of war, is dedicated to Winston Churchill.

The co-authors threw themselves into the war effort. Saunders, who had returned from Geneva to England after the death of his first wife in 1937, became a highly effective official propagandist. He subsequently served on the staff of Air Chief Marshal Sir Trafford Leigh-Mallory, Commander-in-Chief of the Allied Expeditionary Air Forces, and in 1940 he was a liaison officer between the British embassy in Paris and the French Ministry of Information. Much of the background to *Eleven Were Brave*, set in France, was based on his personal experience during the collapse of France and his own narrow escape from Paris. He then wrote *The Battle of Britain*, an officially commissioned popular account that sold 300,000 copies on the first day of publication, and three million copies thereafter. *Combined Operations*, a similarly successful official account, became a best-seller in the United States in 1943. Later on, he wrote inspirational histories of the Parachute Regiment, the Royal Air Force, and the wartime Boy Scout movement.

Palmer's war was distinctly less glamorous, although not without a curious twist of its own. Until his death in 1944 he worked at a routine job at the Ministry of Information, housed in the Senate House of the University of London, a tall, heavy, 1930s building that could easily have belonged in Moscow or Berlin. Here, behind a door marked "Editorial", Malcolm Muggeridge briefly shared a room with him before graduating to SIS. In *Chronicles of Wasted Time* he provided a portrait of Palmer, "a somewhat pale, staid figure", difficult to square with the image of a co-author of thrillers of international intrigue.

We neither of us had much to do, but when I girded against this, Palmer gently rebuked me. Such, he said, had been his lot on the League [of Nations] Secretariat for years past. He had grown used to it, and saw no reason why I should not in time come to do likewise. It was a perfectly permissible and acceptable way of life. Palmer had, indeed, as I saw, developed in himself a sort of Buddhistic power of contemplation as he sat at his desk staring in front of him; expenditure of energy being reserved for things like getting stationery, paper-clips and other clerical impedimenta together, taking control of the opening and shutting of our window, and seeing that his blotter was changed from time to time, and supplies of ink replenished.

From time to time, presumably at duller moments, Palmer would speak to Muggeridge about his partner Saunders. "Palmer clearly held Saunders in considerable awe as a man with sparkling gifts born to shine in a world to which he, Palmer, could not aspire. Mixed with his veneration," noted Muggeridge, "I thought I detected a strain of envy, and perhaps resentment." Letting his imagination roam, Muggeridge later wrote a novel of his own, *Affairs of the Heart*, inspired by the Beeding partnership, in which one of the authors murders his partner, leaving only a single clue hidden in the manuscript of the last novel they were writing together.

The real-life authors, ignorant of the fantasies they inspired, continued to collaborate on the Granby series throughout the war, often introducing real-life characters and events into the fiction and barely concealing the voice of official propaganda. *Not a Bad Show* (1940) sees Granby sending an agent into Germany to find the formula of some secret weapon; the agent ends up spending some time in Buchenwald, which convinces him that "there can be no salvation for normal men and women except by the final destruction of Nazi Germany." The perfidy of Vichy France provides the backdrop to *The Twelve Disguises* (1942), while *There Are Thirteen* is set in France at the time of the Dieppe raid. Here Saunders drew heavily on his wartime experience, for he had been personally commissioned by Lord Mountbatten to write a detailed post-mortem of the raid for high-level circulation in Whitehall. It is as typical a late Beeding as any, with the hero obliged to take strong measures against the treachery of an oleaginous Frenchman, and Dieppe presented as a significant turning point of the war. But while it is a fast-moving tale—"It's the pace that counts," proclaimed the advertising for the Beeding series—it marked the end of an era. "I was still new to the game," the hero John Orton, Granby's right-hand man, muses at one point:

> ...and still inclined to assume that immediate and vigorous action was the daily bread of men in the service. But I was gradually coming to realise that in our profession little good ever came of hurry or excitement. It was the quiet, day-to-day work that counted, the methodical accumulation of evidence, patient watching, attention to detail, the digestion of endless official papers.

The Beeding books had originated in the romantic tradition of the early British spy novel, and Colonel Granby's exploits had been those of traditional derring-do. But the Second World War had injected a new dose of realism, heralding an age in which intrepid agents were replaced by experts who sat in safety behind their desks, patiently unravelling the mysteries of codes and ciphers. It was a world, too, that would have little room for the ironic flippancies of such secure patriots as Granby.

CHAPTER EIGHT

Merchants of Death

Patriotism is for the café.

Eric Ambler

I

"I'm not without a social conscience...I do have something to say. Early in my life and books, I was a little to the left, and I haven't changed much...what I believe in is political and social justice. There is too little of that around, in one's own country or internationally." Thus, in 1981, to the *New York Times* cultural correspondent Herbert Mitgang, Eric Ambler explained his novels of the 1930s, which broke decisively with the cloak-and-dagger tradition. The protagonists are no longer monocled gentlemen of influence but outsiders struggling to survive; their terrain is no longer the velvet-draped corridors of clubland but the sordid reality of dark streets and cheap hotel rooms.

Ambler is the favourite writer of professional intelligence agents on both sides of the Atlantic. It is easy to see why. Although he has always denied any professional involvement with espionage, his novels seem authentic. He is meticulous about detail, and his knowledge of technical and scientific matters is convincing. Phillip Knightley, author of *The Second Oldest Profession*, once said that Ambler's were the only spy novels that adequately conveyed what he had learned about the world of espionage during his researches into the Philby case.

Ambler, more than any other single writer, created the modern spy novel. He built on the foundations laid by Maugham, and has long recognized *Ashenden*'s influence on his early writings. "Ambler," Julian Symons wrote in the *New York Times Book Review* in 1981, "added to Maugham's avoidance of sentiment and coolly realistic style his own unstrained humour, an interest in technical detail that was new...and immense skill in handling the intricacies that most spy stories demand." Espionage, Ambler tells us, can be slow, tedious, and unglamorous—although his protagonists are rarely jaded like Ashenden and are never professional secret agents. Ambler relies little on sex and violence, or on playing up to readers' paranoia. Instead, he draws from the detective novel to present his readers with a guessing game in which layers of deception are peeled away. At the same time his novels are anchored firmly in a contemporary social and political context.

Part of Ambler's gift may be explained by his own background. Born in South London in 1909 of parents who were semi-professional musical entertainers, he grew up in a "two-up two-down no-bathroom house", where his earliest memories were of Zeppelin raids over London and vigorous family debates over the merits of various small-time show-business performers. Doris and Elsie Waters, later to become stars on British radio, were close friends of his parents. At Colfe's Grammar School in Lewisham, founded in 1652 "for the sons of Gentlemen", Ambler found allies against boredom in characters such as Long John Silver, A.J. Raffles, and Rupert of Hentzau, and soon began to dream of becoming a playwright. But he was also intrigued by science, fascinated by emergent wireless technology, and at age sixteen won a scholarship to a London engineering college. Soon bored again, he left to become a trainee salesman for the Edison Swan Electric Company, where he quickly acquired a lot of basic knowledge about electrical engineering. Soon he graduated to the company's publicity department, and just as the Depression began he landed a well-paid job at a London advertising agency.

"Students of the period," Ambler has noted in his autobiography, *Here Lies Eric Ambler*, "have been known to describe the copy departments of the big London advertising agencies of the early thirties as hotbeds of Far-Left conspiracy and fellow-travelling communism. It is an understandable error. The techniques of commercial persuasion may be seen from the outside as differing only slightly from those of political subversion [but] if our copy department was any sort of hotbed it was a literary one." Soon Ambler began to write plays. He also travelled to Europe. On one visit he and a friend were almost arrested in Rome for showing insufficient respect at an exhibition celebrating a decade of Fascism. In Marseilles a year later, after a barman had cheated him at a game of poker dice, he idly spent a day fantasizing how to murder the man by shooting him from the hotel balcony. By coincidence he had chosen the exact spot where a few weeks later a Croat assassin murdered King Alexander of Yugoslavia and the French Foreign Minister, Louis Barthou. "I saw the newsreel several times," Ambler recalled. "I felt oddly guilty, but also pleased. In the Mediterranean sunshine there were strange and violent men with whom I could identify, and with whom, in a way, I was now in touch."

Ambler's fascination with the turbulent politics of southern Europe, his familiarity with technology, and his urge to write finally came together in *The Dark Frontier*, published in 1936. The plot revolves around the construction of an atomic device. This was nine years before Hiroshima and Nagasaki, but Ambler had kept himself well informed about the developments in physics—the main thing he got wrong was the enormous economic and industrial infrastructure required to build such a bomb. "My solemn nightmare of fascist plotters in a Balkan state using atomic blackmail," Ambler has written since, "was flawed by my ignorance."

But critics were impressed. "He has knowledge, and he has speed," remarked the *Observer*. On the advice of a publisher's reader, Ambler studied *Ashenden* and other Maugham short stories, and for the first time read Compton Mackenzie's *Extremes Meet* and *The Three Couriers*. Encouraged by the reception of his next book, *Uncommon Danger* (*Background to Danger* in the United States), Ambler quit his job, signed a contract with his publisher for six more books, and moved to France. By now a haven for refugees from central Europe and the Balkans, and itself torn apart by political passions of the Popular Front era, France was a goldmine for an author seeking to capture the mood of Europe in disintegration. In a back-street *pension* in Nice he encountered a community of Turkish exiles who gave him the idea for *The Mask of Dimitrios* (*A Coffin for Dimitrios* in the United States), still the most famous of his novels. And in Paris in September 1938 Ambler caught the mood of fear that gripped the Continent at the time of the Munich conference. On its last day, before the result was announced, he joined the crowds who had flocked to the cafés of the Boulevard St. Michel. "At about ten minutes to twelve," he said, "everyone gradually drifted away from the café tables and moved out into the street to look up at the sky. We all wanted to catch a first glimpse of the huge fleet of German bombers that had been sent to destroy us...all were prepared for an apocalyptic Armageddon in the style of H.G. Wells."

When Armageddon finally did come, a year later, *The Mask of Dimitrios* had just appeared as a *Daily Mail* book-of-the-month choice in Britain. And *Journey into Fear*, his next book, was published just as the Third Republic collapsed and the Battle of Britain began.

The war set Ambler's career on a new course. "It was," he said, "an interesting and in many ways stimulating war." For a while he served in the Royal Artillery, a period distinguished by duty on the special anti-aircraft battery assigned to protect the Prime Minister's country retreat at Chequers. Once invited to join Churchill's private birthday viewing of a Hollywood movie, Ambler found himself seated next to the Prime Minister in the front row. Soon he became aware of a low, strange noise emerging from the famous siren suit. "Was the Prime Minister asleep?" Ambler wondered, leaning slightly forward to find out. What he heard was Churchill quietly rehearsing a speech. "I could not distinguish words," Ambler recalled, "but what I could hear were the rhythms and cadences of delivery being hummed in a nasal tonic sol-fa of his own."

Ambler was soon rehearsing his own scripts. Assigned to the Army Kinematography Unit responsible for army training films, he wrote his first feature script for a film entitled *The Way Ahead*. Peter Ustinov was his co-writer, Carol Reed was the director, and the film starred David Niven. Later on he wrote *United States*, for which he won a Bronze Star. The film was designed to enlighten British troops about the fighting allies from across the Atlantic, one of many wartime movies required to dispel the negative effects of sudden and unaccustomed Anglo-American cultural contact. *Time*, with its customary generosity, described it as "the best single contribution to Anglo-American understanding in recent years." As an interlude, Ambler worked with director John Huston on a film for the Psychological Warfare Division of the Office of War Information in Italy—an attempt, Ambler has said, to show how the Allies were capturing the "hearts and minds" of the newly occupied Italians. The film was not a success, but it provided Ambler with firsthand experience of war and death as the film unit moved with Fifth Army forces into devastated villages abandoned only hours before by the retreating Germans.

Ambler finished the war as assistant head of the Army Kine-matography Unit and with a myriad of contacts in the film world, where he soon began to flourish. He wrote the screenplays for such major films as *Yangtse Incident*, *A Night to Remember*, and *The Cruel Sea*. But, as he had already learned during the war, "writing for the screen and writing to be read are crafts that have almost nothing to do with one another." Tired of Hollywood, he returned to Europe in 1968. The place he chose to live was Vevey, in Switzerland, the site of Ashenden's exploits. It marked the beginning of a new and more creative period in Ambler's writing.

Although he owes much to Maugham in style, Ambler writes from a significantly different political angle. By class, education, career, and conviction he is an outsider to the British scene, and he has lived abroad for almost three decades. Both his wives have been Americans. His opinions are decidedly anti-establishment and his powerful sympathy for the underdog is reflected in the kinds of characters he creates. His protagonists in the early novels are people such as journalists or writers, usually with what he now describes as "rather wishy-washy liberal views". But with the Hungarian refugee Josef Vadassy, in *Epitaph for a Spy* (1938), he introduced what has become almost the classic Ambler character: the stateless person with no clear national identity, who probably carries several passports— or no passport at all—and who is equally at home— or not at home—in several cities. Indeed, the railway, the frontier, and the passport play a significant part in the early Ambler novels, reflecting a Europe fractured politically and psychologically by the upheavals of the First World War. Ambler is interested in the survivors of the twentieth century's national and political revolutions—the *émigrés*, the refugees, those whose survival depended on living by their wits. In Ambler's world, everyone needs highly trained survival skills.

His novels fall into two distinct periods. The pre-war novels break self-consciously with the Bulldog Drummond tradition and are strongly marked by left-wing idealism. Ambler was the first spy writer to attack capitalism. "Sapper was writing solid right wing. He was an outright fascist.... Buchan was an establishment figure.... I decided to turn that upside down and make the heroes left wing and popular front figures." Ambler also broke with formula conventions in another way. "It was the villains who bothered me most," he once confessed. "Power-crazed or coldly sane, master criminals or old-fashioned professional devils, I no longer believed a word of them.... As I saw it, the thriller had nowhere to go but up."

Alfred Hitchcock, writing the introduction to *Intrigue*, a collection of Ambler's pre-war thrillers, saw Ambler's choice of villains as inspired: "...a strange and motley crew indeed. There are big business men and bankers; the cheap scum of the low cafés of the ancient Continental cities; the professional, suave, well-heeled gangsters whom we have learned to recognize as the incipient chiefs of Gestapos and fascist conspiracies. In brief, they are not only rich people, they are actually the kind of people who have generated violence and evil in the Europe of our times."

Ambler's first novel was published in the year the Spanish Civil War broke out and Hitler marched into the Rhineland. *The Dark Frontier* was intended to be a parody of the Le Queux/Sapper tradition. Professor Barstow, a scientist, suffers concussion in an accident and begins to imagine that he is Conway Carruthers, secret agent. Carruthers—the name of Childers' accidental agent in *The Riddle of the Sands*—is little more than a caricature of Duckworth Drew, and other characters are obviously drawn from the cloak-and-dagger world. Although the book was not a great success and few readers even noticed the parody, it introduced a theme that Ambler was to exploit successfully for the next few years. "Wars were made," muses Professor Barstow at one point, "by those who had the power to upset the balance, to tamper with international money and money's worth."

The power of international capitalism was to be Ambler's principal target in his next five novels: *Uncommon Danger*, *Epitaph for a Spy*, *Cause for Alarm*, *The Mask of Dimitrios*, and *Journey into Fear*. International conspiracy was certainly not new to the spy thriller, and both Buchan and Sapper had dwelt on the power of international finance. But in taking a Marxist perspective, Ambler broke with the anti-Semitic and xenophobic themes of his predecessors. The enemy now was capitalism in the guise of international cartels; together with their interlocking directorates, they pulled the strings of international affairs. "The big businessman was only one player in the game of international politics but he was the player who made all the rules," concludes Kenton, the journalist who narrowly escapes death in central Europe in *Uncommon Danger*.

That international business in general, and arms manufacturers in particular, were responsible for war was a commonplace idea in the 1930s. In 1934–35 a Senate enquiry in the United States, fuelled by isolationist sentiment seeking explanations for the American entry into the First World War, had probed the operations of armaments firms. The League of Nations Union in Britain held a referendum in 1936 on the abolition of the private arms industry which received overwhelming public support, and shortly afterwards the British government established a Royal Commission to look into the industry. The shadowy figure that emerged from both enquiries was that of Sir Basil Zaharoff, who had made a fortune from commissions in the arms trade before and after the war. Zaharoff became the symbol for all private arms dealers and the target of considerable public hostility. Publicity surrounding his death in November 1936 only served to make the arms manufacturers loom even more significantly in the demonology of the Left—and occasionally, too, of the Right: both *Bulldog Drummond at Bay* (1935) and Valentine Williams' *The Fox Prowls* (1939) star villainous merchants of death.

Ambler has denied suggestions that Dimitrios, the shadowy central figure in his famous pre-war novel, is modelled on Zaharoff, although both were from the environs of Constantinople and both veiled their lives with mystery. What would be difficult to deny is that the arms industry looms behind all Ambler's pre-war novels, and furnishes a key to his explanation of international relations in the Fascist era.

Ambler's books chart the collapse of political liberalism over the last fifty years and tell us about the amoral way people and governments behave in our totalitarian age. Latimer, the hero of *The Mask of Dimitrios*, describes Dimitrios as "a unit in a disintegrating social system". He is not evil, Latimer concludes, but "logical and consistent; as logical and consistent in the European jungle as the poison gas called Lewisite...." Evil, Ambler's fiction tells us, is systemic. His protagonists learn this on personal journeys from innocence to knowledge. They are not professionals, but individuals caught up by accident in the whirlwinds of history. Unlike the accidental heroes of Childers or Buchan, they are not inspired by patriotic feeling or personal heroism. "Patriotism is for the café," says one of them. They act out of fear, or to survive, and in doing so develop a sense of outrage at the international manipulators who make money out of misfortune and social injustice. In *Uncommon Danger* and

Cause for Alarm this leads them to co-operate with two Soviet spies, the Zaleshoff brother and sister. This affable couple is now barely credible, especially when we remember that Ambler was writing at the height of the Stalin purges, and that George Orwell in *Homage to Catalonia* had already unmasked the ruthless behaviour of Soviet agents during the Spanish Civil War. But the theme of Soviet benevolence is evidence of Ambler's commitment to the notion of an anti-Fascist popular front to fight Nazism, not of his political percipience about the U.S.S.R.

It is striking that none of his pre-war novels deals directly with the Nazi regime. Presumably Ambler felt that in denouncing the power of international capitalism he was also attacking its supposed puppet in Germany. This was political innocence of an extreme kind. "I was certainly naive," he has since admitted. "For that reason most of my later books are about the loss of innocence."

II

Ambler has had no official connection with espionage services and the authenticity of detail is the product of careful research. But not everyone has been convinced. Following publication of *Cause for Alarm*, Ambler received a summons from the Foreign Office. He was asked how he had discovered escape routes between Yugoslavia and Italy. "Oh, by working it out from maps," he replied. Likewise the ruthless world in which his characters move reflects his own perception of modern international relations. But he is not the only writer to use the spy novel as a vehicle for the discussion of loyalties in an ideological age. By the late 1930s he had been joined by Graham Greene.

The novels of both writers bear the imprint of the Fascist era. They centre on themes of economic depression and the threat of war, and their characters are often political, economic, or social refugees: people crossing frontiers, looking for jobs, scanning the headlines about international crises, or worrying about the correct documentation to satisfy the police. Greene, writes critic George Woodcock, "was a typical man of the Thirties in the way he symbolized political or ethical conflicts in terms of frontiers and police, of gun-battles and no less lethal betrayals, of life on the run...."

Unlike Ambler, however, Greene belongs to the tradition of the spy writer professionally employed in intelligence work. In his first autobiographical work, *A Sort of Life*, he says that he supposes every novelist "has something in common with a spy: he watches, he overhears, he seeks motives and analyzes character, and in his attempt to serve literature he is unscrupulous." In Greene's case, it is difficult to know when the writer stops and the spy begins. Nor does Greene really want us to know, for he has followed the trail blazed by Le Queux, and deliberately drawn smokescreens across his tracks.

As early as the age of nineteen he was involved in what in *A Sort of Life* he disarmingly describes as "a small affair of what might have become espionage". While studying at Oxford he offered his services as a propagandist to the German government to counter French efforts to establish a separatist government in the Rhineland. Somewhat to his surprise, the offer was accepted, and he soon found himself travelling to Germany, spending part of the trip in the company of a German intelligence officer. After his return he offered to spy on the French separatist organization, and then toyed with becoming a double agent by selling his information to the French embassy.

This serio-comic affair, finally terminated by the Locarno Agreement, the international settlement over Germany reached in 1925, was only the first of Greene's entanglements with the world's trouble-spots. On many subsequent journeys in his life of restless travel he has been suspected of being a spy. A member of the Secret Intelligence Service during the Second World War, he worked in West Africa and London. Later, he was to be found in Vienna during the frigid period of Four-Power control, in Prague during the 1948 Communist coup and again after the 1968 Russian invasion, in Indo-China while the French fought the Viet Minh, in Malaya and Kenya during the Communist and Mau Mau insurgencies. He was in Poland in 1955, in Cuba on the eve of Castro's revolution, in the Congo during the independence crisis, in Israel in 1967. All legitimate journalistic assignments, of course—for Greene has never given up journalism—and all "ways of escape" (the title of his second autobiographical memoir) for a man drawn to melodrama. But the boundaries between professional espionage and what Baden-Powell would have called amateur reconnaissance are not always clearly drawn.

Greene was recruited into the Secret Intelligence Service by his younger sister, Elisabeth. Although Greene intimates that this was in 1941, he is not very precise about the details. Fellow author Malcolm Muggeridge has been more forthcoming. The two men got to know each other while first working, early in the war, in the Ministry of Information, and sometimes they would go out together to watch London in the blitz. Summoned to an interview with SIS, Muggeridge later recalled that it "was a consequence of a plot long before hatched with Graham Greene, whose sister, Liza, worked for someone important in the Secret Service. We hoped that she would recommend us both to her boss as outside representatives, and be able to pull the requisite strings to get us accepted."

After the war, Greene retained many of his SIS friendships and contacts, among them Alexander Korda, the film producer and legendary father-figure of the British film industry with whom Greene made *The Third Man*. (It was in Vienna, while working on *The Third Man*, that Greene was first told about the extensive sewer network and its literally underground police force by an intelligence contact in the British mission.) Korda also worked for SIS, allowing it to use his company, London Films, as cover for SIS officers travelling abroad. Sir Claude Dansey, one of the service's quixotic characters, sat on the company's board of directors and became a close friend of Korda, and Greene admits that on one occasion the two of them sailed down the Yugoslav coast in Korda's yacht on an espionage mission. It's no wonder that Greene was put under surveillance by the French authorities during his many visits to Indo-China during the war against the Viet Minh. Indeed, General De Lattre once openly accused him of being a British spy; Greene had, after all, spent time touring obscure corners of the north with the British consul in Hanoi, an old wartime colleague. His two post-war spy novels, *Our Man in Havana* and *The Human Factor*, ring so true because they are built on a foundation of personal experience.

Greene's early novels share the ideological outlook of Ambler's. Briefly a Communist at Oxford (an affiliation which for many years gave him problems in getting a visa for entry to the United States), in the thirties he sympathized openly with the Left. His first dramatically successful thriller, *Stamboul Train* (*Orient Express* in the United States), published in 1932, a story of frontiers, passports, and Balkan intrigue—the very stuff of the inter-war thriller—shows Greene's sympathies lying clearly with Dr. Czinner, the exiled Social Democratic leader who returns home to a useless martyrdom. The 1936 novel *A Gun for Sale* (*This Gun for Hire* in the United States) introduces the obligatory period devil-in-the-top-hat in the shape of Sir Marcus of Midland Steel, a man "with the faintest of foreign accents and of mysterious origin", who sets off a war scare in Europe through a political assassination in order to increase his profits. Greene, like Ambler, was impressed by contemporary inquests into the power of the merchants of death, and even attended sessions of the Royal Commission on the private manufacture of weapons that met in London in 1935.

There are further echoes of Sir Marcus in *The Confidential Agent* (1939). Since his first brush with espionage in 1924 Greene had wanted to write a spy thriller in the Buchan mode, and *The Confidential Agent*—despite its rejection of conventional patriotism—bears a strong Buchan imprint. It shows partly in the transformation of the protagonist from hunted to hunter, but more especially in the ironic contrast between the peaceful surface life of England's familiar scenes and the dramatic adventures of the novel's protagonist. "The best highbrow thriller I have read in a long time," commented a critic in the *New Statesman*.

Set against the background of the Spanish Civil War, *The Confidential Agent* was written in six weeks under the shadow of the Munich Agreement. "D.", an agent of a government of a country embroiled in civil war, has been sent to England to negotiate a deal with Lord Bentwich, a coal magnate, who is concerned only with selling his commodity regardless of political consequences.

Working to foil D. is "L.", a Francoist agent. D. survives an assassination attempt, is framed for a murder, has his credentials
stolen and loses his contract to L., fails in his attempt to foment
a protest strike among the coal workers, and in the end escapes
from England with the sole satisfaction of knowing that L.'s
contract has been cancelled because of political complications.

Into this story Greene weaves the twin themes of the man
alone and the perils of socio-political commitment. D., as the
agent of one side in an ideological struggle, neither trusts himself
nor is trusted by his own side. This bears strong echoes of the
times. By 1939 it was hardly a secret that massive purges of
dissidents had occurred within the world Communist movement.
Stalin had murdered the majority of the Old Bolsheviks and half
the officer corps of the Soviet army, while in Spain the purge
wreaked devastation within the Spanish Republican camp, as
revealed clearly in Orwell's 1939 exposé, *Homage to Catalonia*.
Here lay the seeds for the disillusionment with ideology that was
later so profoundly to affect Greene's generation. D. is an early
harbinger of those who confessed that their God had failed. As
he arrives on the steamer bringing him to Dover, the prospect of
being in peacetime England brings him no security. Is he being
watched by his own side, he wonders.

"The ideology was a complex affair," he meditates, "here-
sies crept in...he wasn't certain that it wasn't right for him to be
watched...in an inner pocket...he carried what were called credentials, but credence no longer meant belief." Later on, after a
series of betrayals, D. notes wryly that no one trusts a confidential agent. No wonder that twenty years later Kim Philby, loyal
to Communism despite the perversions of Stalinism, quoted the
novel in self-justification. For D. takes sides as an act of faith,
fully aware that he may dissent from the actions of his own side,
but none the less remain loyal to a cause.

Shortly afterwards, Greene himself became a confidential
agent, working for SIS in the war against Nazi Germany. "Only
after recruitment," he recorded in *Ways of Escape*, "did I realize
the meaning of all those parties, given by a mysterious Mr. Smith,
to which I had been invited in London where, in spite of the
blitz and the rationing, there seemed no lack of liquor and where

everybody seemed to know each other. I was being vetted."
Admitted as a wartime amateur to the silent game, Greene found
himself early in 1942 stationed in the steamy tropical port city of
Freetown, Sierra Leone, across the border from French Guinea.
Here his principal task was to keep an eye on hostile Vichy
French activities aimed at the huge Allied shipping convoys
sheltering in Fourah Bay.

Like Maugham, Greene found that most of his work consisted
of dull routine. Every morning at seven, he recounts in *Ways
of Escape*, "I would take my little Morris car and drive into
Freetown, do my shopping at the stores—P.Z. or Oliphant's—
and collect my telegrams at the police station to which I was
fictitiously attached by my cover employment of C.I.D. Special
Branch. They arrived in a code unintelligible to the police.... I
would drive home and decode the telegrams and reply to them as
best I could, write my reports or rearrange the reports of others
into an acceptable form—work was over by lunchtime, unless
an urgent telegram arrived or a convoy had brought a bag to be
opened and dealt with."

The outward monotony hid some creative flashes. Kim Philby
back at SIS headquarters in London recalled at least one lively
contribution that Greene apparently forgot. "I do remember...a
meeting," he recorded in *My Silent War*, "held to discuss a
proposal of his to use a roving brothel to frustrate the French and
two lonely Germans suspected of spying on British shipping in
Portuguese Guinea. The proposal was discussed quite seriously
and was turned down only because it seemed unlikely to be
productive of hard intelligence."

Greene was imaginative in other ways, too. In "The Soupsweet
Land", a piece in his 1968 *Collected Essays*, he recalled that,
being quite incompetent in technical matters, he accidentally
locked his code books in the combination safe and was then unable to reopen it. In desperation, using a laborious book code, he
told London that the safe had been damaged in transit and could
they please send out another? The codes themselves produced a
challenge that he was unable to resist, for they contained unex-
pected words in their limited vocabulary. "I wondered how often
use had been made of the symbol for 'eunuch'," he recorded,

"and I was not content until I had found an opportunity to use it myself in a message to my colleague in Gambia: 'As the chief eunuch said I cannot repeat cannot come.'" At other times the monotony was relieved by exchanging cipher messages by one-time pad with Muggeridge, his fellow noviciate who had been sent as SIS man to Lourenço Marques in Mozambique.

After a year, by which time he had concluded that all was a waste of time, Greene was posted back to London. Here he worked with Philby in SIS's Section V, counter-intelligence, where he was placed in charge of Portuguese affairs. "He had a good time sniping at OSS," Philby recorded, "and his tart comments on incoming correspondence were a daily refreshment."

Greene, indeed, quickly found rich material for satire in the wartime SIS, and like Compton Mackenzie before him soon realized that even in war the silent game had its comic and farcical side. Abwehr officers in Portugal, he learned, were sending completely erroneous reports back to Germany based on information from imaginary agents. In return, they received payment for the agents that went straight into their own pockets. In the field, Greene himself had once sent to London an agent's report about a tank storage shed on a Vichy airfield in French Guinea with a cover note saying that he thought the agent unreliable—from other, better sources he believed that the shed contained old boots. London surprised him by congratulating him for a "most valuable" report. "I had learned," Greene drily noted, "that nothing pleases the services at home more than the addition of a card to their intelligence files." Thus, out of his SIS experience, was born the idea that eventually became his marvellous satire of secret service, *Our Man in Havana*.

"An early hero of mine was John Buchan," wrote Greene, "but when I reopened his books I found I could no longer get the same pleasure from the adventures of Richard Hannay.... Patriotism had lost its appeal, even for a schoolboy, at Passchendaele...while it was difficult, during the years of the Depression, to believe in the high purposes of the City of London or of the British Constitution. The hunger-marchers seemed more real than the politicians. It was no longer a Buchan world."

Nor was it a Le Queux world, as Greene made wonderfully explicit in *The Ministry of Fear*, the novel he wrote in his spare time in Sierra Leone. Greene sailed to West Africa on a small 5,000-ton Elder-Dempster cargo ship carrying a load of TNT. At 2:30 p.m. on December 9, just two days after Pearl Harbor and with German armies encircling Moscow and Leningrad, the ship left Liverpool and sailed down the Mersey into the deadly waters of the North Atlantic. By day, the twelve passengers helped to man the submarine watches and learned how to fire the guns, and Greene described the sense of danger being tangible, "like nausea". Like the others, he followed the chief steward's advice to leave the door of his cabin hooked ajar, always slept in trousers, shirt, and pullover, and ate his meals wearing a lifebelt. At night, lying in his bunk, half expecting the torpedo that never came, he read from a long list of books he had taken with him for Africa. It included a number of Trollopes, the Old and New Testaments, several books of verse, a Michael Innes thriller, and the inevitable anthology of Shakespeare. But the book he began reading the day he set off on his twenty-six–day ordeal was Eric Ambler's *The Mask of Dimitrios*.

It's not clear what effect this chilling story of multiple deceit and murder had on Greene's peace of mind as he braved the German submarine threat and prepared for his secret intelligence work. But what we do know is that shortly after he arrived in Sierra Leone as SIS Agent 59200 he began to write *The Ministry of Fear*, a book which he has called his favourite "entertainment" (an idiosyncratic designation Greene uses to "distinguish them from more serious novels"), and which Fritz Lang turned into a Paramount movie in 1944 starring Ray Milland.

In it, Arthur Rowe, a man once imprisoned for the mercy killing of his dying wife, becomes accidentally entangled with a fifth column of German spies in London. To foil him, they convince Rowe that he is wanted for murder, and he becomes a hunted man, wandering through the streets of London devastated by the German blitz, before finally helping to destroy the enemy conspiracy. An uneven and certainly not very funny novel, it is of interest principally because of its explicit claim that the world had finally caught up with the fantasies of William Le

Queux—that life was at last imitating art. ("There are times," he told Marie-Françoise Allain in a 1979 conversation, "when I'm inclined to think that our entire planet gravitates inside a fog-belt of melodrama.")

Rowe, on the run from the police during a German bombing raid on London, seeks refuge in an underground shelter and falls asleep. Here he dreams of his mother and the pre-war world of innocence in which she and her generation lived:

Rowe thought: this would be a dream, too, to her; she wouldn't believe it. She had died before the first great war, when aeroplanes—strange crates of wood—just staggered across the Channel. She could no more have imagined this than that her small son in his brown corduroy knickers and his blue jersey with his pale serious face—he could see himself like a stranger in the yellowing snapshots of her album—should grow up to be a murderer. Lying on his back he caught the dream and held it—pushed the vicar's wife back into the shadow of the pine—and argued with his mother.

"This isn't real life any more," he said. "Tea on the lawn, evensong, croquet, the old ladies calling, the gentle unmalicious gossip, the gardener trundling the wheelbarrow full of leaves and grass. People write about it as if it still went on; lady novelists describe it over and over again in books of the month, but it's not there any more."

His mother smiled at him in a scared way but let him talk; he was the master of the dream now. He said, "I'm wanted for a murder I didn't do. People want to kill me because I know too much. I'm hiding underground, and up above the Germans are methodically smashing London to bits all round me. You remember St. Clement's—the bells of St. Clement's. They've smashed that—St. James's, Piccadilly, the Burlington Arcade, Garland's Hotel, where we stayed for the pantomime, Maples and John Lewis. It sounds like a thriller, doesn't it, but the thrillers are like life—more like life than you are, this lawn, your sandwiches, that pine. You used to laugh at the books Miss Savage read—about spies, and murders, and violence, and wild motor-car chases, but dear, that's real life: it's what we've all made of the world since you died. I'm your little Arthur who wouldn't hurt a beetle and I'm a murderer too. The world has been remade by William Le Queux."

(Greene makes a similar acknowledgement to Le Queux in *The Spy's Bedside Book*. This small classic, chosen with an affectionate eye for the absurd, is dedicated "To the immortal memory of William Le Queux and John Buchan.")

III

Ambler and Greene brought the sombre mood of the 1930s into the mainstream of spy fiction. So did a third writer who continued to produce novels until close to his death in 1988. At the depth of the Depression, a young man who had recently returned to Britain after several years abroad placed an advertisement in the Appointments Wanted column of the *Times*. Shortly afterwards he found himself summoned to the advertising office by a senior clerk. What did he mean, he was asked, and was he aware that his advertisement was open to misunderstanding? The cause of the *contretemps* was that he had described himself as "an Englishman with no national prejudices." The incident tells us something about England in the 1930s. It tells us even more about the author of the offending advertisement, Geoffrey Household.

Household made his name as a novelist with *Rogue Male*. Like the other best-selling thriller of 1939, *The Mask of Dimitrios*, it has become a classic, and has rarely, if ever, been out of print. (It was published simultaneously in the United States by Little, Brown, Household's American publisher since 1938. The latest Penguin reprinting was in 1984.) It is the story of an unnamed but prominent Englishman who attempts to assassinate Hitler by shooting him with a telescopic-lensed rifle. He is caught, tortured, left for dead, and then escapes back to England. Pursued by Nazi agents, he takes refuge in the English countryside where he literally goes to ground, burying himself like a fox in a burrow. He finally kills his pursuers, and as the novel ends we find him returning to Germany determined to succeed a second time.

"I shall not get away alive," he says, "but I shall not miss." (Some forty years later in *Rogue Justice* Household gave us the sequel, in which we learn more about the hero's mission, discover his subsequent fate, and even learn his name: Raymond Ingraham, whose forefathers fought at Agincourt, Waterloo, and the Somme.)

It was later claimed—although never by Household—that *Rogue Male* almost changed the course of history. Colonel Noel Mason-Macfarlane, the British military attaché in Berlin in the 1930s, claimed after the war to have been inspired by the plot to conceive a similar plan to assassinate Hitler. Although Mason-Macfarlane was idiosyncratic enough to have talked rather wildly of doing so to a *Times* correspondent, this was at the time of Munich, a good year before Household's novel saw the light of day, even before he began to write it.

Critics, as well as Household himself, acknowledge strong affinities between *Rogue Male* and the Buchan thrillers, with hunter and hunted, the sense of danger in the midst of the familiar, and the detailed description of a landscape that is integral to the chase. When Penguin Books published their first paperback edition of the novel, they proclaimed it the most exciting novel of adventure since *The Thirty-Nine Steps*. Yet in most other respects Household's novels sharply contrast with those of Buchan. Household heroes are uninterested in power or influence, and would care nothing about earning a column in the *Times*. Distrustful of patriotism and other contemporary ideologies, they are instinctive anarchists. Like Ambler's characters they are never creatures of the state, but individuals caught up in the whirlwind of twentieth-century history. Many are not English at all. When they act, their motive is love and human decency. "I distrust patriotism," confesses the hero of *Rogue Male*, "the reasonable man can find little in these days that's worth dying for. But dying against—there's enough iniquity in Europe to carry the most urbane decadent into battle."

Resistance to the abuse of authority and a strong pan-European sentiment have provided the hallmarks of Household thrillers ever since. In 1939 the hero of *Rogue Male* set out to kill Hitler in revenge for the death by Gestapo torture of his Jewish fiancée, and to put an end to the man who threatened the peace of Europe. Some forty years later the heroine of *The Last Two Weeks of Georges Rivac* (1978) conspires, assisted by a strong personal motive, to save Europe from war and destruction in the face of superpower confrontation.

As the incident of the *Times* advertisement suggests, Household is the most English and yet the most cosmopolitan of the writers so far considered, the least likely to measure the foreigner to the familiar and find him wanting. Until his early twenties, however, he followed a conventional path that could well have taken him onto the highroad of British xenophobia. Born in Bristol in 1900, the son of a barrister, Geoffrey Household attended Clifton College in the same city before entering Magdalen College, Oxford, where he won a first-class degree in English literature. Seizing the opportunity presented by a friend, he opted for adventure over safety, and accepted a job with the Ottoman Bank in Bucharest, thus beginning a picaresque career as a businessman in several European countries that lasted until the eve of the Second World War. Sowing wild oats with abandon, he learned to speak several languages, and discovered, as he put it in *Against the Wind*, his autobiography, "the European within him".

After five years in Bucharest he abandoned his banking career and moved to Paris, and then to Bilbao, where he worked for the banana importers Elders and Fyffes. Shortly before the Great Crash he arrived in the United States, having once again left his job, this time in the hope of finding work as a screenwriter in Hollywood. Instead, he ended up in New York, where he soon landed a relatively lucrative job writing articles for a children's encyclopaedia. Much of this restless travel was in the relentless pursuit of Marina Kopelanoff, an American from Los Angeles whom he had first met in Bucharest. She took seven years to accept his offer of marriage, only finally succumbing in 1930. For the next two years Household travelled constantly between the east and west coasts, during which time, of all things American, practically the only thing he came to enjoy was the American breakfast. "The dead years," he later described this period in America. But the chase for Marina had one good aspect.

"It was at the age of twenty-nine, eager to achieve financial independence which would allow me to follow Marina, that I first hurled myself at writing," Household recalled. "Money was the driving force." He wrote a series of short radio dramatizations for Columbia Broadcasting before returning to Europe in 1933 and becoming a commercial traveller for a printing ink firm. His travels now took him to central Europe, the Middle East, and South America, but increasingly he turned to writing. *The Atlantic* accepted a number of his short stories, and with the success of his first novel, *The Third Hour* (not a thriller) in 1937, he finally settled down to earn his living with the pen.

But the world quickly intruded. With *Rogue Male* completed and in the hands of the publisher, Household prepared for war. "In August 1939 I had all the attributes of peace except any desire for it," he wrote in *Against the Wind*. "I had watched the gropings of my Europe back towards the lights which had gone out in 1914, and had dared to believe that between the economic depression and Hitler's occupation of the Rhineland they had again flickered into life, if only for a few hours and in a few favoured streets. My feeling for Nazi Germany," he added, "had the savagery of a personal vendetta." Appreciated by few of those who admired the passion and tension of *Rogue Male* was the fact that Household's wife was Jewish, and that his early Romanian experience had first exposed him to real anti-Semitism and had converted him into an avowed enemy of institutionalized racism.

The ink was barely dry on the Hitler–Stalin Pact that heralded the onslaught on Poland when Household was summoned to the War Office by letter. "It was a mysterious letter," he remembered, "for it was not franked *On His Majesty's Service* but bore a stamp." It came from a secret department of the War Office known as M.I.R. (Military Intelligence Research), a special unit set up after the *Anschluss* of 1938 to explore guerrilla and unconventional warfare. Later, merged with other clandestine organizations, it was to become the top-secret Special Operations Executive (SOE), which infiltrated hundreds of secret agents into Europe and inspired several post-war fictions about secret agents, most notably those of Ian Fleming. M.I.R. thought

Household useful because of his knowledge of Romania, and shortly after war broke out he was in place, under civilian cover, in Bucharest. M.I.R. was (wrongly) convinced that Germany was economically vulnerable, particularly because of its reliance on oil imports from still-neutral Romania, and plots to disrupt these supplies were given high priority by Household's masters during the so-called Phony War. With two other British colleagues, both, like himself, businessmen-turned-agents, Household was given diplomatic cover at the Legation in Bucharest. Here, according to Household, they severely disconcerted the staff "by playing casually with detonators in [their] office and drinking very much more than was good for them."

Their mission, to sabotage Romanian oil wells should they be threatened with a German takeover, was fraught with delicacy. One plan assumed the active help of the Romanian authorities, but a contingency arrangement was made in case they refused. Working with the British manager of the Unirea oilfield at Ploesti, Household had to tread carefully. There were German agents everywhere, the Americans and Dutch oilmen were neutral, and the Romanian authorities were suspicious. After plans were laid there was little to do but wait, and Household and his friends led a life of idle luxury, dining out in the best restaurants of Bucharest. "We felt like parasites," Household wrote, "upon the unhealthy back of war." The disastrous collapse of France and the Dunkirk débâcle drastically changed the picture. With the Romanians now even more closely tied to the Germans, it was clear that they would not co-operate in the sabotage of their own wells, and Household put the alternative plan into motion. But twenty-four hours before the sabotage was to be carried out, the Romanians posted two military sentries on every well. "Who betrayed us we never knew," he wrote. "Such indications as there were suggested that the leak was not in Bucharest or Ploesti, but through the Roumanian Legation in London. It is possible that someone in authority had forgotten that the allegiances of major oil companies cannot, even in war, be too closely defined."

Shortly afterwards Household left Romania for Cairo, where he joined the Field Security Police to spend six years in Greece, Egypt, Jerusalem, Beirut, and Baghdad writing security and intelligence reports. This, combined with his Romanian adventures, provided rich raw material for his post-war fiction.

By the time Household was up to his neck in acts of his own derring-do in Bucharest, *Rogue Male* had been published to critical acclaim in Britain and the United States. But Household had almost forgotten it. "Truth at the time seemed so much more provocative," he recalled in his autobiography. "Which, by any definition of the real, was nearer to reality I do not know. The attack upon the oil fields petered out into a dining club for diplomatic clerks. *Rogue Male* is still in the present."

For all his individualism and distrust of the state, Household had joined the tradition of the writer-become-spy. That it was clearly established as tradition by the late 1930s is nicely illustrated by what happened to Household *en route* to Bucharest in 1939. Having decided to become a writer, he felt justified in describing himself on his passport as an author, but he was told that this would not do. Authors, he was sternly informed, were suspected by every foreign security officer. Thus, Household noted in *Against the Wind*, "Compton Mackenzie and Somerset Maugham had destroyed our reputation as unworldly innocents forever." Instead, his new passport described him as an insurance agent. Yet another turning point had been reached in the bizarre relationship of fact and fiction. The world of Le Queux now formed a closed chapter in the history of the silent game.

CHAPTER NINE

Special Relations

England may have been bled pretty thin by a couple of World
Wars, our Welfare State politics may have made us expect too
much for free, and the liberation of our Colonies may have gone
too fast, but we still climb Everest and beat plenty of the world
at plenty of sports, and win Nobel Prizes...there's nothing wrong
with the British people....

Ian Fleming, *You Only Live Twice*

The Second World War should have put an end to the traditional
spy novel. The most villainous fictional spy could hardly compete with Reinhard Heydrich or Heinrich Himmler. The triumphs
of wartime intelligence lay in the interception and analysis of enemy codes and ciphers, a prosaic and backroom task, painstaking
work worlds removed from the derring-do of the descendants of
Duckworth Drew. We have seen how this transformation affected
Colonel Granby. We left him in the last of his adventures musing
that little good ever came of excitement, and that what counted in

the great game was the slow and methodical digestion of official papers.

Granby's retirement was premature. The key players might indeed have been the master-minds who gave us Auschwitz, Ultra, and Hiroshima, but these same giants spawned a multitude of shadow warriors. Their accomplishments far outmatched most spy fiction in inventiveness and gave us a multitude of heroes. The silent game, indeed, was brought to a new pitch of refinement in the Second World War, creating an entirely new league of players. In Britain, the Special Operations Executive (SOE) infiltrated hundreds of secret agents and guerrilla fighters into occupied territory. Other equally secret agencies indulged in deception, the manipulation of double agents, psychological warfare, and a multitude of other dirty tricks. In the United States, the Office of Strategic Services (OSS) introduced Americans to the intricacies and excitements of the game. They learned quickly. When OSS was disbanded, the shadow warriors created the Central Intelligence Agency, one of the richest post-war hunting grounds for spy novelists in search of raw material. It has rarely failed them, whether writing romance, farce, or tragedy. Above all, post-war superpower confrontation and the threat of mass destruction have helped to create some of the best spy fiction the century has seen.

I

The war itself produced a predictable crop of traditional spy novels. Many of the detective writers of the 1930s transformed their heroes into counter-intelligence agents, saving Britain and the Empire from Nazi subversion. Thus Michael Innes had Inspector Appleby of the CID tackling foreign spies in *The Secret Vanguard* (1940), while Margery Allingham published *Traitor's Purse* (1941). They were joined by other writers such as John Creasey, Marthe McKenna, Helen MacInnes, Dennis Wheatley, and Peter Cheyney, most of whom had been writing in other genres in the 1930s.

Creasey was a publishing phenomenon of heroic proportions who made Edgar Wallace look like a dilettante. Born in London and married to an American writer of westerns, and with two homes, one in England and the other in Arizona, he wrote 562 novels under more than twenty names, taking an average of ten days to produce each one and selling over eighty million copies of his books. In the 1930s he produced the "Department Z" series about foreign espionage in Britain, and then in 1939, under the name "Gordon Ashe", created the Patrick Dawlish series. Dawlish is an agent in the Bulldog Drummond tradition, frequently parachuting into Nazi-occupied Europe to organize resistance against the occupier.

Marthe McKenna, too, had written about German spies in Britain during the 1930s; she and Helen MacInnes were the two women authors who established reputations as spy authors in this period, and she was the first woman to belong to the "agent-turned-author" club. Born in Belgium in 1893, she spied for the British in her occupied native land during the First World War, when, as a nurse in a German military hospital, she cajoled senior German officers into revealing items of military use to the Allies. Eventually caught, court-martialled, and condemned to death, McKenna was saved only by the armistice in 1918.

After the war she married a British officer and settled in Britain. Two volumes of memoirs, *I Was a Spy* (1933) and *Spies I Knew* (1934), followed, and thereafter she turned to fiction. Her novels were in the Le Queux tradition, hinting strongly that the fiction disguised fact and that enemy (German) spies were swarming over the country. Thus, in the preface to *Lancer Spy* (1937), she warned her British readers that "potential enemy agents are again in your midst, casting envious eyes on your prosperity and surveying with jealous hate your world-wide possessions. They percolate into every walk of life, and whilst they labour with secret intent, the while having soft words of praise and of friendship, they seek your ruin utter and complete." And in *Set a Spy* (1937), starring Lieutenant Peter Thames of the secret service, a tall and handsome man whose twinkling, deep blue eyes could in an instant "harden into adamantine reserve", the reader learns that "London is flooded with spies and international espionage agents...taking advantage...of the tolerant laws of a free country...these dark invaders pursue their insidious tactics."

McKenna took the phrase "dark invaders" from the title of a best-selling book published in the mid-1930s recounting the wartime exploits of a German spy in the United States, Captain Fritz von Rintelen, who had eventually been trapped by a joint Anglo-American intelligence operation. Likewise, she modelled her fictional head of Britain's secret service on its real-life director, Admiral Sir Hugh ("Quex") Sinclair, successor as C to Cumming, who had died in 1923. (The last man to see Cumming alive, oddly enough, was Valentine Williams. Calling on him in his rooftop lair above the spires of Whitehall, Williams chatted amicably with Cumming about the latter's approaching retirement, then left him comfortably ensconced in the corner of his sofa. Shortly afterwards, when Cumming's secretary entered the room, she found the old man dead. "He had died in harness, as he would have wished," noted Williams.) McKenna inherited Williams' veneration for the service, similarly worshipped Cumming's heir, and, along with the professionals, deplored the cut-backs that affected SIS once the war was over.

Satirized as N, the secret-obsessed service chief in Compton Mackenzie's *Water on the Brain*, Sinclair, the man behind Mackenzie's prosecution, was a former Director of Naval Intelligence with a colourful personality to match that of Cumming. He had a reputation as a *bon vivant*, smoked cigars that he kept in a crocodile-skin case, was a divorcé with a stormy private life, and conspicuously drove around London in an ancient open Lancia. To McKenna, Sinclair, "Vice-Admiral George Kingston—'G.K.' to his intimates", in *Set a Spy* carried Britain's fate on his powerful and reassuring shoulders, bringing to the silent game the centuries-old tradition of the "Senior Service", Britain's Royal Navy. "Behind him," she told readers,

> was a superb Service of a centuries-old tradition [that] had served England gloriously and faithfully during mankind's upheavals and Nature's bitterest wrath. And whether it was battling against a raging storm on the bosom of their sexless Mistress, the Sea, where a murmured decision meant the safety of hundreds of

their fellows, or a battle in war which would decide the fate of a world empire, here was that solid dependence, that undying courage handed down through a long line of heroic men. Men who had given their all quietly, asking nor expecting nothing in return, only the well-being of the land they loved as a mother, and were honoured to serve.... A reforming government whittled down their establishment. Good! They who remain must work wonders. With the neglect of peace and a false security, a miserly pittance was meted out to the Service. Good again! With what little there was miracles were wrought. And thus, ready for the hour, that wonderful tradition has been handed on, for those men knew that, as sure as the sun rises over the restless waves, Britain will again sorely need that unsleeping Service.

The ever-wakeful Kingston, indeed, is the only man who understands the dangers threatening Britain, for "only he knew the rampant insolence of covetous dictators and drivelling foreigner reformers when it had become realized that the lion was practically toothless." And only he, as he reveals to young Peter Thames before sending him on his perilous mission abroad, appreciates the blindness of the so-called "wise men" who argue that triumphant statecraft lies in successful operations on three fronts—political, economic, and military. "But always," he tells Thames, "[they] ignore the all-important Fourth Front— Intelligence Service [without which] political perspicacity will grope in the dark."

McKenna was not without some political perceptiveness herself, suggesting in 1937 that Britain would have to fight against Italy, Japan, and Germany simultaneously and that the "Bolshevik threat" was merely a device being manipulated by Hitler and his allies as a smokescreen to keep the German masses docile and to fool his opponents. Beyond that, however, her novels about the Nazis that continued to appear throughout the war were little more than conventional patriotic tracts. They are of interest primarily because, in their linking of the silent game with the traditions of the Royal Navy, they presage the romantic heroism of Ian Fleming and James Bond.

Another woman who first made her mark at this time was Helen MacInnes, who went on to become a tremendously successful author with such works as *The Venetian Affair* and *The Salzburg Connection*, and earned the title of "the Queen of Spy Writers". A Scot, she immigrated to the United States in 1937 and later became an American citizen. Gilbert Highet, her husband, a classical scholar who held the Anthon Professorship of Latin Language and Literature at Columbia University, joined William Stephenson's New York–based British Security Co-ordination in 1940 to work in its special operations section. So there were some raised eyebrows when MacInnes's *Assignment in Brittany* appeared in 1942 with its tale of a secret agent spirited into France by the then-still-novel technique of the parachute drop. Some inside knowledge of Allied behind-the-lines operations was suspected, and MacInnes later discovered that after D-Day many veterans had vainly tried to trace some of her imaginary locations.

Straightforward adventures of good against evil, MacInnes's post-war novels mostly echoed Cold War rhetoric. "I'm against totalitarians in general—national or religious, extremists of the right or left," she said in a 1978 interview. "If I can be labelled anything, I am a Jeffersonian Democrat." Not surprisingly, along with William Buckley, Jr., she became the favourite spy writer of at least three former directors of Central Intelligence, and by the time of her death in 1985 in New York her books had sold more than 23 million copies in the United States alone.

Ian Fleming, however, was more directly influenced by another of the writers who flourished during the war, Peter Cheyney, a failed songwriter and journalist of working-class origins from the East End of London. In the early 1930s Cheyney supported Oswald Mosley's British Union of Fascists, and was an ardent patriot who, according to Donald McCormick in *Who's Who in Spy Fiction*, "would challenge to a duel anyone who sneered at Britain or the Royal Family." The first British writer to attempt to imitate the hard-boiled American thriller, in 1936 Cheyney invented his American G-man, Lemmy Caution. He wrote badly, but sold well in both Britain and the United States, where he shared the publisher Dodd, Mead with Agatha Christie.

His wartime series of spy novels, for obvious reasons known as the "Dark" series—all had such titles as *Dark Duet*, *The Stars Are Dark*, and *Dark Hero* — enjoyed an enthusiastic readership, and by the end of the war he was selling more than a million and a half copies a year. Often they came dangerously close to being self-parodies. Gestapo interrogators torturing British secret agents actually say things such as "We have ways of making you talk." In *Dark Duet* (1942), which its publisher claimed was the first British novel to be openly on sale in Paris after the Liberation (thanks to Resistance efforts), Cheyney self-consciously gives the game away. Ernie Guelvada, the Belgian tough guy who does the dirty jobs (such as killing) for British Intelligence, finds himself in wartime neutral Lisbon, that hotbed of spies. "This is the best hotel in Lisbon," he notes. "It has everything. It even has fat blonde German spies all dressed in black velvet gowns hiding behind the palms in the lounges. It only needs William Le Queux here to write a book about it. It's a scream, *n'est-ce pas?*"

Indeed it is, for Cheyney's world is that of Le Queux merely updated for the idiom of a later age. His agents catch the villains, win the women, and save the country. In doing so they build a bridge to the world of Fleming. Violence, sex, and murder are important ingredients, all tinged with sadism. Cheyney's heroes are tough men fighting in a tough world, saving the country for the unthinking masses and a too often decadent and sybaritic upper class. "Without Cheyney and his broad popularity in the forties and fifties," writes LeRoy Panek, "Ian Fleming's novels would have only part of their content."

Dennis Wheatley was a more interesting case. Like the others, he had established his reputation as a writer in the 1930s and was a man of prolific output, writing some sixty books with a sale of more than 37 million copies. As a child he was an avid reader of popular literature, and his mind, in his own words in his memoirs, *Stranger Than Fiction*, was "steeped in stories of international intrigue." During his teens he devoured historical romances and spy stories by such writers as Oppenheim, Le Queux, and A.E.W. Mason.

Wheatley was born in 1897, the son of a wine merchant, and was educated at Dulwich School. After first training as a naval cadet, he fought during the First World War with the Ulster Regiment, and after being gassed was invalided out of the army. From 1919 to 1931 he helped to run the family business, and then sold it to begin a writing career. A man of conservative instincts ("the demand for equality in all things is the parrot cry of the modern age"), he is another writer who was closely involved in secret government activity.

In the 1930s he became a close friend of Maxwell Knight, the first M.I.5 man he had met, and through him was introduced to such men as Vernon Kell, Knight's boss, who directed M.I.5 from its beginnings in 1909 to his sudden dismissal by Churchill in 1940, and Tom Driberg, the well-known journalist and M.I.5 informer on the Communist Party of Great Britain. Wheatley became involved in some of Knight's operations, and, early in 1939, facilitated his penetration of German *émigré* circles in London by hiring one of Knight's informers, an Austrian refugee named Frau Friedl Gaertner, as a part-time research assistant. Another of Wheatley's assistants was a man called W.H. Tayleur, who happened to be a Fascist sympathizer. At one of Wheatley's frequent pre-war parties, Tayleur brought along the British Fascist William Joyce, the infamous "Lord Haw-Haw", later hanged by the British for his wartime broadcasts from Berlin. Joyce, Wheatley recalled later, told him that Hermann Goering was a great fan of Wheatley's books and hoped that he would visit Germany to meet the top Nazi leaders. Joyce himself evidently had a high opinion of Wheatley; when he fled Britain at the outbreak of war he left behind stacks of papers, among which was a file on Wheatley revealing that Joyce had reported him to Berlin as having great potential as an excellent collaborator after a German invasion and a man who "would make a first-class *Gauleiter* for northwest London." Only Wheatley's friendship with Knight saved him from turning into a prime police suspect.

The affair certainly proved no obstacle to his wartime career. Despite his best efforts, M.I.5 refused to employ him; however, in 1941 he succeeded in joining the Joint Planning Staff in Whitehall, and soon began to work within one of the most secret departments responsible for Deception Planning. He helped to plan such well-known operations as "The Man Who Never Was" (the planting of false documents on a corpse with a fictional biography deliberately left to drift ashore in Spain and fool German agents about Allied planning for the invasion of Italy) and "Monty's Double" (the sending of a double of General Montgomery to Gibraltar to fool the Germans about the real general's whereabouts). In his last and posthumously published book, *The Deception Planners: My Secret War* (1980), he gave an extensive account of his wartime career.

Beginning in 1934, Wheatley had introduced the upper-middle-class secret agent Gregory Sallust into his fiction. Sallust's first adventure, in *Black August*, is to fight against a Communist revolution in Britain, but he appears in several of Wheatley's wartime novels, such as *The Scarlet Imposter*, *Faked Passports* (1940), and *"V" for Vengeance* (1942). In *Code-word—Golden Fleece*, which appeared in 1946, Wheatley drew heavily on his knowledge of the plans to disrupt German oil supplies from Romania (in which Household had been involved). In *Stranger Than Fiction* (1959) he claimed that "to provide accurate background for the stories I had to keep abreast with every development of the war and secure through such sources as were available to any ordinary citizen, as much factual information as I could...." But, as we have seen, he had an insider's knowledge of the silent game and had been involved at the highest levels of British Intelligence.

For all that Wheatley's characters believed in Britain and the Empire, and despite his well-earned expertise in the secret world of intelligence and deception, it was another denizen of the Whitehall world of secrets who reaped the rich dividends that flowed from the reservoirs of patriotic sentiment created by the war. Appropriately enough for a genre that exalted the amateur gentleman, this was to be the reward of a man who had not written a single book before he began his career as the most successful spy writer of the twentieth century.

II

In October 1959, not long after the London *Sunday Times* had passed from the hands of Lord Kemsley into those of Canadian press magnate Roy Thomson, the newspaper's foreign manager boarded a BOAC Comet bound for Hong Kong. He had armed himself with what he described as "the perfect book for any journey": Eric Ambler's *Passage of Arms*, his thriller about arms smuggling in South-East Asia. Ian Fleming's route took him via Beirut, Bahrein, New Delhi, and Bangkok, and although Ambler's novel failed to distract him from noticing the dirt, squalor, and smell of the Middle East and India, he immediately fell in love with the Far East. This was just as well, for Fleming had been sent there to write a series entitled "Thrilling Cities" for his newspaper, and nothing takes the edge off a good thrill more than a bad smell. Of all the places he visited, he loved Hong Kong best, describing it as "the most vivid and exciting city I have ever seen...[and] a pure joy to the senses and spirits." To his surprise, wedded as he was to traditional English food, he found Chinese food delicious. To his even greater delight he discovered the women charming. He noted that they had an almost inexhaustible desire to please, and that every encounter left him with a better opinion of himself. "How very different," he observed with pleasure, "from the knocking we all get in the West where women—and this applies particularly to America—take such ferocious delight in cutting the men down to size."

Despite the personal pleasures he found in his travels, though, Fleming brought back a sombre message for his British readers when he finally returned to London via Honolulu and the United States:

It was a source of constant depression to observe how little of our own influence was left in that great half of the world where we did so much of the pioneering. I cannot remember meeting a single Briton all the way from Hong Kong to New York, with the exception of the British consul in Hawaii...it is a measure of our surrender that there are, I think, only three staff correspondents excluding Reuters covering the entire Orient for the British press...a trip round the world, however hasty, brings home all too vividly the fantastically rapid contraction of our influence, commercial and cultural, over half the globe....

Thrilling Cities, later published as a collection, provides an excellent introduction to the Fleming/Bond phenomenon. It reminds us that Ian Fleming was not just the creator of the most famous secret agent of the twentieth century, but also a professional journalist who watched with dismay the rapid shrinking of British influence in the two decades after the Second World War, a cutting down to size of the British Empire as distressful to Fleming as the deflating effect of American women on his fragile ego. For most of the year he could be found at Kemsley House in London, directing his team of foreign correspondents and writing his regular "Atticus" column for the *Sunday Times*. But each January he would fly off to his Jamaican retreat of "Goldeneye" for two months' holiday to write his annual Bond novel, returning with a complete manuscript for his publishers in March. It was a ritual that had begun with his first novel, *Casino Royale*, in 1952, and it continued until his death of a heart attack at the Royal St. George's Golf Club in Kent in August 1964.

To understand James Bond we have to understand Fleming's character and career. For at bottom James Bond *is* Ian Fleming, as he was or as he would have liked to be, and each of the novels can be seen as an instalment of what John Pearson, Fleming's biographer, has called "the autobiography of dreams". Their clear reflection of Fleming's personality, fantasies, and convictions gives the novels their unique power (and makes them so hard to imitate). Fleming wrote his first Bond adventure in a mere seven weeks, at the age of forty-three. By the time of his death the Bond novels had sold over 40 million copies and were beginning to appear as some of the most successful movies ever. Only a man writing about himself, motivated by strong personal desires and frustrations, could have had such an impact.

So who was Ian Fleming, and how did his life come to result in his extraordinary alter ego?

Fleming was a child of privilege; the Britain which he loved, and for which James Bond fought, was foreign territory to the vast majority of its subjects. He came from a wealthy and landed Anglo-Scottish background. His Scots grandfather, Robert Fleming of Dundee, was a self-made millionaire who virtually invented the modern investment trust and later established the private bank of Robert Fleming and Company in the City of London. When his elder son Valentine married in 1906, Robert Fleming, by then settled in the lush pastures of southern England, gave him a quarter of a million pounds to enable the new couple to buy a spacious country house in Oxfordshire. Their first son, Peter, was born the next year. Less than twelve months later, in 1908, their second, Ian Lancaster Fleming, made his appearance. When Ian was only two his father became a Tory Member of Parliament and the family moved to a large Georgian mansion on Hampstead Heath formerly owned by the Earl of Chatham. Seven years later, Valentine Fleming was killed by a German shell on the Western Front, and it was his fellow M.P. and brother officer in the Oxfordshire Yeomanry, Winston Churchill, who wrote a generous tribute to him in the *Times*.

A dead hero as a father, his mother a very wealthy widow, and his brother an outstanding scholar and athlete, Fleming, for all his material security, developed into a rebellious adolescent, a potential black sheep of the Fleming clan. Leaving Eton early under a cloud, he went to the Royal Military College at Sandhurst, hated it, and dropped out. At this point his concerned and exasperated mother sent him abroad to be straightened out by an eccentric couple, Captain Forbes Dennis and his wife, Phyllis, who ran a language-cum-finishing school at Kitzbühel, in Austria.

Intriguingly, Forbes Dennis was also a member of the British secret service. During the war he had been an intelligence officer in Marseilles, and after the Armistice had been transferred to Vienna as SIS Head of Station under the traditional cover of Passport Control Officer. Even more intriguing, his wife was also involved in the game, publishing a spy novel entitled *The Lifeline* in 1946 under her own name of Phyllis Bottome. Under the guidance of those two players in the silent game at Kitzbühel, Fleming acquired some stability and maturity. Phyllis encouraged him to write. Under her direction he produced an unpublished short story with the title "Death, on Two Occasions", and to the end of his life Fleming remained deeply grateful to her for having set him on the path as a writer. Whether or not they also set him on the path towards intelligence work is difficult to say, but at the very least it must have helped Fleming's later *entrée* into the small club of those who played the silent game to have spent four formative years in the hands of two of its practitioners. By the time he returned to England in 1931 he had certainly acquired some useful practical skills. He was fluent in German and French, and also knew some Russian. He had also developed a cult of personal toughness, seen in frequent tests of endurance he set for himself in mountain climbing or skiing in difficult terrain, that was later to find expression in the personality of Bond.

Fleming had set his sights on the Foreign Office, but badly failed the entrance exam. Instead, shortly afterwards, he found a job with Reuters News Agency in London. Brilliantly successful in reporting the dramatic trial of six British engineers on charges of espionage in Moscow in 1933, and living up the experience for all it was worth, he appeared to have a promising career as a popular journalist ahead of him. But suddenly, after only two years, he quit to enter the world of merchant banking and stockbroking in the City of London. As Europe slithered towards war, Fleming enjoyed the life of a young man around town, lunching regularly at his club, meeting with Old Etonian friends, and having plenty of money and women at his disposal.

Yet the forces that brought Fleming and the world of intelligence together were already in motion. On his return from the Moscow trial he had been debriefed by some "anonymous men" in the Foreign Office, and suddenly, in the spring of 1939, he returned to the Soviet Union again on its behalf, this time under cover as a correspondent of the *Times* accompanying a trade delegation. Although his biographer makes no mention of the Secret Intelligence Service, it seems highly probable that it was behind the mission. Certainly this was the impression of Sefton Delmer of the *Daily Express*, who said that Fleming "seemed to be acting the part of one of the Secret Service men he had read about in E.

Phillips Oppenheim." *Pravda* held the same view, later denouncing Fleming as a spy for British Intelligence. And on his return to London, his first act was to produce an extensive report on his estimate of Soviet strength in a forthcoming war, a document that, in Pearson's words, was written with true "Buchanesque relish".

Fleming's intelligence mission provided a foretaste of what was to come. Almost immediately after this second Moscow visit he was signed up to serve in naval intelligence, and even before the declaration of war was working secretly at the Admiralty on a part-time basis. By September 1939 he was intimately familiar with the machinery of naval intelligence and its place in the labyrinths of Whitehall, and as soon as war broke out he stepped into the job for which he had been carefully groomed: personal assistant and chief intelligence planner to Rear Admiral J.H. Godfrey, the Director of British Naval Intelligence.

The next phase of Fleming's life was crucial in the birth of James Bond. Admiralty intelligence had achieved outstanding successes in the First World War under "Blinker" Hall, and while most of its work had been in the realm of code and cipher breaking through "Room 40", some had also involved cloak-and-dagger work. As we have seen, A.E.W. Mason had been on Hall's payroll, and in Buchan's *Greenmantle* the American Blenkiron had declared to Hannay that if ever he had a really big job to handle he'd plump for the help of British Naval Intelligence. Fleming was at the very heart of this organization during the Second World War, acting not only as Admiral Godfrey's personal assistant but also as his representative on many Whitehall committees. Some of these were directly involved in sabotage and subversion, where Fleming learned at first hand about many of the skills he later passed on to James Bond. His most important contact in this respect was with the Special Operations Executive. His older brother, Peter, was already involved in its work in the Middle East, and emotionally at least Fleming entered the realm of SOE, planning fantastic missions of derring-do and submitting them with enthusiasm to a skeptical higher authority.

A further decisive step in Fleming's evolution came in the summer of 1941, when he accompanied Admiral Godfrey on a top-secret mission to the United States to strengthen Anglo-American intelligence links. In New York City Fleming met William Stephenson ("Intrepid"), the Canadian millionaire who ran British Security Co-ordination out of Rockefeller Center. Stephenson represented both the Secret Intelligence Service and the Special Operations Executive in the Western hemisphere, and at the time of Fleming's visit was giving strong backroom encouragement to "Wild Bill" Donovan. Stephenson was a First World War ace fighter pilot and a lightweight European boxing champion who had made his first million before he was thirty. Fleming, always a hero-worshipper, took to him immediately, throwing himself eagerly into the task of helping Stephenson persuade the Americans to establish their counterpart organization, which would cement the special relationship at the secret level.

Through Stephenson, Fleming met Donovan, who was at that point soliciting advice about the shape of his new agency. Fleming did not hesitate, and in two days he put down on paper everything he thought Donovan should know about the financing, organizing, controlling, and training of a secret service. Later in life, Fleming would mythologize his role in the birth of the OSS, especially when talking to American fans of his Bond novels such as CIA chief Allen Dulles, claiming that what he had produced was the original charter of the OSS. This was fantasy, typical of the later Fleming, but there was sufficient truth to his relationship with Donovan for the latter to present the young Englishman with a .38 Colt revolver inscribed "For Special Services". Inevitably, Fleming would show it to friends, hinting darkly that it was for services of a more deadly and practical kind. And by the time he and Godfrey returned to London, President Roosevelt had appointed Donovan Co-ordinator of Information—America's first head of central intelligence.

Fleming's American visit added more fuel to the growing fires of his fantasy life. Stephenson, described later by Fleming as "one of the great secret agents of the war", presided over an intelligence empire in North America that included "Camp X", an SOE training school for secret agents on the Canadian shore of Lake Ontario. Here, putative agents learned many of the basic James Bond skills required by their deadly profession. Fleming in later life would hint, and his biographer would claim, that he himself had taken the Camp X training course, thus bringing professional expertise to his characterization of Bond. Historical evidence about Camp X contradicts the apparently authentic detail embellishing the story, and it seems to be yet another Fleming fantasy. But it points to something important. Fleming undoubtedly knew about the camp, and it excited his imagination to believe that he might have been trained as a secret agent. In short, this North American adventure marked yet another step towards the creation of Bond.

Back in war-torn Britain, there were more adventures. Shortly after returning to his desk-bound existence in Room 39 at the Admiralty, he established a small unit, under his own supervision, which uniquely combined intelligence and commando functions. This was No. 30 Assault Unit, which Fleming proudly referred to as "my Red Indians", its job being to capture enemy intelligence data during Allied raids. The training course — designed personally by Fleming— drew heavily on his own knowledge of codes, ciphers, and specialized naval gadgetry. The unit was frustrated in its first mission at Dieppe, but during the North African landings in 1942 it succeeded in ransacking the Italian naval headquarters in Algiers and carrying off a huge amount of intelligence material. Fleming mostly supervised the unit from afar, defining its targets and carefully planning the details of each operation, much as "M" would later prepare the way for James Bond. But typically, Fleming wanted to get as close to the action as possible. He watched the abortive mission at Dieppe from offshore and accompanied the unit on one of its very last missions, the rescue of the entire German naval archive from incineration at a castle in Würtemburg. He also followed the unit into France after D-Day, and it was here, sitting by a Normandy roadside with a friend, that he announced what he would do after the war was over. He was going, he said, to "write the spy story to end all spy stories." It was another seven years before he lived up to his promise.

Later on, Fleming would claim that he wrote his first Bond novel to take his mind off the shock of his impending marriage to Ann, Lady Rothermere. This was a typically flippant and cynical remark, concealing more than it revealed. The prospect of marriage undoubtedly disturbed Fleming's equilibrium, and he was also anxious about money and approaching middle age. His brother, Peter, the eternal sibling rival, had just published a light-hearted spy thriller of his own entitled *The Sixth Column*, dedicated to "my brother, Ian". And his post-war career with the Kemsley newspaper empire had been a disappointment. All contributed to the creative burst of energy that produced James Bond, and *Casino Royale* was written without research or notes, flowing uninhibitedly from a combination of memory and imagination. In his imagination Fleming re-created himself as a younger man of action. But in memory, he returned to the ever-fertile pastures of the war, and the unfulfilled life of the man of action that had passed him by.

The Bond books were a cultural as well as a literary phenomenon. They generated imitations, parodies, comic strips, commercial products, and movies as well as much vehement critical comment. There was even a Communist answer to James Bond: Avakum Zakhov, the secret agent in *Zakhov Mission* (London, 1968), by Bulgarian novelist Andrei Gulyashki. Some critics saw Bond as a cause as well as a symptom of cultural decay, denouncing the novels for their sex, violence, snobbery, and blatant materialism. One critic dismissed Bond as a "jazzed up Richard Hannay". *The Catholic World* published an article entitled "007—The Gentleman in Decline", and the *Ladies Home Journal* published a piece alarmingly titled "How James Bond Destroyed My Husband". Mordecai Richler denounced the books for their sanitized racialism, and their author as "an appalling writer", while British author Kingsley Amis robustly proclaimed them healthy good fun and went on after Fleming's death to write one of his own Bond novels, *Colonel Sun*. Critics also disagreed about the books' literary merits. Some described Fleming as a third-rate hack or the writer of "wild penny dreadful improbabilities". Others were more flattering, seeing the Bond saga in terms of ancient myths skilfully re-created in modern idiom, technological fairy tales for twentieth-century readers. It took Eric Ambler, a skilled craftsman himself, to make the obvious point. "Critics," he noted, "rarely remark on how well-written the James Bond stories are. I suppose with a man so civilized and amusing as Mr. Fleming, good writing is taken for granted."

Fleming once boasted that he wrote his novels for "warm blooded people in railway trains, aeroplanes and beds...I aim for total stimulation of the reader all the way through, even to his taste buds." He succeeded beyond his wildest dreams, finding inspiration in the fictional territory he had explored as a schoolboy, where such writers as Buchan and Sapper had been basic ground cover. One of his earliest and most enduring memories of his private school was of the headmaster's wife reclining on a sofa after supper in a room full of boys, a favourite pupil stroking her feet while she read out loud from the latest Bulldog Drummond adventure. But Fleming was also a perceptive journalist who captured vividly the cross-currents of tradition and change that revolutionized Britain and its place in the world during the post-war years.

The Bond novels draw on Fleming's wartime experiences in some very obvious ways. Bond, like Fleming himself, enjoys the rank of commander in His Majesty's Navy, and specific incidents can be related to Fleming's experience at the Admiralty. For instance, Bond's claim to have won his licence to kill after shooting a Japanese through the eye in Rockefeller Center is clearly related to some cloak-and-daggery that Fleming discussed with William Stephenson at BSC Headquarters in New York. The office was one floor above the Japanese Consulate General, and one night—at least according to the myth—Fleming accompanied Stephenson and others in a burgling operation to steal Japanese ciphers.

More important, the entire structure of Bond's universe pivots on the Second World War. Although young men of Fleming's social rank and privilege declared at Oxford in 1933 that they would not fight for King and Country, those who survived emerged with a heightened sense of pride about Britain's role in the war and her position in the post-war world. The Royal Navy still symbolized British power, and a romantic like Fleming could easily imagine in his wilder flights of fancy that the

Victorian Pax Britannica had been restored. For all his European education, Fleming remained insular in his prejudices and tastes. All this rubbed off onto James Bond. The outward trappings of Bond's life carry the message that "British is best"—from the 4 1/2-litre Bentley and the seventy hand-rolled Morlands cigarettes he smokes a day to the carefully tailored handmade shirts and the comfort of Blades, his West End club—and that only the worst can be expected of foreigners. The villains are invariably foreign and, like those in Le Queux, Sapper, or Cheyney, are invariably deformed or grotesque. Some have Semitic features, and a high proportion are ex-Gestapo or SS men.

But there is more to Bond than a simple-minded patriotism asserting the effortless superiority over lesser breeds that so delighted Fleming's fans and enraged his critics. Read as episodes in an international soap opera, the Bond novels provide a commentary on the slow and steady decline of British power in the post-war world. Fleming was far too intelligent and well informed not to see what was happening to Britain, and the dispiriting conclusions he drew from his visit to the Far East were already implicit in his fiction.

Take, for example, *Casino Royale*, the first Bond novel, written during the winter of 1952. The most obviously biographical, it also provides an allegory for Britain's experience in the Second World War. Bond is sent to France to destroy Le Chiffre, one of the chief agents of the Soviet agency SMERSH, by defeating him at the gambling tables. And what happens to Bond on this lone mission? He loses steadily to Le Chiffre and is rescued only by a massive infusion of money slipped to him by his American friend, Felix Leiter of the CIA. No sooner is he saved than he falls into the hands of Le Chiffre. But the latter, it transpires, has gone freelance and is now *persona non grata* with his Russian masters. Just as he is about to administer the *coup de grâce* to Bond he is eliminated by a SMERSH hit man and Bond is saved. Britain, in short, is saved by the benevolence and financial largesse of the United States (Leiter) combined with the physical intervention of the U.S.S.R. (the SMERSH hit man): the story of the Second World War, and not a comfortable one to a thinking patriot.

After this backward glance, Fleming adopted a more obviously Cold War outlook, and the theme of the Anglo-American alliance, so vividly brought home to Fleming during the visit of 1941, dominates the early Bond novels. In these, Fleming delivers his encomium to the special relationship in Bond's friendship with Felix Leiter. In *Live and Let Die* (1954), the second novel, Bond's mission is to neutralize Mr. Big, "the most powerful Negro criminal in the world", who is also an agent of SMERSH helping to finance Soviet espionage in North America. The action takes place almost entirely in the United States, and Bond works closely with the FBI and the CIA. And although Felix Leiter is badly mauled when he falls into Mr. Big's shark-infested fish tank, he recovers to rescue Bond while the latter is successfully foiling the plot to capture Fort Knox in *Goldfinger* (1959). *Thunderball* (1961) is also an Anglo-American operation involving Leiter, and the American is still around in the last, and posthumously published, Bond novel, *The Man with the Golden Gun* (1965).

It's no wonder that the United States has provided an enormous and enthusiastic market for Bond. Fleming worked hard for this in his lifetime, and the movies have guaranteed Bond's place in the American imagination. The breakthrough came in 1961, when in an article in *Life* magazine on President Kennedy's reading habits, *From Russia, with Love* appeared in the top ten list of his favourites. "It would be hard to over-estimate its importance in the development of the cult of James Bond in the United States," writes John Pearson. "From that moment the American boom really began." Another great Bond fan was Allen Dulles, the Director of Central Intelligence, who was given a copy of *From Russia, with Love* by Jacqueline Kennedy. Later, he met Fleming at a dinner in London. "We had quite a night of it," Dulles said. "Fleming was a brilliant and witty talker, with ideas on everything. Before we got through, we had pretty well torn orthodox Intelligence to pieces. We talked of new tools that would have to be invented for the new era.... Ever since that night, I kept in constant touch with him." Dulles, despite his gung-ho reputation, claimed he had no illusions about Bond's resemblance to real-life agents. "I fear that James Bond in real life would have had a thick dossier in the Kremlin after his first exploit," he wrote, "and would not have survived the second." But he took seriously some of Bond's secret gadgetry, and once instructed the CIA to work on developing the kind of homing device that Bond often places on his opponents' cars.

The CIA may also have missed much of the irony in Bond and/or Fleming. In Washington in 1960 at a dinner with Kennedy, who was the Democratic presidential candidate at the time, Fleming suggested that already Americans were taking Fidel Castro far too seriously. Instead of inflating him, why not deflate him? "How?" asked Kennedy. With great seriousness Fleming proceeded to elaborate a spoof proposal to bring Castro down by appealing to the Cubans' love for money, religion, and sex. First, American planes should scatter Cuban notes over Havana as a gesture of friendship; second, from their Guantanamo base, they should somehow project a gigantic cross into the sky forcing the Cubans constantly to look skyward; and third, they should convince the Cubans that radioactivity in the atmosphere settled and lived longest in men's beards. This would convince Cubans to shave off their beards. And without bearded Cubans, Fleming announced triumphantly, there would be no Cuban revolution. The dinner party apparently took all this in the spirit it was intended. But half an hour after it broke up, Dulles was on the phone to one of the party asking for more details. One of his top aides, John Bross—ironically, a former OSS man who had been trained at Camp X—had been one of the guests at the dinner and had reported Fleming's plans back to Dulles. What a shame, the director lamented, that he hadn't been able to hear more of Fleming's ideas in person. Clearly, the irony had passed Dulles by, and the CIA went on to concoct plans for Castro's demise that belonged essentially to the fantasy world of Bond.

Kennedy's presidency, marked by the great East–West confrontations of the Berlin Wall and the Cuban missile crisis, brought the world to the brink of war and served to emphasize how relatively weak Britain now was as an independent power. Fleming knew that the rhetoric of the special relationship concealed the end of an age, that the British Empire was giving way to the Pax Americana, and his feelings about the United States were accordingly deeply ambivalent. By the time of his death they had turned into criticism and resentment. What begins as a celebration ends as a requiem.

In *Casino Royale* (1953), with Churchill back as Prime Minister and the coronation of Queen Elizabeth about to be crowned itself by the triumphant conquest of Everest, Felix Leiter confesses to Bond that "Washington's pretty sick that we're not running the show." This is the last time that Leiter has to say it, for it soon becomes apparent that Britain is not running any important shows either. In *Moonraker* (1955) Bond faces off against Hugo Drax, an ostensible patriot with high political connections being financed by the British government to build the Moonraker nuclear missile, "to give Britain an independent say in the world." But Drax, it turns out, is an ex-SS man, and his missile is secretly targeted on London—"a giant hypodermic needle ready to be plunged into the heart of England." Bond, of course, foils Drax's plot, but not before Drax has taunted him that the British are "too weak to defend [their] colonies, toadying to America with [their] hats in [their] hands." The sentiment is echoed by Bond himself in *From Russia, with Love* (1957), in which he confesses to his Turkish friend Kerim that "as for England, the trouble today is that carrots for all are the fashion. At home and abroad. We don't show teeth anymore, only gums."

Britain had been hideously revealed as a toothless tiger in the jungle of world affairs during the Suez Crisis of the preceding year, a massive humiliation that delivered a mortal blow to lingering illusions of imperial greatness. Fleming's Jamaican retreat provided a temporary refuge for the British Prime Minister Sir Anthony Eden, who resigned after the crisis, but while Fleming had personal sympathy for Eden, he thought Suez a major disaster. "In the whole of modern history," he said, "I can't think of a comparable shambles created by any single country."

So all was by no means well with Britain even during Bond's prime. In *Goldfinger* (1959), for example, Britain is in desperate need of gold as it suffers through yet another currency crisis. Things went downhill at an increasing pace after 1960. The superpower confrontations were followed by the era of *détente* and decolonization, and former American Secretary of State

Dean Acheson declared that Britain had lost an empire but not yet found a role.

The confusion and the loss of bearings are amply reflected in *Thunderball* (1961). In the first place, SMERSH has been replaced by SPECTRE, a freelance international gang headed by Ernst Stavro Blofeld. Although often at the service of the Kremlin, it is less menacing than SMERSH and 007 begins to lose some of his edge. Things are not going well with Britain either. There are marches against the H-bomb, and the welfare state is sapping the moral fibre of the country. Bond himself is ingesting fibre at a health farm to cure his body of the poisons of good living. When he finally gets into action he confesses to Leiter that, while Cold War tensions are easing off, "the war just doesn't seem to have ended for us," and he lists a dreary succession of post-war colonial crises such as Cyprus, Kenya, and Suez.

Bond is even more demoralized by the time we find him two years later in *On Her Majesty's Secret Service*. Deprived by M of his licence to kill, he has sent in his resignation, and at the end hints at retirement by marrying Teresa (Tracy) Draco, daughter of the head of the Union Corse on whom Bond has relied for information about Blofeld's hideout. It is only Tracy's murder by Blofeld *en route* to their honeymoon that saves Bond from the death that all secret agents since the days of Duckworth Drew have suffered when entering into matrimony. It is thus with a strong personal hatred for Blofeld that Bond sets out for his Far Eastern adventure in *You Only Live Twice* (1964). Not that his mission begins as a personal one. Significantly, his task is to get from the Japanese intelligence service information about Soviet cryptographic secrets. But why does he have to go to Tokyo for these? Because the CIA refuses to pass them on to the British in the wake of a series of British spy scandals. Dulles is no longer head of the CIA, and the old special relationship is dead. Worse, Bond has to listen to a sermon from "Tiger" Tanaka, M's opposite number in Japan, about a Britain that has become the pitiful ruin of a once-great power. Bond protests; but he is forced to recognize the truths that lie behind Tanaka's words.

What, then, remains for this secret agent of an offshore European island deprived of its influence in Washington? Not much, must be the answer, and it is difficult to see how Fleming could have continued the series if he had lived. *The Man with the Golden Gun* (1965), the posthumous 007 novel, is also the least convincing. It begins with a Bond who has been brainwashed by the KGB into attempting to kill M, and once deprogrammed he is sent off to chase one of the least interesting of Fleming's villains, Scaramanga, another freelance killer, who is mixed up with the KGB and the secret police of Castro's Cuba. Although Bond recovers "the old fierce hatred of the KGB and all its works", there is no recovery of the Anglo-American alliance. Felix Leiter makes an appearance, but is now working for Pinkertons. The mood has turned sufficiently sour for Bond to be overtly critical of the United States. Its strident anti-Communism, he says, is merely driving the Cuban people further behind Castro. If Americans were more pragmatic and less hysterical, Bond argues, Castro would fall of his own account—a clear echo of Fleming's dinner-table discussion with Kennedy some five years before. Clearly, with such hard words for old allies, it was time for Bond to quit. His moment had passed, the fertile fields of memory and imagination rendered sterile by a world that had changed since the halcyon days of Ian Fleming's war.

Yet this is not quite the end of the matter. *Casino Royale* contains some intriguing references to a theme that has since played an increasing part in spy fiction, that of Soviet penetration of the Secret Intelligence Service.

Apart from the brutal torture scene in which Le Chiffre beats Bond's testicles with a carpet beater, the most shocking event in *Casino Royale* is the revelation that Bond's personal assistant, Vesper Lynd, has all along been a double agent working for SMERSH, and that "the real enemy had been quietly, coldly, without heroics, right there at his elbow." Although Vesper eventually falls in love with Bond, she then kills herself in a fit of remorse over her treachery.

Vesper Lynd is an intriguing figure, not just because she is the first of a succession of Bond girls, nor because she is the only one to be a double agent. She intrigues because Fleming uses her to comment directly, if codedly, on events that had shocked Britain in general and the intelligence services in particular only the year before.

In May 1951 two British diplomats, Guy Burgess and Donald Maclean, defected to the Soviet Union. The significance of both was played down in public, although Maclean had occupied sensitive Foreign Office positions both in London and in Washington. Even more sensitive was the suspicion that the two men had been tipped off about investigations into their loyalty, and that there remained a "third man" yet to be unmasked. Four years later the name of Kim Philby, a high-ranking member of the Secret Intelligence Service, surfaced in public for the first time. Cleared by the then Prime Minister, Harold Macmillan, it was not until his defection to Moscow in 1963 that Philby confirmed the suspicions that he had long been a Soviet mole.

When Fleming was writing *Casino Royale*, however, the doubts about Philby were confined to a tight inner circle of the Anglo-American intelligence community. In the aftermath of the Burgess–Maclean affair, Philby had been immediately recalled from Washington, where he was the SIS link man with the CIA, put through several interrogations, and then officially retired from the service. It marked the end of a remarkable career in SIS that had seen Philby rise rapidly during the war to the position of rumoured heir apparent to the legendary "C". By the time the Third Reich collapsed and Soviet armies entered Berlin, Philby had become head of the anti-Soviet section of the SIS, a powerful and influential position that gave the Kremlin access to some of Britain's most sensitive intelligence secrets. *Casino Royale*, a work of apparently idle fiction, took its own view on Philby's guilt. For what was Vesper Lynd's position before working for Bond? None other than personal assistant to the head of the anti-Soviet section of the SIS. She has obviously been betraying secrets for some considerable time, and Bond reflects on the ghastly consequences: "the covers which must have been blown over the years, the codes which the enemy must have broken, the secrets which must have leaked from the centre of the very section devoted to penetrating the Soviet Union." These were the thoughts of a large number of people in the British intelligence community at the time. In pointing the finger through Vesper Lynd at the anti-Soviet section of the SIS, Fleming was taking sides in an insiders' war and proclaiming his own conviction about Philby's guilt.

To the average reader, however, Vesper Lynd was significant in providing Bond with his very *raison d'être*. At an early point in the novel he had confessed to Mathis, his French opposite number in the Deuxième Bureau, that "this country right or wrong business is getting a bit out of date." Such hesitations quickly dissolve in the face of treachery. Bond recognizes that there is indeed an enemy to fight, and that his life must now be devoted to destroying SMERSH and all its works. Conceived during the Second World War, Bond was finally presented to the world in the chill delivery room of the Cold War.

Why did Fleming not make more of the theme of Soviet penetration of the secret service in his later novels? Partly because the issue never became public until the very end of Fleming's life, and partly because James Bond, the man of action with a love of foreign adventure, was hardly cut out for the painstaking hunting down of moles. But it was also a matter of class and class loyalty. Fleming was not the man to confront the full implications of the Philby affair, being too loyal to the very England that so long attempted to conceal the scandal's full dimensions. For all Fleming's frequent protestations of being non-political, his England, as Kingsley Amis has said, is substantially right of centre. Bond's newspaper—the only one he ever reads—is the *Times*, he reveres Churchill and the monarchy, and he dislikes both the masses and the welfare state. Whereas Buchan's respect for the established order was that of an outsider who wished to get in, Fleming's was that of an insider who never had the slightest wish to get out. Those who did, like Philby, were beyond comprehension.

CHAPTER TEN

"Put Not Your Trust in Princes"

I don't care a damn about men who are loyal to the people who pay them, to organisations...I don't think even my country means all that much. There are many countries in our blood, aren't there, but only one person. Would the world be in the mess it is if we were loyal to love and not to countries?

Graham Greene, *Our Man in Havana*

Despite Fleming's declining enthusiasm for Anglo-American relations, the Bond novels remained firmly anchored in Cold War rhetoric. This was not true for three writers who first made their mark on spy fiction in the 1930s. Instead, Eric Ambler, Geoffrey Household, and Graham Greene dissociated themselves from the world of superpower confrontation to cast a critical eye on the world of power politics.

I

"Nowadays...we don't hear the phrase 'merchants of death' very much. It's all very sad. The idea that the act of selling arms somehow tricked people into making wars they didn't want never really stood up to very close inspection, did it? But it was good to have a fine, top-hatted bogeyman to put all the blame on. The trouble is we've learned a thing or two since nineteen thirty-nine. Now we can't even blame the politicians—not with much conviction, anyway. The real bogeyman crawled out of the mud with our ancestors millions of years ago. Well, we all have a piece of him, and when we start to put the pieces together, it's like one of those nuclear-fission things—when the mass reaches a critical point, a chain reaction starts, and poof!"

With these words from the mouth of Colonel Soames, the Singapore police inspector in his 1959 novel, *Passage of Arms*, Eric Ambler marked out the distance travelled since his classic novel about Dimitrios some twenty years before. Both the Second World War, with its revelations of the horrors that man can wreak on fellow man, and disillusionment with Stalin's Russia were responsible. Together, they furnished Ambler with the dominating theme of his post-war novels: the loss of innocence in a world of increasing violence and big-power domination.

As we have seen, the war provided Ambler with a rapid and concentrated education in the inventiveness of man's inhumanity to man, and insights which ensured that his post-war fiction could never be the same as that of the 1930s. As he said in "The Lizzie Borden Memorial Lectures", collected in *The Ability to Kill* (1963), "Our Anglo-Saxon culture is built on studious denials of the existence within us of the primitive. The revelation that there is, after all, an ape beneath the velvet, is perennially fascinating."

After his return to Europe with his second wife—the producer Joan Harrison, who for many years worked closely with Alfred Hitchcock—Ambler recovered his old form to write some of his best novels. To visitors to his apartment overlooking Lake Geneva, spacious, comfortable, its walls decorated with nineteenth-century lithographs, he appeared as the very epitome of the English gentleman—quiet, civilized, and impeccably courteous and well dressed. Critic Gavin Lambert wrote of him in *The Dangerous Edge*, "Wary and spectacled, his eyes suggest that the longer you study appearances the more deeply you distrust them." One American said later that Ambler resembled "a cross between an Oxford don and a successful banker." Ironically, Ambler's characters are often the antithesis of the English gentleman, but the comment tells us something about Ambler's mature novels. Ironic and urbane, they exhibit a fascination with the labyrinths of human motive and explore the complexity of interests in Byzantine international dealings. They combine the mastery of facts ideally found in the Oxford don with the shrewdness of the successful banker. And while full of action, they are mainly exercises in the unravelling of human character in games of subtle calculation.

There was a twelve-year gap between *The Mask of Dimitrios* and Ambler's first post-war novel, *Judgment on Deltchev*. This, published at the height of the Cold War, produced the first hate mail he had ever received. "The letters I received about the book were all more or less abusive," Ambler recalled. "I was a traitor in the class war struggle, a Titoist lackey and an American imperialist cat's paw. One message was a single piece of used toilet paper. The single piece," he added, "was a delicate touch I thought; it spoke of careful premeditation."

Judgment on Deltchev was Ambler's response to the Communist show trials in Eastern Europe when, as he later told critic Clive James, he realized that after clearing out the Nazis "there were still all these other shits around." Set against the thinly disguised events of the Petkov trial in Bulgaria (Nikola Petkov, leader of the Bulgarian Peasant Party, was executed after a show trial in September 1947), it reveals the cynical manipulations within a ruling Communist party and a society living in fear of the secret police. But unlike other popular writers who turned this theme into Cold War propaganda, Ambler's novel was no uncritical homily on the virtues of Western democracy.

Deltchev, the victim of the show trial, is no hero. Persecuted by the regime, he is also a victim of his own weaknesses and far from the courageous "freedom fighter" depicted by Western propaganda. Directed against the totalitarianism of the left, *Judgment on Deltchev* was also levelled against the crude simplicities of the anti-Communist right.

Ambler played with a similar theme in his next novel, *The Schirmer Inheritance* (1953). In his search for the heir to an American multi-million-dollar fortune, the lawyer George Carey travels across post-war Europe to end up in a Greece devastated physically and psychologically by a decade of occupation and civil war between Communist and non-Communist. Rather than align with either the right or the left, Ambler introduces prototypes of characters who become increasingly prominent in his later fiction: Sergeant Schirmer, the ex-Wehrmacht soldier, and Arthur, an ex-British soldier, who join forces to profit from the absurd world around them. Their Marxist patter provides merely a carefully contrived façade behind which they manipulate events to their own advantage. "What do I want with causes?" asks Arthur at one point, answering with one of his favourite biblical injunctions: "Put not your trust in princes." Sergeant Schirmer agrees. "I think, Corporal, that in future we must trust only ourselves."

Since then, Ambler's views have become even less congenial to the ideology of the superpowers and more obviously sympathetic to the underdog—whether it be the small nation overshadowed by an alliance with one of the great powers, a struggling Third World country seeking to remain independent, or merely the individual struggling against the bureaucratic and computerized world of officialdom. One of the most tautly written and effective of his post-war thrillers is *The Night-Comers* (*State of Siege* in the United States), published in 1956, in which Ambler recovered the best of his pre-war form. Ian Fleming, reviewing it in the *Sunday Times*, noted with relief that "There are not many authors one can automatically buy sight unseen, and it seemed for a time after the war that Eric Ambler had crossed himself off the short list. With *The Night-Comers*...we can again buy Ambler blind."

Written after an extended trip that Ambler made to Asia, and set in post-independence Indonesia, the novel offers an unsentimental look at a nationalist government in which incompetent rulers are faced with rebellion from Muslim extremists. Major Saputo, who protects the protagonist, the expatriate engineer Fraser, from death during the rebel seizure of the capital, serves the rebellion in order to betray it. "We must choose between evils," he reflects. "The Nasjah Government is corrupt and incompetent...but with them at least the machinery of representative government is preserved and gradual change is possible. In the end, if the Americans and you British don't interfere, there will be fresh, healthy growth. But we must have time and patience." And in response to Fraser's inevitable response that it may not be the Americans and British who do the interfering, Saputo reveals that he is far removed from the spirit of the Cold War. "Communism?" he says. "That is your bad dream, not ours."

Equally sympathetic to Third World aspirations and skeptical of growing American involvement in South-East Asia is *Passage of Arms*. Greg Nilsen, an American businessman on holiday, becomes involved in arms smuggling from Malaya to Indonesia. The weapons are arms from Red China used by the defeated Malayan Communist insurgents, now being shipped to Indonesia for use against Communist guerrillas. The irony appeals to Nilsen's crusading democratic zeal, but he gets badly burned in the process and ends up a wiser and poorer man. Like Fowler in Graham Greene's *The Quiet American*, Nilsen is a secular missionary in a culture of which he is dangerously ignorant. Indeed, Ambler consciously evokes Greene's 1955 novel in a scene set in Saigon, where a taxi driver shows Nilsen and his wife the café where the quiet American had set off his bomb. Distressed that people should take the novel for fact, Nilsen indignantly points out that the Americans are pouring in millions of dollars of aid. He is even more distressed after Monsieur Seguin, a French civil engineer, speaks frankly about American motives. "It is sad," Seguin says, "you Americans give away billions of dollars to defend yourselves against Communism, but you ask everyone to believe that you give it because you are good and kind.... America is rich, and behaves like the rich always behave. When they begin to fear death, they become philanthropists."

The main message of Ambler's novels in this period seems to be that, in a world divided between the imperialism of the rich and the totalitarianism of the impoverished, the individual can do worse than pursue his own self-interest. The real hero of *Passage of Arms* is Girija Krishnan, the Indian clerk on a Malayan rubber plantation who discovers the former Communist arms cache and with the profit establishes a fleet of commercial buses.

Ambler then created his likeable villain and small-time con artist, Arthur Abdel Simpson, whose adventures in *The Light of Day* (1962), filmed as *Topkapi*, and *Dirty Story* (1967) extolled the merits of survival in the face of "the dumb beast, authority." Described in his Interpol dossier as a chauffeur, pimp, guide, pornographer, waiter, and interpreter, and armed with his favourite aphorism that "Bullshit baffles Brains", Simpson lives a life of international larceny. "Your life," a British official notes with disapproval, "is nothing but a long dirty story." But the story has a reason. Simpson's exploits are motivated by the desire to acquire a regular passport and fixed residence, for, like many an Ambler character, he is of mixed parentage and falls between the gaps created by the rigid structures of officialdom and the national state. As one critic noted, "Here, in the guise of a series of exciting fables, is the century of uncertainty and fear, blundering and irresponsibility, through which all of us are groping our way."

Ambler is too ironic to make such claims for himself. Irony, indeed, has often been accompanied by facetiousness. In "Spy-Haunts of the World", an essay in *The Ability to Kill*, Ambler suggested in the late 1950s that the old-fashioned Orient Express spy was becoming extinct. The solution? "What I propose," he penned, "is nothing less than the setting up of an International Spy Reserve, to be called 'The E. Phillips Oppenheim Memorial Park'." He recommended the Ile du Levant, off the Riviera coast, part of an eighteenth-century coastal defence system dotted with forts. "Their appearance," noted Ambler, "is superb. It would be a pleasure to spy on them...garrisons of disabled army veterans could easily be provided for the spies to outwit. Escapes by boat to the mainland could be made at dead of night.... There is not a moment to lose."

In 1968 Ambler finally left the United States and settled in Switzerland. From this neutral state in the heart of Europe he then produced *The Intercom Conspiracy* (1969), an ironic novel written in dossier style that sees him once again bereft of faith in the virtues of either of the superpowers. "What I did in that book," he told this author in 1981, "was to exchange the capitalist-in-the-top-hat villain for the two superpowers. They've become the enemy now. Jointly." The intelligence chiefs of two small west European members of NATO, sharing a common dislike of American and Soviet domination of Europe, decide to go freelance. Both have been active in the wartime resistance and wonder again about Europe's future. "In a gloomy moment they saw themselves reduced to the role of passive onlookers, of village policemen stationed at minor crossroads on a secret war battlefield where the only effective forces engaged were the big battalions of the CIA and KGB." Through a small magazine called *Intercom*, Colonels Jost and Brand begin to leak secrets embarrassing to both the Americans and the Russians. Both the CIA and the KGB try to suppress *Intercom*, and eventually one of them—it is not clear, nor does it matter, which—succeeds. Before then, however, both Brand and Jost have made small fortunes. Their con artistry aligns them with the smaller-time dealings of Arthur Simpson, but Ambler also pursues an older and favourite theme. "A realist," says Brand at one point, "is one who assumes that most of the secrets we guard so jealously are already well known to the other side...[but] the conventions must be observed and the pretences maintained."

Ambler's return to Europe gave a sharper edge to his novels. *The Levanter* (1972) provides a skeptical look at the pretensions of terrorist groups in the 1970s, while *Doctor Frigo* (1974) dissects a coup against a Central American dictatorship with analytical precision. Michael Howell, the main character of *The Levanter*, becomes unwittingly involved in plans for a Palestinian terrorist attack in Israel and eventually foils it. All that terrorism requires, Howell notes, apart from the explosive, is "a touch of megalomania fortified by the delusion that campaigns of terror can end in happiness ever after." Fairytale endings are equally dismissed in *Dr. Frigo*, in which Dr. Ernesto Castillo, the *émigré* son of an assassinated politician, unwillingly gets enmeshed in a plot to stage a coup in his native country, assisted by the CIA and the French intelligence service who are interested in oil reserves off its coast. His apolitical skepticism and contempt for most of the politicians involved, including the man implicated in his own father's death, find an echo in the political ruthlessness and cynicism of the guerrilla leader El Lobo, who is wrongly believed to have been successfully co-opted into the conspiracy. The two men reach an understanding of events that sets them apart from the vanities and pretensions of the politicians around them—and Castillo is only too happy to leave once the coup is over and return to his mistress and medical practice in exile. In the aftermath of Vietnam and Watergate, and with the massive U.S. Senate inquiry into CIA wrongdoings under way, *Dr. Frigo*'s message struck a powerful chord of recognition. At its 1975 annual banquet in New York the Mystery Writers of America gave Ambler its Grand Master award; Julian Symons regards it as Ambler's finest work; the *New Yorker* declared it "A novel of intrigue and a comedy of a high and conspicuously intelligent order."

"Politics have become so shabby in many places...perhaps they always have been. Perhaps you have to be young to believe in them...," Ambler said in conversation with the author in 1981, when he published *The Care of Time*. The remark provides a commentary on most of his later work, just as the novel provides an epitaph to Ambler's writing career. Narrated by Robert Halliday, a New York ghost writer, it presents the story of the Estonian-born Zander, a high-level fixer of international deals who wishes to come in from the cold with a new identity and protection in the West. In exchange, he offers his services as mediator in secret contacts between Western intelligence services and a ruler of one of the small states in the Persian Gulf. Zander is a survivor of the kind that Ambler has consistently written about and admires, a man whose wits and abilities enables him to adapt to cultures utterly foreign to those of his youth. "I admire the survivors," Ambler told the author. "These seem to be the most striking human beings...America and Canada are full of people who have moved and survived...because if they'd stayed behind, they would have gone under.... Of course, it's part of being young, part of having the courage to do something tomorrow that you are not doing today, to take a step, to move." The real theme of *The Care of Time* is that Zander—the German word for that voracious and predatory fish, the pike—is beginning to falter as he ages, and is now a survivor for whom age is becoming hard to ignore. He only just survives, and it is clearly time for him to retire and leave the field to a younger generation.

"What I'm frightened to death about today," Ambler told Herbert Mitgang when the book was published, "is the kind of thinking that leads to an attitude of 'my armoury is bigger than your armoury'." For almost fifty years Ambler has written novels to entertain, advise, and make aware: a "continuous fable of international politics...since 1937", Paxton Davies once wrote in the *Hollins Review. The Care of Time* served as Ambler's farewell to the genre he had dominated for nearly four decades, the final instalment of his fable.

II

If the war eventually helped to take Ambler to Hollywood, it led his compatriot in the 1939 thriller best-seller stakes, Geoffrey Household, back to Britain.

After the collapse of the Romanian sabotage plans, House-hold had eventually landed up in Cairo, where he joined the Field Security Police with the task of defending the army against the attentions of enemy agents. For the next five years this job took him all over the Middle East. In Jerusalem and Teheran, Beirut and Baghdad, Athens and Haifa, he rapidly learned the complexities of counter-intelligence. On one occasion he masqueraded as a Nazi agent, in full uniform, in the hope of entrapping an Arab informer. On another, he exchanged information with the chief of the Hagana, the Israeli intelligence organization, and on yet another found himself wrestling with the problems of keeping the peace between Vichy and Gaullist factions among French troops in Syria. Those five years in the army, besides equipping him with a wealth of raw material for his fiction, also tempered his restlessness, "gathering me again to my own countrymen", as he put it in *Against the Wind*. In addition, he was happier. In 1942, his tempestuous marriage to Marina over, he had married again, this time an Hungarian woman, Ilona Zsoldos-Gutman. The war ended, and with two children to care for, Household put down his roots in Britain.

Ironically, he found it "a foreign country". He had sympathized with the Republicans in the Spanish Civil War, and his dislike of Nazism was visceral. But the feelings were personal, deriving from experience—a Jewish wife, direct contact with the poverty of Spain—rather than ideological, and he "was infuriated by the fact that volunteers were engaging themselves for the sake of Democracy or Communism or some confounded panacea for the toiling masses, and not one of them for love of Spain." Such dislike for formulas and panaceas left him out of step with the quiet revolution of post-war Britain, and the Welfare State and its inevitable bureaucracy found in him an instinctive antagonist. "Since the individual and his free development are precious to me," he wrote, "I loathe the state control which is inseparable from socialism.... I am probably," he added, "an anarchist." But an anarchist with Whig leanings, looking to the traditionalist and hierarchical values of rural society as a counterbalance to the power of the state.

The individualism and anti-authoritarianism of this passionate and unconventional Englishman permeate his post-war novels. In *The High Place* (1950) the action revolves around the plans of the World Opposition, a secret organization based in a refugee community in Syria and dedicated to resisting the growth of state control throughout the world. The hero, Eric Amberson, believes that "our civilisation is rushing towards an antheap discipline and welfare, and that progress must be checked if any recognizable human spirit is to survive", and up to the point where it becomes clear that it is contemplating violence Household presents the community in a sympathetic light. The next novel, *A Rough Shoot* (1951), distancing itself from the extreme polarizations of the Cold War then reaching its climax, has the hero foiling a super-patriotic and quasi-Fascist plan for a *coup d'état* that, in the words of the narrator, "for me and my like [would mean] that the flag over the concentration camp would be white instead of red." Similarly, in *Fellow Passenger* (1955), which presents a central character who makes both the English authorities and the Communists look ridiculous, Household dissociates himself from the fashionable anti-Communism of the McCarthy years. "I was weary of the melancholy confessions of ex-communists," he noted, "and it seemed to me that any of the fiery young men whom I had known in the early nineteen thirties—when a lad of generous spirit was no more to blame for catching communism than any other intimate disease—would be far more ready to laugh at himself than to beat a dreary breast with Germanic polysyllables. And communism itself is so gloriously inefficient...that I can never fear it, as I did Hitler, to the point of hysteria." Understandably, the book sold less well in America than in Britain—the first time this had happened. In *Watcher in the Shadows* (1960) Household returned to the *Rogue Male* theme of personal vengeance and rural chase for the sake of a woman tortured and killed by the Nazis.

In the atmosphere of *détente* during the 1970s Household, like Ambler, began to identify the superpower conflict as the major threat to human decency and the survival of Europe. In *Red Anger* (1975) the English hero finds himself the victim of both the CIA and the KGB. When the violent climax comes, as it so often does in Household, in the tranquillity of the English countryside, the hero is shot during a chase between what are described as "two gangs of infidel trespassers". If there are no illusions about the brutalities of the KGB, there is much soul-searching about the Americans. British allies, they have acquired the morals of the KGB and trample over England with the same imperialist ruthlessness as the Russians elsewhere.

That both Marxist left and capitalist right are sources of tyranny, Household states more explicitly in *Hostage—London* (1977); here the narrator also dissociates himself from a group of New Left terrorists who threaten to destroy London with a nuclear device, although he is not unsympathetic to their rejection of the tyranny of state and commerce. And in *The Last Two Weeks of Georges Rivac* (1978) the heroine is the daughter of a Hungarian colonel shot after the 1956 uprising; she provides the British secret service with information about potentially mutinous elements of the Warsaw Pact forces. This is not for the sake of some abstract ideology, still less out of sympathy for the Americans. It is because "whatever the fears and intrigues of the superpowers, war that involved the two happily compatible halves of Europe was blinding idiocy." Here, some fifty years after he first crossed the English Channel and discovered the European within him, was the true world of Geoffrey Household.

III

"If we enlarge the bounds of sympathy in our readers we succeed in making the work of the State a degree more difficult. That is a genuine duty we owe society, to be a piece of grit in the state machinery." The sentiments could be those of Household, but they are the words of Graham Greene in an address entitled "The Virtue of Disloyalty", given to the University of Hamburg on his receipt of the Shakespeare Prize in 1969. The thought was not new. Greene had used almost identical words in an exchange of views with Elizabeth Bowen and V.S. Pritchett, published in 1948 under the title "Why Do I Write?".

Greene's war, as we have seen, involved work with the Secret Intelligence Service, first in West Africa and then, when he returned from Sierra Leone in 1943, in the Iberian subsection of Section V. From this experience he wrote *Our Man in Havana* (1958), the sharpest spy novel since *Water on the Brain* in the early 1930s.

John le Carré has revealed that for this novel Greene came close to meeting the same fate as Compton Mackenzie for *Greek Memories*: an appearance at the Old Bailey for breach of the Official Secrets Act. One day, while working for SIS, le Carré bumped into the lawyer for "The Firm" in the office canteen, with a mint-new copy of *Our Man in Havana* in front of him. "I said I envied him his luck," recalled le Carré, "but he only sighed.

The fellow Greene would have to be prosecuted. Greene, an ex-officer of the Service, had accurately portrayed the relationship between a head of station in a British embassy and his agent in the field. It wouldn't do."

Greene escaped prosecution, but the SIS lawyer was right to recognize the voice of an ex-SIS man drawing on his experience with the Firm, for Greene obviously drew heavily upon his wartime career. He may have taken cynicism into the service with him. Certainly he left with an increased dose.

Wormold is a vacuum cleaner salesman for a British export company. A widower living in Havana, he has one commitment: to the future financial well-being of his only child, Molly, an adolescent girl who has caught the roving eye of Captain Segura, head of the Cuban secret police. It is a future hardly assured by Wormold's own dismal business prospects, for there is no great demand for his product—nor do its sales lie close to Wormold's heart. Unaccountably approached by Hawthorne, the regional representative of the British secret service, a man carrying with him "the breath of beaches and the leathery smell of a good club", Wormold at first balks at the prospect of becoming an agent, but then warms to the idea. ("The elegant Hawthorne owes a little, in his more imaginative flights," Greene wrote in *Ways of Escape*, "to an officer [in SIS] who was at one time my chief.") To please his superior, Wormold invents agents and networks, and finds to his delight that he has discovered a way to bankroll Molly's future by claiming expenses for his fictional creations. When he is carried away by enthusiasm and reports the presence of mysterious and gigantic constructions in the mountains, he is asked to provide drawings. Grasping at straws, he submits plans based on the model of vacuum cleaner he is currently attempting to sell. This marks the humorous climax of the novel, and one of the funniest scenes is that in which secret service chiefs pore over the plans in London with full seriousness while Wormold's control suppresses his sickening realization of the truth in order to preserve his own credibility. After that, however, the farce turns to tragedy. Wormold's fictions turn sour as they make him an all too real target of a rival service, and his only friend, Dr. Hasselbacher, is killed. He runs afoul of the secret

police and receives veiled warnings from the sinister Captain
Segura. Then there is an attempt on his life, and Wormold is
finally forced to kill an enemy agent. It is time for him to confess
the truth. Recalled to London, he expects the worst. Instead, he
finds himself being awarded the OBE and the job of lecturing
new recruits into the service—the only way SIS can think of to
save its own face and hush up the scandal. So Wormold gets to
keep his money, Molly's future is assured, and Wormold himself
marries Beatrice, the agent whom London had sent out to Havana
to help him with the burden of his work.

The novel is a powerful satire on the follies, gullibilities,
and sensitivities of the secret service world, set squarely in the
tradition of *Water on the Brain*. But it also contains a powerful
political bite. Greene spent a lot of time during the declining days
of the Batista dictatorship enjoying the delights that Havana then
had to offer. Witnessing the developing civil war that brought
Castro to power in 1959, he was dismayed by British refusal
to recognize political realities. By the time he finished *Our
Man in Havana* he had no regrets. "It seemed to me," he said,
"that either the Foreign Office or the Intelligence Service had
amply merited a little ridicule." But if he mocked the British, he
also offended the new Cuban regime. The satirical tone of the
novel had the effect of minimizing the black underside of the
Batista regime, thus making Greene enemies on both sides of the
political fence.

Greene's post-war journey has marked him out, like Ambler,
as a bitter opponent of both power blocs. In particular, Greene
has earned a reputation as anti-American. Certainly he has
bitterly opposed American policies in the Third World, most
recently its policies towards Nicaragua.

But the record goes back to even before the Second World
War, dating from Greene's first visit to the United States in
1937–38 prior to his going to Mexico to research the persecution
of the Catholic Church. "I have always felt ill at ease in the
States," he told Marie-Françoise Allain in *The Other Man*; "the
terrifying weight of this consumer society oppresses me." As
for American foreign policy, Greene was quite frank. "I will
go to almost any length to put my feeble twig in the spokes

of American foreign policy," he told his interlocutor. *The Quiet American* (1955) is perhaps the best known of his fictional critiques of American policy, and it reads like the report of a highly perceptive intelligence officer predicting impending American disasters in Vietnam. Its central figure, the agent Pyle, presented as a man of dangerous because naïve idealism, is based on one of the CIA's covert operations officers encountered by Greene on one of his visits to the country.

Soviet imperialism has also drawn Greene's ire. When the Kremlin imprisoned dissident writers Daniel and Sinyavsky he tried to block Russian translations of his novels, and after the 1968 invasion of Czechoslovakia he accepted an invitation from Josef Skvorecky and the Writers' Union to go to Prague and make a protest speech. This does not mean that Greene is politically neutral. In 1971 he went to Chile to see the newly elected Salvador Allende. Explaining why he was there, he told the doomed Marxist that it was "because I'm forever searching for...Communism with a human face." "But," he explained to Allain, "one concludes that Communism is unlikely ever to escape from Stalinism or dictatorship."

That individual loyalties must mean more than loyalties to any particular state or ideology is central to Greene's creed. As Beatrice tells Wormold in *Our Man in Havana*, "I don't care a damn about men who are loyal to the people who pay them, to organisations...I don't think even my country means all that much.... Would the world be in the mess it is if we were loyal to love and not to countries?" Along with Ambler and Household, Greene believes that loyalty to the state is a luxury we can no longer afford and that the writer should always be ready to change sides at the drop of a hat. "Loyalty," he once said, "forbids you to comprehend sympathetically your dissident fellows." The most notorious dissident fellow known personally to Greene was, of course, Kim Philby. When Philby's memoirs, *My Silent War*, were published in England in 1968, Greene refused to join in the chorus of denunciation. Instead, he wrote a sympathetic foreword comparing Philby's loyalty to the Soviet Union with that of English Catholics who in the reign of Elizabeth I worked secretly for the victory of Spain.

Inevitably, given Greene's relationship to Philby, Philby's defection should be seen as the inspiration for Greene's last spy novel, *The Human Factor* (1978). Philby's shadow falls sharply across this desolate and compassionate novel of human frailty, and Greene indeed abandoned it at one point for fear that it might be seen as a *roman à clef*. Two minor characters whose commitment to the Communist cause remains intact in spite of the course of Soviet policy might be seen as analogues of Philby: Carson, the South African Communist who "survived Stalin like the Roman Catholics survived the Borgias", once saving the protagonist's wife and son from the South African secret police; and Hallyday, the English contact for whom Stalin is no more reason for doubting the cause than Hiroshima might be for abandoning democracy. But Maurice Castle, the agent who defects, is motivated not by ideology but by love. A middle-aged man, "brilliant at the files", he is deeply and fearfully in love with his younger black South African wife, Sarah. Because of this love, and because he helped her and her son Sam escape from the evils of apartheid, he is prepared to provide the Soviet Union with information about British and American collaboration with the South African regime. Naïvely, he believes that he can limit his co-operation with the Russians: Castle is not a Communist, and never could be. "I'll fight beside you in Africa," he tells his control, "not in Europe." The denouement is a human tragedy. Believing he is about to be unmasked by British counter-intelligence, he defects to Moscow, expecting his wife and son to follow him. But he has been doubly deceived. The Russians' sole use for his African intelligence has been as part of a wider deception campaign they are playing against the British. And because his wife's son is not on her passport she cannot leave Britain to join him without abandoning the child. The novel closes with Castle, alone in his comfortless Moscow apartment, speaking to the disembodied voice of his wife on the phone. As they speak, and as the novel closes, the line goes dead.

When Castle confesses his treachery to Sarah, she replies—as Beatrice replied to Wormold—"Who cares, we have our own country. You and I and Sam. You've never betrayed that country, Maurice." But in defecting, he loses it, and perhaps he has betrayed it, too. Perhaps, also, the novel betrays Greene's realization of the flaw in his defence of Philby. For Maurice Castle possesses motives radically different from those of Philby, far closer to those Greene has always praised—love and the commitment to another person.

Greene has expressed dissatisfaction with *The Human Factor*. He had wanted, he claims, to write a novel of espionage free of the conventional violence of the James Bond type, one which showed that the daily routine of the secret service was like that of any other profession. It is odd that he should have expected to accomplish this given his strong liking for melodrama. Of course he fails. Dr. Percival, the SIS doctor who poisons the initial suspect in the case, Castle's colleague Davis, is a fairly melodramatic figure, and the violence of his intervention is quite inconsistent with the aim that Greene set himself. As Philby himself wryly told Greene after he had read the novel, the doctor must surely have been imported from the CIA.

Greene's spy novels are neither peripheral to the rest of his own work nor marginal to the history of spy fiction. He has used the figure of the spy not merely to explore the secret world itself but also to pursue his favourite themes of loyalty and betrayal. He belongs to the line of writer-agents whose experience in the game commends his fiction to other professionals in the business, and whose writing has strongly influenced both readers and other writers. Greene's strongest link is with the world of John le Carré, and it was le Carré who successfully completed the mission that Greene set himself: to show members of the service going about their daily office work like any other professionals. It was le Carré, too, who first explored the territory of treachery and betrayal through which Fleming in the 1950s had feared to tread.

CHAPTER ELEVEN

The Dream Factory

Was not Bill also betrayed? Connie's lament rang in his ears: "Poor loves. Trained to Empire, trained to rule the waves.... You're the last, George, you and Bill." He saw with painful clarity an ambitious man born to the big canvas, brought up to rule, divide and conquer, whose visions and vanities all were fixed, like Percy's, upon the world's game, for whom reality was a poor island with scarcely a voice that would carry across the water.

John le Carré, *Tinker, Tailor, Soldier, Spy*

Ian Fleming's world was that of the special relationship on which he hoped the sun would never set. Le Carré's revolves in the chill shadows of post-imperial decline. In the 1960s Britain entered a prolonged period of self-reflection about its diminished status in the world, and often painful inquests about those who had steered the ship of state with such self-assurance over the preceding century. Were these the leaders Britain needed in a new Elizabethan age? How had they served the Empire and nation whose leadership they took for granted? Did they perceive Britain's true interests in a new and dangerous world dominated by the nuclear superpowers, and did they understand the ideological dimensions of twentieth-century politics?

These questions help to explain why le Carré's novels have enjoyed such an enthusiastic following on both sides of the Atlantic. Britons can squirm pleasurably beneath the flagellation of a headmaster's report on the state of the school. Americans may enjoy the spectacle of the corrupt and inept British ruling class once again demonstrating the superiority of the American way of life—a particularly gratifying and diverting exercise, given the beginnings of America's own imperial decline.

Le Carré's spy novels, beginning with the much underrated *Call for the Dead* (1961), represent a decisive break with the romantic and swashbuckling figure of James Bond. Le Carré despised Bond, in a BBC interview once describing him as a "consumer goods hero" who exploited the privileges of power and wealth in a completely amoral way. "You could take James Bond," le Carré said, "and given the prerequisites of the affluent society, given above all an identifiable villain of whatever kind—and weak people need enemies—you could dump him in the middle of Moscow and you would have a ready-made Soviet agent...the really interesting thing about Bond is that he would be what I call the ideal defector. Because if the money was better, the booze freer and women easier in Moscow, he'd be off like a shot. Bond is the ultimate prostitute." Bond, in short, represented the very worst that Western society had to offer.

Le Carré redressed the balance and created the anti-heroic figure of George Smiley. Eternally middle-aged and breathtakingly ordinary, this small and pudgy man with the faithless wife and a taste for German literature represents the very antithesis of Bond and the fantasy world in which he operates. The reality of East-West espionage is quite different. The rapid expansion of the West's intelligence services in the Cold War produced muddle and chaos, often at the expense of agents' lives and safety. "While many of these serious human tragedies were taking place," le Carré pointed out to his PBS audience of viewers for the American serialization of *Tinker, Tailor, Soldier, Spy*, "all that literature could supply at that time was a hero who was really fighting the Cold War with the same ethic and single-mindedness with which he fought the hot war. Ian Fleming's James Bond.... I felt it was a miserable failure of literature that we had supplied so little of the real harshness of the scene." Not without reason, Steven Marcus in the *New York Review of Books* once described le Carré as the Graham Greene of the Cold War.

Le Carré speaks with personal experience about the world of espionage and has conveyed more convincingly than any other writer the complex labyrinths of its interior bureaucracies. For many years he denied that he had been a member of Britain's Secret Intelligence Service, denials that rang hollow against the known facts of his career and the plausibility of detail and feeling in his fiction. He has now given up the attempt, openly acknowledging that he belongs to the school of the writer-agent in the honoured tradition of Maugham and Greene.

Le Carré's first experience of intelligence work came during his period of national service with the Intelligence Corps in Austria in the early 1950s, where his job was to interrogate refugees fleeing from Czechoslovakia and Hungary. This followed a year at Bern University in Switzerland, and prior to that several unhappy years at private and public school culminating at Sherbourne.

When le Carré's most recent novel, *A Perfect Spy*, was published in 1986, the world learned in full what le Carré had previously hinted at: that over his schooling and youth—indeed well into middle age—there had hung the dark shadow of a family scandal. Ronald Cornwell, his father, fictionally portrayed in *A Perfect Spy* as Rickie Pym, was a high-rolling convicted embezzler and con man who lived on a grand scale, and from whose chaotic business and emotional life the young David Cornwell— le Carré's real name—was sheltered by relatives and boarding school (his mother left his father and the family when her son was only three years old). "Ronnie's life accomplishments," le Carré told readers of the *Sunday Times*, "if unorthodox, were dazzling: a string of bankruptcies spread over nearly fifty years and accounting for several millions of pounds; literally hundreds of companies with grandiose letterpaper and scarcely a speck of capital; a host of faithful friends who smiled on his business ventures even when they themselves were the victims...foreign travel in the grand manner, smart cars, custom made suits and shoes, and such a lavish way with hospitality, provided always that he could sign for it, that even the most conscientious of his circle gave up trying to pay for it." On one spectacular occasion, on the eve of le Carré's first marriage, Ronald Cornwell went bankrupt for over £1 million.

Le Carré was eighteen when he first learned of his father's criminal record, and for many years the two men were deeply estranged from each other. The wounds had a profound and transparent effect on le Carré's life and fiction. They turned him into a solitary and introspective figure well able to measure the attractions of the self-enclosed institution of the secret service for those seeking shelter from the outside world. "In a shifting childhood punctuated by the ups and downs of my father's windy life," le Carré has said, "hurrying from temporary mother to temporary school, I began to dream of a secret centre to the world which, if I ever reached it, would reveal the purpose behind our mad pursuit."

After national service le Carré went up to Lincoln College, Oxford, where he obtained a First Class degree in modern languages in 1956, the year of Hungary and Suez. Magnus Pym, son of con man Rickie, and the double agent protagonist of *A Perfect Spy*, is portrayed at Oxford as infiltrating left-wing groups and reporting back to M.I.5. When asked by Joseph Lelyveld, chief of the London Bureau of the *New York Times*, if this too was autobiographical, le Carré ambiguously replied that "he didn't think it would have been a respectable thing to do." He then worked as an assistant schoolmaster at Eton for two years before entering the Foreign Office in 1959. Fans of George Smiley will recall that he was first recruited into the secret service by Jebedee, his Oxford tutor. Was le Carré himself recruited for SIS at Oxford? Or, as *A Perfect Spy* suggests, had the call come earlier, in Austria, or perhaps even Bern? Whatever the answer, le Carré's Foreign Office profile between 1959 and 1964, when he resigned following the financial success of *The Spy Who Came In from the Cold*, furnished what is known professionally as "light cover" for five years' direct involvement in secret intelligence work. From 1960 to 1963 this was under the guise of Second Secretary at the British embassy in Bonn, and in 1964 as British consul in Hamburg.

The early 1960s saw the Cold War come to a climax over Germany and Berlin. In 1958 Nikita Khrushchev gave the West an ultimatum over the fate of the city, and the Berlin Wall went up in August 1961, closing the last gap in the Iron Curtain—an instant symbol of a divided Germany, a divided Europe, and a divided world.

Working in Bonn, le Carré visited Berlin frequently. He has talked about the experience on several occasions, usually in connection with the novel that made his name a household word, *The Spy Who Came In from the Cold*, which begins and ends at the Wall. "I lived and worked and moved in its shadow," he has said, "and became profoundly shocked by the image of a physical division through a living city which symbolized the sterility of the Cold War and which cut people off, one from another, and from the warmth of human contact."

Le Carré's brief career as a secret intelligence agent also coincided with some of the great betrayals within SIS. Directly or indirectly, they have yielded much of the raw material for his fiction, which he has supplemented by intensive reading into the background of major espionage cases such as those of Gouzenko and Petrov. (Igor Gouzenko, a GRU cipher clerk in the Soviet embassy in Ottawa, defected in 1945. Vladimir Petrov, a KGB agent, defected in Canberra in 1954.)

The first great betrayal was that of George Blake, who in April 1962 was sentenced at the Old Bailey for spying for the Soviet Union. Blake was of Egyptian, Dutch, and Jewish origin, and had escaped from Nazi-occupied Holland to Britain, where he assumed his Anglicized name. He then worked for British Naval Intelligence and SOE, and at the end of the war joined SIS. After language training at Cambridge he was posted to Seoul under consular cover, and here in 1950 was captured, along with the rest of the British Legation, by the North Koreans. Released from internment in 1953, he returned to London and was transferred to the highly sensitive position of Deputy Director of Technical

Operations in the SIS Berlin headquarters. For more than four years he was privy to some of the closest-kept secrets about CIA and SIS operations behind the Iron Curtain. In 1959 he returned to SIS HQ in London, and then in 1960 was sent to Beirut. It was from here in 1961 that Blake was recalled to London for interrogation as a suspected Soviet agent, and then tried in camera the following year. He received a forty-two –year sentence, but escaped from a British prison in 1966. He later surfaced in Moscow and was awarded the Order of Lenin, the Soviet Union's second-highest decoration.

It has been said that each year of Blake's sentence represented an agent he had betrayed to the Russians. This may be true, for he had extensive knowledge of British intelligence secrets and promiscuously gave them to the Russians. He certainly informed them about Operation Gold, the tunnel built under the Berlin sector boundary to tap Red Army cables; he gave the KGB vital information about East German defectors to the West; and he betrayed a number of British networks within eastern Europe. The scale of human disaster was monumental, and it shook SIS to its core. Le Carré, working within SIS on German affairs, was acutely aware of the consequences for those hapless agents caught in the cold by betrayal at home.

It was against this background that he wrote *The Spy Who Came In from the Cold* (which in 1965 was made into a major film starring Richard Burton, Claire Bloom, and Oskar Werner). It opens with a British agent in Berlin witnessing at the Wall the death of yet another member of his intelligence network in East Germany. But it is the deception of an agent by his own side, rather than betrayal by an enemy agent, that provides the main theme of *The Spy*, still the best le Carré novel. Tautly and carefully constructed, it breathes with a strong moral outrage, and still has the power to shock. It is a passionate and bitter book, the work of an idealist first confronted by the human costs of the machiavellian intrigues and corruptions of the world of international politics.

The Spy was widely greeted as introducing a welcome note of realism into spy fiction after a decade of Bond. Graham Greene, whose *Our Man in Havana* had stated similar claims for the individual against the state, welcomed it as the best spy novel he had ever read. Julian Symons in *Bloody Murder* placed it in the realist rather than romantic school of spy fiction, saying that "here the story [of betrayal] is most bitterly and clearly told, the lesson of human degradation involved in spying most faithfully read." Yet among professionals reactions were mixed. Some enjoyed the authentic flavour that le Carré brought to bureaucratic and personal rivalries within the secret world, but others derided the notion of realism. Kim Philby, for example, described the whole plot of *The Spy* as basically implausible, and from the opposite end of the ideological spectrum Richard Helms, Director of the CIA, strongly disliked it. These reactions were predictable. Helms objected to the book's mood of defeat, despair, and human isolation, while Philby—who defected to Moscow the year the book was published—was certainly echoing the official Moscow denunciation of the novel as a piece of Cold War apologia. Denunciation from both sides of the ideological divide is not the least of the arguments in its favour.

Le Carré's spy fiction can be divided into two phases. The first begins in 1961 with *Call for the Dead* and concludes with *A Small Town in Germany* (1968). The second begins with *Tinker, Tailor, Soldier, Spy* (1974) and ends with *A Perfect Spy* in 1986. In the first, the dominant theme is the moral corruption that is inseparable from espionage. However noble the objective, and however moral the agent, espionage inevitably involves those who work within it in the suppression of their humanity. In these early novels le Carré speaks directly from his own experience. He once said of Eton and the Foreign Office that both were institutions so isolated from the outside world that they were incapable of human contact with the people they were meant to govern. And on another occasion he confessed that he had taken up fiction writing as a useful antidote to the *déformation professionnelle* of a service he much admired. The theme is rendered explicit in his first novel. "It's an old illness you suffer from, Mr. Smiley," says Elsa Fennan in *Call for the Dead*, "...and I have seen many victims of it. The mind becomes separated from the body; it thinks without reality, rules a paper kingdom and devises without emotion the ruin of its paper victims...[then] the files grow heads and arms and legs, and that's a terrible moment, isn't it?... When that happens I am sorry for you." The world of the "Circus", le Carré's term for SIS headquarters, is a masculine one populated by those who see love as a weakness to escape or to exploit. Here, le Carré's fiction follows convention, for women symbolize feeling and emotion, and are therefore either dangerous or dysfunctional. In *Call for the Dead*, Elsa Fennan is both. As a woman she can feel the inhumanity of Smiley's secret bureaucratic world, and she can generate the love in her husband that makes her his controller in the theft of Foreign Office documents. All subsequent le Carré novels are coloured by the theme of love's betrayals. The inhabitants of the Circus are escaping from, or have been abandoned by, their wives. Smiley's Achilles' heel is his errant wife, Ann, and Karla, Smiley's rival at Moscow Centre, is eventually brought down by love for his daughter. Connie Sachs, the archivist whose knowledge of the records makes her a key figure in the Circus, is the exception that proves the rule. For Connie, as becomes explicit in *Smiley's People*, is a decidedly masculine lesbian; and she too will sacrifice her love in order to rejoin the game.

The Looking Glass War (1965) is the most desolate novel of this first phase, portraying men who, to fill the emotional emptiness of their lives, devise an operation behind the Iron Curtain that is merely a futile exercise in nostalgia for the heroics of the Second World War. They launch it as part of their rivalry with a sister secret agency—there are strong echoes here of the wartime SOE–SIS rivalry—and fall victim to its superior skills. Borrowing an ethic from the past, they live within a dream factory of the present where they plan heroism for the future. Their operation is doomed from the start, but their empty rituals still demand a human sacrifice in the form of the agent Leiser, whom they then abandon in the cold. Theirs is a shadow war, a looking-glass war, and all are dupes of the illusion that the once-great game for which they were trained has any relevance in the contemporary world of the Cold War. It is scarce wonder that many of his former "Foreign Office" colleagues dislike this book most of all, seeing it as a personal betrayal. At a diplomatic dinner many years later, one of them yelled at le Carré, "You *bastard*, you utter bastard."

Less successful but equally passionate, *A Small Town in Germany* cannot have improved this mood. Set in the British embassy in Bonn, where le Carré had served for three years, it bitterly dissects British willingness, sometime in the "recent future", to deal with a neo-Nazi popular leader and thus to betray Leo Harting, the half-Jewish local employee who has uncovered incriminating facts about the leader's Nazi past. It is the task of Alan Turner, the hard-bitten security officer sent from London, to trace Leo before his secrets become public knowledge. "Externally," le Carré once explained, "Leo and I lived in the same house, worked in the same building, ate in the same canteen, drank at the same parties, and we felt perhaps, for different but related reasons, the same intense alienation from the environment of which we were a part. But there," he concluded, "the analogy ends. Perhaps I have more in common with Alan Turner, and have set one part of my nature in pursuit of another."

The pursuit between contradictory sides of his personality shortly spilled over into le Carré's personal life. The heady financial success that followed publication of *The Spy Who Came In from the Cold* enabled le Carré and his wife and three children to leave England and live in Crete. But shortly after their return to England a few months later, the marriage broke up amidst considerable publicity about le Carré's affair with the wife of another author. Eventually he remarried and had another child. Since then he has lived a secluded life in Cornwall, from which he emerges for the occasional interview.

The emotional turmoil of those years is captured in the underestimated but highly autobiographical romantic adventure entitled *The Naive and Sentimental Lover* (1972). Taking Schiller's distinction of personality types and behaviour between the naïve and the sentimental, the natural and the learned, the innocent and the corrupt, le Carré explores the relationship between Aldo Cassidy, a successful but distinctly sentimental businessman trapped in an unhappy marriage, and the self-styled poet Shamus de Belvedere and his mistress, Helen, who live in a late sixties haze of serendipitous naïvety. A *ménage à trois* evolves, but eventually Cassidy returns to the sentimental and civilized world to which he really belongs. He has found his place, but forever after suffers a sense of loss. "For in this world, whatever there was left to inhabit," concludes the novel, "Aldo Cassidy dared not remember love."

If not love, then certainly passion, ebbed from the second phase of le Carré's spy fiction, which began with the publication in 1974 of *Tinker, Tailor, Soldier, Spy.* This firmly established his international reputation as the dominating figure of contemporary spy fiction, and was greeted with extravagant hyperbole. "The spinner of spy stories and the poet of fantasy have met to produce a novel that shoulders its way into the front rank of the art," wrote a critic in the London *Times. Newsweek*, always generous, proclaimed le Carré "a master of the spy novel". *L'Express* of Paris suggested comparisons with Balzac and *La Comédie Humaine.* Elsewhere he was proclaimed, ludicrously, as "the Solzhenitsyn" of the genre. Since then a successful TV serialization seen in both Britain and North America has inspired a transatlantic enthusiasm for le Carré that even Fleming would have envied.

Tinker, Tailor explores the labyrinths of the secret bureaucratic world with consummate skill. In its depiction of the working of power and its effects on the individual, as well as for its introduction to the arcane tradecraft of espionage, it is a minor masterpiece. Its real fascination, however, and one reason for its widespread popular appeal, lies in its obvious fictionalization of the case of Kim Philby.

The Philby affair has assumed the dimensions of parable, metaphor, and legend. His career as a Soviet agent within the Secret Intelligence Service exemplified the smooth highroads to power for those born of the right social pedigree, and the cover-up that protected him for so long testifies to the self-protective barriers that the British establishment so rapidly constructs against those who would pursue its errant and criminal members. The foreign-born and half-Jewish Blake received a sentence of forty-two years; Philby, born to rule in the Raj, was allowed to escape. His career is a richly textured tale about the old-boy networks from which the defenders of Empire were drawn.

He was born in India of British parents and spoke Hindi before English. His father, civil servant Harry St. John Philby, later became a famous Arabist and maverick who during the Second World War was interned for Fascist sympathies. Young Harold Philby quickly acquired the nickname "Kim". It was to remain one of the supreme ironies of his long career as a Soviet agent that he should always be known by the name that Kipling had given to the boy hero of his classic novel who spied against the Russians in the great game.

He was sent to Westminster School and then on to Trinity College, Cambridge, which he entered in 1929. It was here, in the left-wing milieu engendered by the Depression and the rise of Fascism, that Philby, like so many others, was recruited as a Soviet agent. It was a loyalty carefully masked by an outward display of conservative sympathies that culminated when he covered the Spanish Civil War for the *Times* as a freelance correspondent with the Nationalist forces of General Franco. He returned to England with something of a reputation as a journalist, and when the war broke out was recruited into Section D of the Secret Intelligence Service. This was a forerunner of the Special Operations Executive, where Philby later worked as an instructor at its agents' training school in Beaulieu. In 1941 he joined the Secret Intelligence Service itself, and was made head of the Iberian desk of its Section V (counter-espionage) where, as we have seen, Graham Greene was a colleague.

Philby did well in SIS. He was able, hard-working, and adept at office politics. Something of a high flyer, he was promoted in 1944 to head of the Soviet Section, one of whose main tasks was the setting up of networks in eastern Europe for use against the Russians. Philby had penetrated to the heart of the secret service he was committed to betraying. He stayed there for two years and was then sent to Istanbul, a key listening post in the early Cold War years. From there, in 1949, he was sent to his most important posting of all, as SIS liaison man with the CIA in Washington. It gave him a unique overview of CIA operations and made him a key figure in several joint CIA-SIS operations directed against the Soviet Union—most notably attempts to infiltrate agents into

Albania, Georgia, and the Ukraine—all of which he betrayed to his masters in Moscow.

Philby might have continued in this sensitive post for some time but for the defection to Moscow in 1951 of the two British diplomats Maclean and Burgess. Both had been spying for the Russians, and Burgess was a known friend of Philby. Recalled to London during the inquest that followed, Philby was interrogated. Nothing was proved against him, but he remained under a cloud. None the less, he was not dismissed but given a number of low-level missions throughout the Middle East in the following decade. His name briefly surfaced publicly in 1955 in connection with allegations about a "third man" who had warned Maclean and Burgess they were under suspicion, but he was officially cleared by the Prime Minister. Finally, in 1963, the evidence of a Soviet defector pointed unequivocally to Philby as a Soviet mole. Faced with the prospect of yet another interrogation, which he could not hope to win, Philby fled to Moscow. He has since received some of the highest Soviet decorations, and is a major-general in the KGB.

How did this man born into the British ruling class survive undetected for almost thirty years as a Soviet agent? How could he have risen so high in SIS, and how was it that even under suspicion he was protected for so long?

There are those who seek an explanation in Soviet conspiracy. Le Carré, more convincingly, believes in conspiracy of another kind. "In the unequal duel between Kim Philby and the British Secret Service," he has written, "a new dimension is added to the relationship between the privileged Englishman and the institution which he collectively comprises." Philby belonged to the very establishment he resolved to betray, and it fostered, nurtured, and protected him. He rose to the heights without any close scrutiny of his political loyalties, and suspicions against him were discounted by his fellow members in the secret club to which he belonged. Kim, after all, was one of them. Le Carré sees SIS as a microcosm of the British condition and of British social attitudes and vanities. SIS not merely defended the Britain of clubland, it also embodied it. "The real conspiracies," le Carré told American viewers of *Tinker, Tailor, Soldier, Spy*, "are the conspiracies of self-protection, of using the skirts of official secrecy in order to protect incompetence, of gross class privilege, of amazing credulity."

Betrayal and treason lie at the heart of *Tinker, Tailor*, as George Smiley hunts down the mole within the Circus. The chase is conducted according to the classic methods of counter-espionage, as Smiley, with the vital help of archivist Connie Sachs, painstakingly cross-checks the voluminous archives of the Circus and foils the less efficient attempts of the mole to destroy the written record. The villain turns out to be Bill Haydon, whose fictional career bears a strong resemblance to that of Philby. Ubiquitous, charming, and unorthodox, he is socially well connected. His sisters have married into the aristocracy and he is a cousin to Lady Ann Sercomb, Smiley's wife. Through hard work and ability he has risen quickly to the top of the service and is in charge of operations into the Soviet bloc. Like Philby, he betrays his colleagues, his friends, his country, and his class. He cuckolds Smiley and exploits Lady Ann to mask his betrayal. He is the ultimate cynic, and yet remains protected by the incompetence of Control and the hopes of his colleagues that their ill-formed suspicions are unfounded.

Smiley, on the contrary, lives by loyalty—to his faithless wife, Ann, his subordinates, his colleagues, and his country. In the end, integrity triumphs over corruption. Haydon—unlike Philby—meets death at the hands of the friend he betrayed, and Smiley, triumphant, assumes control of the Circus. Good defeats evil and Smiley emerges from *Tinker, Tailor* as a hero in the best tradition of the popular novel. It's scarce wonder that Smiley has become almost as legendary a figure as Philby, for *Tinker, Tailor* with all its outward verisimilitude, constructs a potent and appealing myth for the class-ridden and post-imperial *Angst* of Britain in the 1970s. That Philby was protected by a conspiracy of class is true enough, but that he was unmasked by a Smiley is not. It was evidence from defectors and strong CIA suspicions that undid Philby, and far from receiving his just deserts, he ended up alive and well in Moscow. *Tinker, Tailor* is a fantasy; George Smiley, a myth.

But on whom is the myth modelled? If Bill Haydon is loosely based on Kim Philby, who is the real George Smiley? There are those who say that it is the late Sir Maurice Oldfield, the dumpy, bespectacled, and music-loving bachelor who as "C" ran SIS between 1973 and 1978. True, there are some superficial similarities with Smiley. A potential academic career was interrupted in 1939, and the fight against Nazism and hopes of building a better post-war world provided Oldfield's formative experience. But this was true for an entire generation, and there is no obvious reason why in 1961, when he invented Smiley, le Carré should have chosen Oldfield as a model. More convincing as a model for Smiley is David Cornwell. Smiley, le Carré has confessed, is a fantasy about himself.

There are sufficient factual, emotional, and psychological similarities between George Smiley and David Cornwell to place le Carré in the camp of spy novelists who since the days of William Le Queux have conceived fantasies about themselves as super agents. The origins of both are somewhat obscure and, at least during the period Le Carré wrote about Smiley, little is known about their childhood. Both go up to Oxford to study German literature, and from there go on to spend a few months improving their language in a small German-speaking city. The war provided Smiley with his formative professional experience, and he spent four years travelling through the Third Reich under cover as the agent of a Swedish arms manufacturer. Le Carré, of course, was too young to serve in the war, but no child who was fourteen years old in 1945 could fail to live imaginatively in its aura for the next few years. And when he entered national service he was sent to Austria, and his first professional SIS posting was in Germany itself.

Here the external similarities between le Carré and Smiley end. But other, more subtle, similarities take over. Smiley's constant dilemma is how to retain his humanity in the service of a cause and profession to which he is profoundly loyal and deeply wedded. Le Carré felt, and still feels, the same ambivalence. Reared in all-male institutions, he understands the attractions and loyalties inspired by such institutions as the Foreign Office. Alienated he may have been by the time he left; he none the less admired the professionalism of the service and respected many of those with whom he had worked. *Tinker, Tailor, Soldier, Spy* is dedicated to two of his colleagues in the Bonn embassy whom he had met a decade before. Smiley, like le Carré, is a quietly passionate man who guards his privacy, and while Smiley smarts with the betrayals of adult love, le Carré bears the scars of childhood betrayal. Both, too, are profoundly English in their attachment to the country of their birth. Smiley is at home only in London, and it seems that le Carré is at home only in Cornwall. Ian Fleming wrote much purple prose about England but could hardly wait to escape to Jamaica and America. Len Deighton, le Carré's contemporary who wrote the immensely successful *Funeral in Berlin*, became a tax exile in Ireland. Le Carré, now holed up in the hedgerows of Cornwall after his brief excursion to Crete twenty years ago, has become a sometime pundit on the state of the nation's health. And it is in this rural, self-enclosed world that le Carré, once the demystifier, has spun the myth of Smiley.

The myth-making continues in le Carré's last two Smiley novels, the first of which, *The Honourable Schoolboy* (1977), is his least successful. Encumbered by its heavily researched background in East and South-East Asia, and self-indulgently elaborate, it depicts Smiley master-minding the defection to the West of a Soviet agent in Peking. It also discusses the theme of idealism betrayed, but lacks the passion to deal with the latter and is unconvincing with the former. *Smiley's People* (1980) returns to the familiar le Carré hunting grounds of central Europe. In a novel of great skill and virtuosity, Smiley engages in his final duel with Karla of Moscow Centre. Smiley wins, and Karla defects to the West by crossing through the Berlin Wall. Smiley once again is the legendary slayer of Goliath, the British St. George to Moscow's dragon. He is, of course, sufficiently self-aware to appreciate that the victory is ambiguous.

"George, you won," says Smiley's colleague Guillam, as the two men observe Karla's crossing. "Did I," replies Smiley, "yes, yes, well I suppose I did." In reality, Smiley knows that he has also lost, for in entrapping Karla by exploiting the Russian's love for his daughter, he has lost a fragment of his own humanity.

Smiley, though opposed to the cause that Karla serves, is forced to respect the opponent who fell into his hands once before and refused every material blandishment to defect. With Ian Fleming, the villains are larger than life, and the closer that Bond gets to them the more awful they become. Not with le Carré, for how does Karla look as he emerges across the Wall? "One little man, hatless, with a satchel...his face, aged and weary and travelled, the short hair turned to white by a sprinkling of snow. He wore a grimy shirt and a black tie: he looked like a poor man going to the funeral of a friend." Such human depictions of the enemy certainly buried the monstrous villains of the age of Bond. For many of le Carré's readers this reduction of the Cold War to its human dimensions provides his strongest appeal.

This has not endeared le Carré to committed ideological professionals, as the comments of Richard Helms, quoted earlier, indicate. Another former CIA member has denounced le Carré for writing "futility chic". At the most extreme, he has been denounced for undermining faith in Western democracy by suggesting a symmetry of good and evil between the two power blocs. Such views rest on a fundamental misreading of le Carré. Nowhere does he suggest anything other than a passionate commitment to liberal values, and *Smiley's People* paints an utterly dismal portrait of Soviet society. Le Carré directs his anger not at Western society but at those missionaries of the Cold War who find in its secret war a substitute religion. Leamas's passionate outburst at the end of *The Spy Who Came In from the Cold* some twenty years ago is as relevant now as it was then. Describing his masters in London, Leamas has this to say: "They don't proselytize: they don't stand in pulpits or on party platforms and tell us to fight for Peace or for God or whatever it is. They're the poor sods who try to keep the preachers from blowing each other sky high."

This is all a far cry from James Bond. But there are hidden continuities between le Carré and his predecessors. Le Carré is a self-confessed patriot, even though a disgusted one, dismayed that so little has changed in Britain since the jingo days of the Empire, and sharing Orwell's old complaint in his essay "The Lion and the Unicorn" that the country is like a family with the wrong members in control. And what, after all, is le Carré's Britain? Is it so far different from that of Fleming? True, it lacks the snobbery and sex and violence, and George Smiley is a far cry from the "consumer goods hero", James Bond. But by the end of his fictional career Smiley has surely won a place in the pantheon of British heroes by carrying off major coups against the nation's enemies that outrank the feats of Bond. Like Britain itself, Smiley may be small, modest, and unprepossessing to look at, but beneath his bespectacled, grey, and toad-like exterior the bulldog virtues of loyalty, integrity, and doggedness pulsate as strongly as ever they did in the heroic days of the great game. Smiley is also a product of Oxbridge, and his physical universe is largely contained by the square mile that encompasses Whitehall. There are occasional forays into the country, but this means, as in Fleming, the Home Counties. The reader of le Carré, like that of Le Queux or Fleming, could remain oblivious of the Britain north of the Trent.

Le Carré is quintessentially *English*. The ambivalence towards America and Americans found in Fleming becomes indifference marked with contempt and hostility in le Carré. In part, this reflects the passage of time since the heyday of Bond. By the early 1960s the special relationship glorified by Fleming was moribund, and the CIA-SIS relationship was badly strained by British spy scandals such as those of Blake and Philby. There is some verisimilitude here, but there is also a tangible cultural antagonism. The Cousins, as the CIA is referred to by the inhabitants of the Circus, are regarded as rivals to be feared or derided rather than as colleagues to work with in a conflict between the "West" and Communism. Control, head of the Circus, despises the CIA "and all their works which he frequently seeks to undermine." Elsewhere, CIA personnel are described as "Fascist puritans". And when Smiley loses out in the bureaucratic struggle for control of the Circus in *The Honourable Schoolboy*, it is to men who believe that the path to strength lies in Britain working closely with the Americans. Smiley, it is clear, does not approve. It is ironic, therefore, that while the most strongly negative attitudes towards le Carré have come from the United States, Americans are also among his most uncritical admirers.

Le Carré made his mark on spy fiction by unmasking the pretensions of espionage and depicting the world of international politics as one of cruel absurdity. He portrayed spying as a largely self-serving exercise played by the immature products of Britain's institutionalized élite who found in their self-enclosed world both a microcosm of and an alternative to the external world. Spies, Alex Leamas cries during the anguish of his betrayal in *The Spy Who Came In from the Cold*, are "a squalid procession of vain fools, traitors, too, yes; pansies, sadists and drunkards, people who play cowboys and Indians to brighten their rotten little lives." Le Carré himself has said that spies should not be seen as loyal or dedicated men firmly believing in some ideology and making great sacrifices for it. Yet le Carré has replaced one mystique with another, while at the same time suggesting that the older territory of the spy novel should be abandoned. Smiley emerges from his fictional career as a super-spy who smites his foes with well-aimed blows from the incriminating files. But who are the foes? Once upon a time it was clear, but now nothing is certain. "So far as I can ever remember of my youth," Smiley muses in *The Honourable Schoolboy*, "I chose the secret road because it seemed to lead straightest and furthest toward my country's goal. The enemy in those days was someone we could point at and read about in the papers. Today, all I know is that I have learned to interpret the whole of life in terms of conspiracy." .

For a quarter of a century le Carré has attempted to come to terms with the decline of Britain as a great imperial power, and with the post-war world of ideological conflict. Born in 1931, he belongs to the generation of Englishmen who during the euphoria of victory over Nazi Germany were assured that the Empire lived on. "It took me a long time to realize that it was a complete illusion," he says, "and this, I suppose, predicates a disenchantment." Then came the Cold War. Three years after victory, pilots who had fought the Battle of Britain and later bombed Berlin were supplying the city with food during the 1948 airlift. "People who'd thought they were destroying evil in the world, through conflict with an absolute enemy...suddenly realized," le Carré told his American TV audience in 1984, "that they were harnessed to a seemingly endless succession of wars and we'd taken part in this seamless transition from the war against Fascism to the war against Communism; and we seemed scarcely to have drawn breath in between.... My anger...is that somehow there was the most massive failure of diplomacy.... And I suppose we are now saddled with the obligation to fight out an ideological war which just possibly need never have been joined."

With George Smiley, le Carré has also debated the morality of espionage. To pay the price of the nasty things that have to be done to preserve democracy, Smiley sacrifices his conscience and bears our collective guilt. But is it all worth it? Le Carré is still not sure. Speaking at Johns Hopkins University in 1986, he seemed to doubt it. "All that sacrifice of moral conscience—was it really noble?" he asked about Smiley. "Is there such a grand difference, in fact, between the man who voluntarily gives up his moral conscience and the man who never had one in the first place?"

His answer echoes the refrain of Graham Greene, fellow exile from the silent game. "It's not the dissenters who have brought havoc to our non-conciliatory world," le Carré told his audience, "but the *loyal* men marching blindly to the music of their institutionalized faiths...real heroism lies, as it always will, not in conformity or even patriotism, but in acts of solitary moral courage."

CHAPTER TWELVE

Empire Blues

Peacetime spy organizations normally develop their reputations when an empire's going downhill... That's what's happened with the British, and now that we're getting screwed up the CIA's getting important just like the British spies did.

Taylor Branch, *The Empire Blues*

Spy writers began to flourish in Britain when they could strike the chord of national vulnerability. The way was then open for the secret agent as hero. In the hands of William Le Queux, spy novels were weapons in a campaign for increased national security and an organized secret service. Other writers also combined instruction with amusement. Erskine Childers warned in *The Riddle of the Sands* of the dangers from an expanding Germany, and even the glitter-of-diamonds world of E. Phillips Oppenheim contained a clear message about dangers to national security. Numerous spy novels had appeared before the formation of the Secret Intelligence Service on the eve of the First World War, and all were the products of apprehensions of decline. "It was in the world of capital that SIS had its traditional heart," John le Carré has written, "in the preservation of trade routes, in the defence of foreign investment and colonial wealth, in the protection of ordered society." The need to defend Empire made sense only when the Empire could already be challenged; the need to defend order only when "society" felt under threat.

After the First World War, there was a change in the relationship between fact and fiction. Recruitment of professional writers into the Secret Intelligence Service bred spy novelists who drew on their experience for the raw material of their fiction, such as John Buchan, A.E.W. Mason, Somerset Maugham, and Compton Mackenzie. The secret agents portrayed in the novels of this early period were single and youthful gentlemen. They fought foreign spies who were certainly not gentlemen, often acting from mercenary motive, and who lacked the grace and charm of their opponents. These agents moved in a man's world in which women were always a threat. Feminine guile of a friendly sort weakened the single-minded resolve needed by secret agents to carry out their patriotic duty, while that of a hostile kind was so cunning and devious that men were defenceless before its onslaught. The secret agent thus embodied the nation in relation to exterior threat. But he also represented the class, and within that class the sex, that ruled Britain with such assurance in the early decades of the century.

The ideological totalitarianism of the 1930s challenged easy assumptions about patriotism and national honour. Good and evil could no longer be defined by class or country, and even in peacetime millions of people's lives were torn up in the maelstrom. Eric Ambler and Graham Greene used the spy novel to represent an alternative view and to portray men caught up in events over which they had little control, victims of world forces moving towards the holocaust, symbols of a society in disintegration.

The Second World War encouraged hopes that the old certainties could be restored. Ian Fleming's James Bond was a linear descendant of the Duckworth Drews, Richard Hannays, and Bulldog Drummonds of earlier years. Fleming was a propagandist of the new Elizabethan age, but its illusions soon passed in the face of Britain's international decline, the dissolution of its empire, and the rise of the superpowers. James Bond was replaced by Alex Leamas in *The Spy Who Came in from the Cold,* a secret agent caught up in a game of the rules of which he himself was ignorant, a victim of his masters who used him as a pawn. Agents like Leamas are no longer gentlemen carrying out their duty from a sense of *noblesse oblige,* but salaried bureaucrats doing a menial job like any other. The grammar school or state school has become the recruitment ground, and agents lack the effortless superiority that carried them through the crises of an earlier age. They are still of course men, but for the first time the masculinity of their world is seen as a flaw, not a strength. With the Burgess-Maclean-Philby-Blunt revelations, it became all too clear in the real world that to be a gentleman is no guarantee of sexual or patriotic orthodoxy. Neither gender nor class can guarantee the integrity of the nation. Irony or cynicism becomes a powerful mood.

Since the revelations of the 1960s about Philby, and more particularly since Sir Anthony Blunt was revealed as a traitor in the late 1970s, the dominant theme in British spy novels has been that of the mole, the highly placed traitor within the secret service who works out of loyalty to the other side. To all appearances he may be an English gentleman. Inside he is a deep-dyed villain. The focus of spy novels has turned inward, to conspiracy within the nation or secret service. Still, external conspiracy remains part of the staple fare. Both help explain the spy novel's immense appeal. In a complex international world people have become both cynical and credulous. Feeling that the nuclear stalemate, with its prospect of sudden annihilation, leaves them little control over their destinies, they look for conspiracies as an explanation. "Conspiracy has replaced religion... it is our mystical substitute," says the Soviet diplomat Anton Grigoriev in le Carré's *Smiley's People.* Brecht said a similar thing many years ago to explain why people read detective novels. "Behind the events we are told about," he wrote, "we suspect other occurrences about which we are not told.... Only if we knew would we understand." Spy novels answer a similar need and simplify the international world. Spy writers know it.

That fears of imperial decline and national weakness provide an especially fertile breeding ground for spy novelists is amply proved if we look at the United States and the recent increase in the number, popularity, and output of American spy writers.

The humiliation of the Vietnam defeat still lies darkly across the collective American psyche. Just as the Boer War dented Britain's imperial self-confidence and strengthened feelings of national vulnerability that nourished the early spy novel, so the American defeat in Southeast Asia, followed by such other humiliations as the Iran hostage situation, sparked a crisis of self-confidence. Hence the brash rhetoric of President Reagan, the 1980s popularity of Rambo, and the brief but intense love affair of millions of Americans in 1987 with Colonel Oliver North, the solo hero from the secret world who singlehandedly took on Communists in Central America and mullahs in Iran. The end of the 1980s then saw a serious and widespread debate conducted in newspapers and learned journals about whether America was a nation in decline. Whatever the answer, the very fervour of the debate indicated a serious mood of critical introspection, and was deeply reminiscent of a similar debate that had raged in Edwardian Britain before the First World War. The subsequent collapse of Communism in Eastern Europe and the apparently rapid weakening of the Soviet Union hardly changes the picture. Americans still feel deeply vulnerable in the face of new "demons" that appear threatening and incomprehensible—especially, at present, in the Middle East. Indeed, the collapse of the predictable bilateral world of the Cold War is likely to increase rather than diminish feelings of insecurity. Not surprisingly, therefore, intelligence has become more and not less important to the United States.

Of course spies began their move long before appearing on centre stage, and U.S. espionage in fact and fiction existed long before the Cold War and the post-Vietnam era. But, as in the case of Britain, there was a great deal of pretence involved about espionage. The mythology of American democracy, like the honour of the English gentleman, seemed inconsistent with the imperatives of espionage. Spies, Americans believed, were products of autocratic and evil regimes. In his war address to Congress in 1917, for example, President Wilson dwelt at length on the theme that only autocracies such as Germany maintained spies and that democratic regimes such as the United States had no need of them. Yet, as he spoke, the United States had a foreign intelligence system in place and at home was stepping up surveillance against domestic radical movements as well as German undercover operations. After the war the system was scaled down. In 1929 Secretary of State Henry Stimson uttered his famous protestation when he learned of the existence of the State Department's code-breaking operation, the Cipher Bureau, more popularly known as the Black Chamber, which secretly monitored the communications of some twenty nations. "Gentlemen," he said in ordering its closure, "do not read each other's mail." But this did not mean that cryptanalysis in the United States stopped. It merely shifted place within the American bureaucracy and took a lower profile. And those who later claimed that inter-war American espionage was virtually nonexistent either were misinformed or were making a case for expansion. When General George C. Marshall told a Senate committee in 1945 that until the Second World War American intelligence abroad was "little more than a military attaché could learn at dinner, more or less, over the coffee cups," he was also preparing the groundwork for the contemporary national security state.

American authors were certainly aware of the possibilities of spy fiction in the years between the world wars. The Harvard-educated Francis Van Wyck Mason, for example, entertained American readers from the 1930s to the late 1960s with numerous exploits of Captain Hugh North, of U.S. Army Intelligence, in novels with such seductive titles as *The Branded Spy Murders* (1932), *The Budapest Parade Murders* (1935), and *The Deadly Orbit Mission* (1968), his final work. John P. Marquand produced his highly popular Mr. Moto series, starring the Japanese secret agent Moto, in the 1930s. Still, spy fiction was largely dominated in these years by British author E. Phillips Oppenheim, whom many readers probably believed to be an American because of his frequent transatlantic visits, his American wife, and his astute American publishers. As a genre, the spy novel remained a minority taste beside the Western or the detective novel.

The creation of a powerful and centralized intelligence establishment in the United States after the Second World War set the stage for the mature American spy novel that appealed to a mass audience. The CIA was formed in 1947, inheriting many of its personnel from the wartime Office of Strategic Services (OSS). The National Security Agency followed in 1952 and the Defense Intelligence Agency in 1961. And in 1960, some thirty years after Stimson's outrage over the activities of the Black Chamber, President Eisenhower heralded a new era in the history of American espionage by openly admitting, after a U2 spy plane crashed in the Soviet Union, that espionage was "a distasteful but vital necessity." Alan Dulles, the longtime Director of Central Intelligence, edited an anthology of spy fiction in 1969—an indication that spying and spy fiction had come of age. As Dulles said, "World War II and the Cold War served to elevate the reputation of spying in the public mind." Spy novels were already selling well, one example being the Matt Helm novels of Donald Hamilton in which Helm, sometimes described as the American equivalent of James Bond, fights a series of battles against a wide variety of villains.

As in Britain, however, it took more than the appearance of a national intelligence system to make the spy novel a fully successful genre. What was needed was a heavy dose of fear about national decline and vulnerability. The trauma of the Vietnam War fueled a desperate need for patriotic reassertion and the denial of imperial decline. This trauma coincided with controversy about the CIA in the aftermath of the Watergate scandal. The unmasking of covert military operations in Southeast Asia, the attack on executive privilege, and widespread allegations of official misconduct for the first time in American history created a national debate about intelligence activities, forcing Americans to confront the realities of international espionage.

One effect of the fallout from Watergate was to stimulate members or ex-members of the CIA to write novels and air internal controversies. The former spy as author thus became part of the American as well as the British scene. The best-known such writer was Victor Marchetti. Marchetti joined the CIA in 1955 and became a Soviet specialist, ending up in the office of the Director of Central Intelligence. He was closely involved in tracking the Soviet Union's policies in Cuba that culminated in the 1962 Missile Crisis, and he worked on analyzing Soviet anti-ballistic missile capability in the 1960s. But the fact that the CIA was less involved in the silent game of intelligence collection and analysis than in the far noisier game of clandestine operations and covert action, particularly the destabilization of foreign governments, disillusioned him; he finally resigned from the agency in 1969 and became its vocal and out-spoken critic. Eventually, after a protracted court battle, he published a censored but major exposé of the CIA in 1974 entitled *The CIA and the Cult of Intelligence*. But he had already spilled many of the beans in his 1971 novel, *The Rope Dancer*. "I sought to put forth my... feelings... in fictional form," he later said, "... to describe for the reader what life was like in a secret agency such as the CIA, and what the differences were between myth and reality in this overromanticized profession." The novel discusses how the assistant to the Director of Central Intelligence defects to the Soviets and reveals a great deal about the inner workings of the CIA. It so alarmed the CIA that the injunction forcing Marchetti to submit later manuscripts for clearance was also extended to any fictional material.

At the opposite end of the political spectrum to Marchetti was another CIA agent, E. Howard Hunt. Hunt had been in the OSS and had worked for the Agency since the beginnings of the Cold War. He was deeply involved in the Cuban Bay of Pigs disaster and, after retiring from the CIA in 1970, played a central role in the Watergate break-in. Hunt began to write spy novels in the 1960s, many under the pseudonym David St. John. Richard Helms, Director of the CIA from 1966 to 1973, gave Hunt permission to publish his work, possibly in the belief that he would build popular support for CIA covert activities. That was certainly the intent, and when Hunt first floated the idea of an American equivalent to the James Bond books, the CIA director agreed that they could be good public relations. Certainly Helms liked Hunt's books—as he also liked Fleming's—and sometimes gave copies to visitors from a small stock he kept in his office.

Hunt's novels were straightforward good guy/bad guy anti-Communist novels in which the Western world was forever being saved from Soviet or Chinese threat by the CIA. Donald McCormick, in his *Who's Who in Spy Fiction*, has described Hunt as "not so much a milestone as a gallows landmark in the history of the spy story," largely because of his novels' awfulness but also because of their "unabashed, vehement ultra-right-wing politics." Like Le Queux, if Hunt couldn't find enemy agents, he fantasized about them or invented them. Eventually, at Watergate, reality caught up with him.

One example of Hunt's right-wing views on the real world is to be found in *The Berlin Ending* (1973), in which he airs the belief—not uncommon in the CIA—that German Chancellor Willy Brandt was a Soviet agent. After his imprisonment for his Watergate misdemeanors Hunt wrote *The Hargrave Deception*, a *roman à clef* significant only because it deals with what has since become an obsessional theme in spy fiction—the search for the mole.

The "Big Mole" theory might be christened "the search for the American Philby." It began with the defection to the United States in 1961 of Anatoli Golitsyn, a high-ranking member of the KGB. In addition to exposing a number of Soviet agents in the West, Golitsyn also hinted at the presence of a top-level mole within the CIA itself. From then until the mid-1970s the Agency was torn by controversy over his allegations. The believers were led by James Jesus Angleton, head of the CIA's Counterintelligence Division, a Yale graduate who had worked in the OSS and then for the CIA in Rome. Sent back to Washington in 1949 as the CIA's liaison with British intelligence, he found that his opposite number was Kim Philby. Angleton's links with Philby added a further twist to his hunt for the mole, and there has been much speculation about their relationship. Beliefs range from the notion that Philby totally duped Angleton through the theory that Angleton, knowing Philby's Soviet loyalty, fed him misinformation to the belief that Philby was a false defector who pretended to be a traitor to fool the KGB. Hunt's *The Hargrave Deception* plays with the latter theory, and Angleton and Philby are its heavily disguised central characters.

A highly-placed mole betraying secrets to the Kremlin was also the theme of the 1967 novel *Topaz* by Leon Uris, although here the action is set in Paris, where a KGB defector reveals that a close advisor to the French President is working for the Soviets. Uris was friendly with the former head of French intelligence in Washington and appears to have used information about Soviet penetration of the French intelligence service as the basis of his novel.

One of the most recent successful American authors of spy novels is Charles McCarry, who now enjoys the reputation of being the "American le Carré." The British spy writer John Gardner, indeed, has even said that McCarry "leads the field in terms of the world league." This judgment, however, seems overstated. A former journalist and speechwriter for President Eisenhower, McCarry joined the CIA in 1958 and spent the next decade in Africa and Asia before retiring to become a freelance writer. His first novel, *The Miernik Dossier* (1973), he constructed like a file, skillfully presenting his readers with the need to examine the raw material like an intelligence analyst. The novel, which dealt with the problem of deciding whether a Polish defector was genuine, received high praise from the old master, Eric Ambler. The principal character of McCarry's novel was Paul Christopher, a CIA agent, a sensitive yet deeply patriotic American who has since become a fixture in McCarry's fiction. His second and best novel, *The Tears of Autumn,* created a stir in official CIA circles by suggesting that President Kennedy was assassinated by a Vietnamese conspiracy in revenge for the CIA-supported coup that had led to the death of President Ngo Dinh Diem of South Vietnam. Paul Christopher carries out a personal crusade to find the truth in the face of opposition from his own superiors. Appearing at a time when the CIA was under maximum attack within the U.S. Senate, the novel was not exactly welcomed by supporters of the Agency. Yet it can hardly be argued that McCarry is out to "get" the CIA, or is in any way breaking out of the patriotic tradition. In *The Last Supper* (1983), for example, he addresses the theme of the mole within the CIA, taking the reader from the Nazi era via the OSS to contemporary Washington to unmask not only the Soviet mole but also the man who recruited him, a dissolute and high-ranking British SIS agent. McCarry has consistently refused to talk about his work in the CIA out of loyalty to his former colleagues.

An American author who comes close to le Carré both in viewpoint and in style is W.T. Tyler, the pseudonym of S.J. Hamrick, a veteran U.S. Foreign Service officer familiar with the world of secret intelligence. His first novel, *The Man Who Lost the War* (1980), is probably his best. Set in Berlin and other cities of central Europe, it explores classic le Carré terrain, and there is a strong resemblance to the English author in his emphasis on mood, landscape, and character. Again, it explores the unmasking of a Philby-type British mole. But, uncharacteristically, it develops a quasi-alliance between the two main characters, one an American and the other a

Soviet intelligence officer, against the cynical maneuverings of their superiors. Both are portrayed sympathetically, each concerned with preserving his humanity despite the pressures of the world that surrounds him. *The Ants of God,* Tyler's second novel, explores the relationship between a freelance American operative who is a Vietnam veteran and two of the women he meets in the course of a covert operation. Like the American central character in Tyler's first book, he is a loner with an unhappy emotional past. So is Reddish, the CIA agent in *Rogue's March;* in this novel Tyler portrays the devastating effects of American and Soviet interference in the affairs of a central African nation racked by internal conflict. Along the way Tyler offers a strong critique of big-power politics and the damage that Cold War assumptions cause to long-term American interests.

The same cannot be said about the novelist recruited for the CIA in 1950 by E. Howard Hunt, who subsequently became his executor and guardian to his children. William Buckley, Jr., is best known as a conservative columnist and commentator, editor of the *National Review,* and host of "Firing Line." He has been a member of the U.S. delegation to the United Nations, as well as a New York mayoral candidate. But added to his list of occupations is that of spy novelist.

"The moral vision of the people who engaged in the cold war was not benighted.... all the ethical egalitarianism with which we've been buffeted in the past fifteen years is an hallucination," Buckley told an interviewer in 1978. His spy fiction unashamedly carries the unapologetic message of the Cold War era. His series' fictional hero, Blackford Oakes, is the Duckworth Drew of the Ivy League set— updated, certainly, in his sexual manners but nonetheless a projection of patriotic schoolboy adventure fantasies. Buckley rarely misses the opportunity to knock the shibboleths of American liberalism, frequently introducing real-life characters such as Allen Dulles or Averell Harriman to celebrate their role as heroes of the Cold War. Most of the novels are set in the 1950s, when Buckley himself worked for the CIA: he was sent as a deep-cover agent to Mexico by Howard Hunt, but boredom got to him and he left after only a few months. In the first, *Saving the Queen* (1976), Oakes is sent to discover the source of high-level leaks of American secrets in—where else?—Britain, and the passages dealing with Oakes's

CIA training are virtually autobiographical. *Stained Glass* (1978) tantalizes the reader with the view that the West could have resisted Soviet domination over East Germany in the early Cold War. Axel Wintergren, a German hero of the anti-Nazi resistance, is the one politician who might reunite Germany. His power threatens Stalin's hold over East Germany, and the Soviet dictator makes his displeasure known to Washington. Afraid of damaging American relations with the Soviets as well as relations with the West German government of Konrad Adenauer, the CIA concocts a plan to assassinate Wintergren. Oakes is the agent and in the course of deciding whether to follow his orders he undertakes much musing on the dilemmas of *Realpolitik*. Since the novel's appearance Buckley has said he wanted to title it *Détente,* because it provides a critique of détente in the 1970s even though it is set in the past. *High Jinx* (1986) is yet another thinly disguised version of the Philby affair, this time revolving around the joint CIA-SIS operation to destabilize Albania in the 1940s that Philby betrayed to Moscow.

Buckley believes that the CIA has the authority and even the obligation to act in the internal affairs of other nations. As might be expected, he is completely unapologetic about his novel's ideological purpose—"to demonstrate," he said in the *New York Times Book Review* in 1978, "that we *are* the good guys and they're the bad guys. I began writing spy novels because I thought the point was worth making in a fluid context that would capture a wider audience." In *Saving the Queen* Blackford Oakes offers his own version of the Buckley doctrine: "We might in secure conscience lie and steal in order to secure the escape of human beings from misery and death. Yet, viewed without paradigmatic moral co-ordinates, simpletons would say simply: *Both sides lied and cheated*—a plague on both their houses." With Buckley, we are firmly back in the world of William Le Queux and Ian Fleming, where right is right and wrong is what the other chap does.

Yet another former CIA officer who has recently entered the ranks of the spy writers is William Hood, whose novel *Spy Wednesday* appeared in 1986. Hood, like many a CIA officer, began his career in the wartime OSS, and then for almost thirty years worked at various CIA stations in Europe. In the early 1950s, at the height of the Cold War, he worked in Vienna, where he took a leading part in running a sensitive operation to help a Soviet intelligence officer defect. *Mole,* his nonfiction book about the affair, appeared in 1982 and was widely praised for the highly realistic view it gave of espionage tradecraft. This is one of the chief characteristics too of *Spy Wednesday,* which concentrates on the familiar theme in recent U.S. spy fiction of the Soviet defector. Like le Carré, Hood has a powerful feel for the inner world of the intelligence community. Harold Trosper, a former CIA officer who left the agency during the troubled 1970s, returns to his old profession not so much out of political belief as out of the loss of belonging. What he missed was "the pressure, the occasional excitement, and even the companionship spawned by the bruising secret war."

If Hood takes a sympathetic view of this secret war, the same can hardly be said for author David Ignatius, whose novel *Agents of Innocence* appeared, to wide acclaim, the following year. Ignatius, a professional journalist with the *Washington Post,* was a reporter in the Middle East for the *Wall Street Journal* during the early 1980s. The novel describes a U.S. operation masterminded from the CIA station in Beirut to penetrate the Palestine Liberation Organization; in fictional form it presents Ignatius's views about the failures and weaknesses of U.S. foreign policy in the Middle East. There are no clearcut answers in the secret world, Ignatius says, because it is a "world painted in shades of gray, rather than black and white, and spy fiction is the fiction of gray." The book's title reflects the real lesson about U.S. intelligence efforts that Ignatius believes he learned from his stint in the Middle East. It is not dissimilar to that drawn by Graham Greene more than thirty years before in *The Quiet American* in observing U.S. policy in Southeast Asia. "Americans are not hard men," says the Arab who helps the CIA in its penetration. "Even the CIA has a soft heart. You want so much to achieve good and make the world better, but you do not have the stomach for it. And you do not know your limitations. You are innocence itself. You are the agents of innocence."

This is not quite how the other superpower sees its own intelligence efforts, of course, though it too has a sense of vulnerability. The Soviet Union is also a declining empire, in this case obsessed with explaining its failures by blaming the machinations of the capitalist world. Spy writers are equally popular there, and the KGB is the front line of the nation's defence. Nothing about *glasnost* and *perestroika* has yet changed that. The top Soviet writer of spy fiction is Julian Semyonov, whose *Tass Is Authorized to Announce* has been made into a highly successful TV series. The book, which has sold over three million copies in the U.S.S.R. and has been translated into English, is set in an African country where a newly elected Marxist government fights off—with the help of the KGB—a CIA plot to restore capitalism. His second novel to be translated into English, *Seventeen Moments of Spring,* is set during the collapse of the Third Reich and features as its hero a double agent recruited to the Communist cause by no less a figure than the real-life Felix Dzerzhinsky, founder of the Cheka and forerunner to the KGB. Semyonov has written over fifty books that have sold more than thirty million copies and is a wealthy man, with a large apartment in Moscow, a dacha in the suburbs, and a villa on the Black Sea. He has close KGB contacts (he is rumoured to be one of its colonels) and exploits obsessions similar to those of his American counterparts: the plot of *Tass Is Authorized,* for example, centres upon a CIA mole passing information to Washington.

British spy fiction since the 1960s has flourished. Beneath the shadow cast by le Carré, an army of artisans has busily been turning the spy novel into a genre that rivals the popularity of the crime and detective story. Len Deighton, whose brilliant early novels *The Ipcress File* (1962), *Funeral in Berlin* (1964), and *Billion-Dollar Brain* (1966) once led Julian Symons to describe him as "a kind of poet of the spy novel," has kept up the production line but at some expense to the poetry. In the 1970s his working-class anti-hero (known as Harry Palmer in the film versions) disappeared, the fascination with gadgetry and technology became more pronounced, and Deighton sometimes overburdened his stories with barely disguised research. Recently, however, he has rediscovered some of his old form.

Deighton's father was chauffeur to the Keeper of the Prints and Drawings at the British Museum, and he grew up in what he calls an "Upstairs, Downstairs world" in which as a young child he closely observed the lives of those from a completely different class. After serving in the Royal Air Force, he went to the Royal College of Art and then worked for an advertising agency in the 1950s. As with many British spy novelists, the Second World War provided him with a basic standard. One of his most successful nonfiction books about the war was in the Le Queux invasion-novel tradition—*SS-GB,* a story of Britain occupied by the Nazis. Deighton was deeply affected by growing up in London during the blitz and watching the reactions of ordinary Londoners to death and destruction. It helps to explain a great deal about his characters. "I think what interests me," he once told the author, "is the mixture of cynicism with patriotism. It's the man who goes to war because he's a patriot, but then plunders an art treasure while he's there, that I find interesting.... I do like to write books in which there are no really deep-dyed villains and no flawless heroes." Sentiments like these were well in tune with the spirit of post-Bond. Like his characters, Deighton seems to have no particular view of the political world around him (although Harry Palmer was vaguely to the left, and certainly no James Bond), and his novels carry no obvious political message. Despite his once-expressed belief that "moles" were of little significance in the Cold War, however, Deighton yielded to fashion. In the "Game, Set and Match" trilogy—*Berlin Game* (1983), *Mexico Set* (1984), and *London Match* (1985)—he turned to the theme of treachery at home and recovered some of his best form as a writer. The central figure, and hero, of the series is Bernard Samson, a man cast in the same mould as the anonymous hero of Deighton's first works. Since completing his first trilogy, Deighton has written another called "Hook, Line and Sinker." Also starring Bernard Samson as its central character, this trilogy takes up the story of deception and betrayal three years after the events described in *London Match.*

Another contemporary British author who shares Deighton's views about the limited value of moles to their masters, yet has chosen them as a major theme, is Ted Allbeury. For him, as for many other writers, the mole obsession became a peg on which to hang a conservative message in tune with the spirit of the 1980s. Allbeury is perhaps the most popular of the large current crop of spy writers; like Deighton, he has until recently drawn heavily from the well of the Second World War. A decade older than Deighton, Allbeury served in the Army Intelligence Corps and ended up as a lieutenant-colonel working in the murky intelligence world of occupied Germany. Allbeury turned to spy writing at an older age even than Fleming. After several years of working in sales and advertising, then running a pirate radio station off the Thames Estuary, at age fifty-four he published *A Choice of Enemies* (1971), which the *New York Times* immediately selected as one of the ten best thrillers of the year.

Allbeury's greatest strength is conveying what it is like to be an agent in the field. "I have tried," he says, "to show that people employed in espionage or intelligence work have private lives, and that the work affects their lives." As critic H.R.F. Keating has said of Allbeury, after reading one of his novels, "one has not only lived excitingly and even wept inward tears for the sadness of things, but one has learnt about individuals and even about national consciousness. One's understanding of what makes the Russians tick, for instance, has been quite simply enlarged.... And this fulfills... a political purpose in alerting readers in the West to a danger that exists for them." Allbeury's recent books are explicit in their anti-Communism and in their hostility to the hard left in Britain. *All Our Tomorrows* (1982), for example, depicts a Britain morally corrupt and politically adrift, governed by self-serving politicians and racked by labour unrest, which agrees to "neutralization" by the Soviet Union. It was not the first of Allbeury's books to stress the dangers to Britain of Soviet-inspired subversion. In both *The Special Collection* (1975) and *Moscow Quadrille* (1976) he depicted Soviet efforts to bring industrial chaos to Britain, and in *The Twentieth Day of January* (1980) he played with the vision of a successful Soviet plot to get their own man in the White House—the prelude to a disastrous American withdrawal from Europe. "I hate books with a message," Allbeury said about *All Our Tomorrows*, "but the message in this one is, 'You can't have total freedom. You've got to decide which freedom you will sacrifice, for the sake of the freedom you really want.'" Despite the recent urgency of his conservative message, not all of Allbeury's novels read like political tracts for Mrs. Thatcher. Many are grounded in his wartime experience; *The Special Collection* (1975) and *The Lonely Margins* (1981), for example, start off with SOE missions to wartime Europe.

Current conservatism finds another author in William Haggard, who has described his books as "basically political novels with more action than in the straight novel." Haggard is the pseudonym of Richard Clayton, an Oxford-educated civil servant who worked during the Second World War in the Intelligence Division of the Indian Army. His series character, Colonel Russell of the Security Executive, who first appeared in Haggard's 1958 novel, *Slow Burner,* is a hard-headed operative with few political illusions, a realist in a world of liberal wishful thinking. Haggard's novels capture the pragmatic and calculating world view that dominates Whitehall—one well attuned to current moods of *Realpolitik.* "He cannot put pen to paper," writes H.R.F. Keating, "without showing in every word one unchippable top-level view of the world."

A similar "Whitehall" view can be found in the spy fiction of Kenneth Benton, C.M.G., whose career provides another example of the strong link between fact and fiction. In the 1930s Benton worked for SIS in Vienna, and then after the *Anschluss* was transferred to Riga in Latvia. After the Soviet occupation in 1940 SIS transferred him to Madrid, and when the war was over he held a series of diplomatic postings until his retirement in 1968. Several novels followed, some of them with an espionage theme. His 1976 novel *A Single Monstrous Act* belongs to the school of cultural pessimism, describing a left-wing plot headed by a university professor willing to misuse his influence over students to take over Britain—a generous compliment to their power that few professors would recognize. Nonetheless, Benton has revealed that the novel was based "to some extent on the research I carried out for a handbook on subversion and counter-subversion." A conservative with more dramatic flair is Alan Williams, a journalist who once worked for Radio Free Europe. For its plots his fiction draws heavily on contemporary events. *Gentleman Traitor* (1975), one of the best known, is built on the career of Kim Philby, and *Holy of Holies* (1981) fantasized on the efforts of the West to rid itself of the menace of Islamic fundamentalism.

The output of a host of other good writers illustrates further contemporary trends. The spy novels of Anthony Price, starring Colonel Butler and David Audley, have been dubbed "the thinking man's spy fiction." In one of his most recent, *Here Be Monsters* (1985), Audley runs up against a highly sophisticated KGB disinformation campaign. Gavin Lyall turns out fast-paced macho novels with plenty of violence, and John Gardner, who created the anti–James Bond comic figure of Boysie Oakes with *The Liquidator* in the 1960s, soon found himself writing the new James Bond novels. These were not especially well received. Bond purists were quick to complain when Gardner modified aspects of Bond's behaviour, and he terminated the effort in the early 1980s. Since then he has directed his efforts at producing a vast trilogy which began with *The Secret Generations* (1985) and has continued with *The Secret Houses* (1988) and *The Secret Families* (1989). The series, described by Gardner as "a work of fiction, set against reality," traces the history of Britain's secret service in the twentieth century. Covering three decades from the founding of the service before the First World War up until the mid-1930s, it tells the story of the aristocratic Railton family that puts its talents at the service of the SIS and at the same time lays the seeds for the great ideological betrayals of the 1930s. Here, again, we see the British obsession with class loyalty and betrayal reflecting itself in contemporary spy fiction.

One writer to emerge in the 1980s was John Trenhaile, with his saga of the KGB agent Stepan Povin in *The Man Called Kyril* (1981), *A View from the Square* (1983), and *Nocturne for the General* (1985). This series too deals with a mole, although here it is the hero himself, a secret Christian (and homosexual), who is passing KGB secrets to Sir Richard Bryant, head of Britain's SIS. And it reflects well, in a sophisticated way, the revived concern of contemporary spy writers with Communism, a trend likely to increase in the era of Gorbachev and *glasnost*. "The real furnace these days—I won't call it a war," says Trenhaile, a former London barrister, "is the ideological conflict between Communism as practiced and capitalism as practiced. People simplify this into East vs. West, Reds vs. Capitalists, and so on. But it's not simple. Until you know who your Communists are, what their grandparents thought and what they had to undergo, you really can't be sure of what you're dealing with today." The 1990s are likely to see such themes continued. Communism may be dead or dying in Eastern Europe, but in the Soviet Union the great issues of Communism versus democracy have still to be confronted. The prediction made many years ago by Julian Symons in *Bloody Murder*—that the spy novel was exhausted—was clearly premature.

On the contrary, John le Carré's recent prediction seems far more plausible. "A spy writer, we are told by someone clever, is as good as his paranoia," le Carré told an audience in the United States. "In a world as tightly wired as our own today, where intricate political decisions are sold like washing powder, and one man's mood can visit instantaneous havoc on the remotest places, these could be the spy writers' vintage years."

Julian Symons once suggested that the spy novel contained two traditions. The first was conservative, supporting authority and asserting that agents were fighting to protect something valuable. The second was radical, critical of authority, claiming that agents perpetuated or even created false barriers between "us" and "them." Ernest Mandel, the Marxist writer, has recently suggested in his social history of the genre, *Delightful Murder,* that the crime story has begun to contribute to the questioning of basic bourgeois values. But what may be true of the crime novel hardly applies to recent spy novels. Spy novelists of the 1960s such as le Carré and Deighton certainly presented the spy as an alienated individual victimized by the system he was supposed to defend. This tradition, built on foundations laid by Ambler and Greene, still exists, as can be seen in Martin Cruz Smith's *Gorky Park* (1981) or W.T. Tyler's *The Man Who Lost the War* (1980). But taken as a whole, recent spy novelists reflect the growing conservatism of the last few years which to many people has been vindicated by the 1989 revolutions throughout Eastern Europe. A case in point is Frederick Forsyth's 1984 novel *The Fourth Protocol,* released as a major film in 1987. The book, besides being a first-rate story, combines conservative pessimism about the left in Britain with fashionable mole phobia to produce a plot in which Kim Philby, safely "at home" in Moscow, conspires with the "hard" left to take over power and turn Britain into a Soviet satellite. Still, this distaste for the left can quickly accommodate itself to changing circumstances. Forsyth's latest novel, *The Negotiator,* deals with the threat posed by a conspiracy of wreckers to growing U.S.-Soviet détente in the early 1990s. The preservation of international peace, and the prevention of nuclear war, will still be the principal goals of fictional agents in the last decade of the twentieth century.

For almost a hundred years British writers used spy fiction to explore the rapidly changing world in which Britain declined from a self-assured empire to an introspective European island beset by serious problems. We can now see a similar process at work in the United States. It is safe to predict that American spy writers have a guaranteed future.

The main object of spy writers has always been to entertain and amuse. But they are always more than entertainers. Spy writers present us with unique orientations about nations and their place in a complex and dangerous world. If we care to look, these commentators of the silent game can inform as well as amuse us.

Select Bibliography

Allain, Marie-Françoise. *The Other Man: Conversations with Graham Greene*. London: Bodley Head, 1983.

Ambler, Eric. *The Ability to Kill*. London: Bodley Head, 1963.

————. *Here Lies: An Autobiography*. London: Weidenfeld and Nicolson, 1985.

————. *To Catch a Spy*. London: Bodley Head, 1963.

Amis, Kingsley. *The James Bond Dossier*. London: Cape, 1965.

————. "A New James Bond". In *What Became of Jane Austen?* Harmondsworth: Penguin Books, 1981.

Andrew, Christopher. *Secret Service: The Making of the British Intelligence Community*. London: Heinemann, 1985.

Atkins, John. *The British Spy Novel: Styles in Treachery*. London: John Calder, 1984; New York: Riverrun Press, 1984.

Baden-Powell, Sir Robert. *My Adventures as a Spy*. London: C. Arthur Pearson, 1915.

Bamford, James. *The Puzzle Palace: A Report on the NSA, America's Most Secret Agency*. Boston: Houghton Mifflin, 1976.

Barley, Tony. *Taking Sides: The Fiction of John le Carré*. Milton Keynes and Philadelphia: Open University Press, 1986.

Barzun, Jacques, and Wendell Hestig Taylor. *A Catalogue of Crime:*

Being a Reader's Guide to the Literature of Mystery, Detection, and Related Genres. New York: Harper & Row, 1971.

Boyle, Andrew. *The Riddle of Erskine Childers*. London: Hutchinson, 1977.

Bryce, Ivar. *You Only Live Once: Memoirs of Ian Fleming*. London: Weidenfeld and Nicolson, 1975.

[Buchan, John]. *John Buchan, By His Wife and Friends*. (Preface by George M. Trevelyan.) London: Hodder and Stoughton, 1947.

Buchan, John. *Memory Hold-the-Door*. Toronto: Musson Book Company, 1941.

Buchan, William. *John Buchan: A Memoir*. London: Buchan and Enright, 1982.

Calder, Robert Louis. *W. Somerset Maugham and the Quest for Freedom*. London: Heinemann, 1972.

Carrington, Charles. *Rudyard Kipling: His Life and Work*. London: Macmillan, 1978.

Cawelti, John G. *Adventure, Mystery and Romance: Formula Stories as Art and Popular Culture*. Chicago: University of Chicago Press, 1976.

Clarke, I.F. *Voices Prophesying War, 1763–1964*. London: Oxford University Press, 1966.

Cockburn, Claud. *Bestseller: The Books That Everyone Read 1900–1939*. London: Sidgwick and Jackson, 1972.

Craig, Patricia, and Mary Cadogan. *The Lady Investigates: Women Detectives and Spies in Fiction*. London: Gollancz, 1981.

Daniell, David. *The Interpreter's House: A Critical Assessment of the Work of John Buchan*. London: Thomas Nelson and Sons, 1975.

Donelly, Peter (ed.) *Mrs. Milburn's Diaries: An Englishwoman's Day-to-Day Reflections 1939–1945*. London: Fontana Books, 1979.

Dooley, D.J. *Compton Mackenzie*. New York: Twayne Publishers, 1974.

Dulles, Allen (ed.) *Great Spy Stories from Fiction*. London and Glasgow: William Collins Sons, 1969.

Eames, Hugh. *Sleuths, Inc.: Studies of Problem Solvers—Doyle, Simenon, Ambler, Chandler*. Philadelphia & New York: J.B. Lippincott, 1978.

Eco, Umberto (ed.), and Oreste del Buono. *The Bond Affair*. London: Macdonald & Co., 1966.

Fleming, Ian. *Thrilling Cities*. New York: New American Library of World Literature, 1964.

Fletcher, Katy. "Evolution of the Modern American Spy Novel". *Journal of Contemporary History* 22, No. 2 (April 1987).

Foot, M.R.D. *SOE: The Special Operations Executive 1940–46*. London: British Broadcasting Corporation, 1984.

Granatstein, J.L., and David Stafford. *Spy Wars: Espionage and Canada from Gouzenko to Glasnost*. Toronto: Key Porter, 1990.

Green, Roger Lancelyn. *A.E.W. Mason*. London: Max Parish, 1952.

Greene, Graham. *In Search of a Character*. London: Bodley Head, 1961.

———. *A Sort of Life*. London: Bodley Head, 1971.

———. *Ways of Escape*. Toronto: Lester & Orpen Dennys, 1980.

———, and Hugh Greene. *The Spy's Bedside Book*. London: Rupert Hart Davis, 1957.

Hagen, A. Ordean. *Who Done It? A Guide to Detective, Mystery, and Suspense Fiction*. New York: Bowker, 1969.

Harper, Ralph. *The World of the Thriller*. Baltimore and London: Johns Hopkins University Press, 1974.

Horler, Sydney. *Excitement: An Impudent Biography*. London: Hutchinson, 1933.

Household, Geoffrey. *Against the Wind*. Boston: Little, Brown, 1959.

Howarth, Patrick. *Play Up and Play the Game: The Heroes of Popular Fiction*. London: Eyre Methuen, 1973.

Hynes, Samuel. *The Edwardian Turn of Mind*. Princeton: Princeton University Press, 1968.

———(ed.) *Graham Greene: A Collection of Critical Essays*. Englewood Cliffs, N.J.: Prentice-Hall, 1973.

Keating, H.R.F. *Whodunit? A Guide to Crime, Suspense, and Crime Fiction*. New York: Van Nostrand Reinhold, 1982.

Knightley, Phillip. *The Second Oldest Profession: The Spy As Bureaucrat, Patriot, Fantasist and Whore*. London: André Deutsch, 1986.

Lambert, Gavin. *The Dangerous Edge*. London: Barrie and Jenkins, 1975.

Lane, Margaret. *Edgar Wallace: The Biography of a Phenomenon*. London: William Heinemann, 1938; New York: Book League of America, 1964.

Le Queux, William. *Things I Know about Kings, Celebrities, and Crooks*. London: Nash & Grayson, 1923.

McCormick, Donald, and Katy Fletcher (eds.) *Spy Fiction: A Connoisseur's Guide*. New York: Facts on File, 1990.

McCormick, Donald. *Who's Who in Spy Fiction*. London: Elm Tree Books, Hamish Hamilton, 1977.

Mackenzie, Compton (Sir Edward Montague Compton). *Aegean Memories*. London: Chatto & Windus, 1940.

———. *Athenian Memories*. London: Cassell, 1931.

———. *Gallipoli Memories*. London: Cassell, 1929.

———. *Greek Memories*. London: Chatto & Windus, 1939.

———. *My Life and Times*. London: Chatto & Windus, 1963.

Mandel, Ernest. *Delightful Murder: A Social History of the Crime Story*. London and Sydney: Pluto Press, 1984.

Marchetti, Victor, and John Marks. *The CIA and the Cult of Intelligence*. New York: Dell, 1975.

Martin, David. *Wilderness of Mirrors*. New York: Ballantine, 1980.

Masters, Anthony. *The Man Who Was M: The Life of Maxwell Knight*. London: Grafton Books, 1986.

Maugham, W. Somerset. *The Summing Up*. London: William Heinemann, 1938.

Merry, Bruce. *Anatomy of the Spy Thriller*. Montreal: McGill and Queen's University Press, 1977.

Monaghan, David. *The Novels of John le Carré: The Art of Survival*. Oxford: Blackwell, 1985.

———. *Smiley's Circus: A Guide to the Secret World of John le Carré*. New York: St. Martin's Press, 1986.

Morgan, Ted. *Somerset Maugham*. London: Cape, 1980.

Muggeridge, Malcolm. *Chronicles of Wasted Time: Part 2, The Infernal Grove*. London: Collins, 1973.

Oppenheim, E. Phillips. *The Pool of Memory*. London: Hodder and Stoughton, 1941.

Palmer, Jerry. *Thrillers: Genesis and Structure of a Popular Genre*. London: Edward Arnold, 1978.

Panek, LeRoy L. *The Special Branch: The British Spy Novel 1890–1980*. Bowling Green, Ohio: Bowling Green Popular Press, 1981.

Parish, James Robert, and Michael R. Pitts. *The Great Spy Pictures*. Metuchen, N.J.: Scarecrow Press, 1974.

Pearson, John. *The Life of Ian Fleming*. London: Jonathan Cape, 1966.

Philby, Kim. *My Secret War*. London: MacGibbon and McKee, 1968.

Powers, Thomas. *The Man Who Kept the Secrets: Richard Helms and the CIA*. New York: Knopf, 1979.

Reilly, John M. (ed.) *Twentieth Century Crime and Mystery Writers*. London: Macmillan, 1980.

Richler, Mordecai. "Bond." In *Notes on an Engendered Species and Others*. New York: Alfred A. Knopf, 1974.

Rockwell, Joan. "Normative Attitudes of Spies in Fiction." In Rosenberg, B., and D. Manning-White, *Mass Culture Revisited*. New York: Van Nostrand Reinhold, 1971.

Rubenstein, Leonard. *The Great Spy Films*. Secaucus, N.J.: Citadel Press, 1979.

Sauerberg, Lars Ole. *Secret Agents in Fiction: Ian Fleming, John le Carré, and Len Deighton*. New York: St. Martin's Press, 1984.

Sladen, N. St. Barbe. *The Real Le Queux: The Official Biography of William Le Queux*. London: Nicholson & Watson, 1938.

Smith, Barbara A. "Themes in British Espionage Fiction of the 1930s." M.A. thesis, University of Waterloo, Ont., 1986.

Smith, Bradley F. *The Shadow Warriors: OSS and the Origins of the CIA*. London: Deutsch, 1983.

Smith, Janet Adam. *John Buchan*. London: Rupert Hart-Davis, 1965.

————. *John Buchan and His World*. New York: Scribner's, 1979.

Smith, Myron J. *Cloak and Dagger Bibliography: An Annotated Guide to Spy Fiction 1937–1975*. Metuchen, N.J.: Scarecrow Press, 1976.

Stafford, David. *Britain and European Resistance 1940–1945*. London: Macmillan, 1980.

————. *Camp X: Canada's School for Secret Agents 1941–45*. Toronto: Lester & Orpen Dennys, 1986.

————. "Conspiracy and Xenophobia: The Spy Novels of William Le Queux, 1893–1914." *Europa* (Montreal) III, No. 3 (1982).

————. "John Buchan's Tales of Espionage: A Popular Archive of British History." *Canadian Journal of History* (Spring 1983).

————. "Spies and Gentlemen: The Birth of the British Spy Novel, 1893–1914." *Victorian Studies* (Summer 1981).

Standish, Robert. *The Prince of Storytellers*. London: Peter Davies, 1957.

Steinbrunner, C., and O. Renzler. *Encyclopaedia of Mystery and Detection.* London: Routledge, 1976.

Stratford, Philip (ed.) *The Portable Graham Greene.* Harmondsworth: Penguin Books, 1982.

Sutherland, John. *Bestsellers: Popular Fiction of the 1970s.* London & Boston: Routledge & Kegan Paul, 1981.

Swiggett, Howard. "Introduction." In Buchan, John, *Sick Heart River.* Toronto: Musson, 1941.

Symons, Julian. *Bloody Murder: From the Detective Story to the Crime Novel, A History.* London: Faber & Faber, 1972.

Taylor, Edmond. "The Cult of the Secret Agent." In *Horizon* 17 (Spring 1975).

Trevelyan, George M. "Preface." In *John Buchan, by His Wife and Friends.* London: Hodder and Stoughton, 1947.

Usborne, Richard. *Clubland Heroes.* London: Constable, 1953.

Watson, Colin. *Snobbery with Violence: Crime Stories and Their Audience.* London: Eyre & Spottiswoode, 1971.

Wheatley, Denis. *The Deception Planners.* London: Hutchinson, 1980.

———. *Stranger Than Fiction.* London: Hutchinson, 1959.

Williams, Valentine. *The World of Action: The Autobiography of Valentine Williams.* London: Hamish Hamilton, 1938.

Winks, Robin W. *Modus Operandi: An Excursion into Detective Fiction.* Boston: David R. Godine, 1982.

Winn, Dilys. *Murder Ink.* New York: Workman Publishing, 1977.

Young, Kenneth. *Compton Mackenzie.* London: Longmans, Green, 1968.

Index